Nancy Weinberg

W9-CZU-201

SEVERE DISABILITIES

Publication Number 921
AMERICAN LECTURE SERIES

A Publication in
The BANNERSTONE DIVISION *of*
AMERICAN LECTURES IN SOCIAL AND REHABILITATION PSYCHOLOGY

Editors of the Series
JOHN G. CULL, Ph.D.
Director, Regional Counselor Training Program
Department of Rehabilitation Counseling
Virginia Commonwealth University
Fishersville, Virginia

and

RICHARD E. HARDY, Ed.D.

Chairman, Department of Rehabilitation Counseling
Virginia Commonwealth University
Richmond, Virginia

The American Lecture Series in Social and Rehabilitation Psychology offers books which are concerned with man's role in his milieu. Emphasis is placed on how this role can be made more effective in a time of social conflict and a deteriorating physical environment. The books are oriented toward descriptions of what future roles should be and are not concerned exclusively with the delineation and definition of contemporary behavior. Contributors are concerned to a considerable extent wtih prediction through the use of a functional view of man as opposed to a descriptive, anatomical point of view.

Books in this series are written mainly for the professional practitioner; however, academicians will find them of considerable value in both undergraduate and graduate courses in the helping services.

SEVERE
DISABILITIES

SOCIAL AND
REHABILITATION APPROACHES

RICHARD E. HARDY, Ed.D.

JOHN G. CULL, Ph.D.

CHARLES C THOMAS · PUBLISHER
Springfield · Illinois · U.S.A.

Published and Distributed Throughout the World by

CHARLES C THOMAS • PUBLISHER

BANNERSTONE HOUSE

301-327 East Lawrence Avenue, Springfield, Illinois, U.S.A.

© 1974, by CHARLES C THOMAS • PUBLISHER

ISBN 0-398-02943-1

Library of Congress Catalog Card Number: 73-10077

With THOMAS BOOKS *careful attention is given to all details of manufacturing and design. It is the Publisher's desire to present books that are satisfactory as to their physical qualities and artistic possibilities and appropriate for their particular use.* THOMAS BOOKS *will be true to those laws of quality that assure a good name and good will.*

Printed in the United States of America

W-1

Library of Congress Cataloging in Publication Data

Hardy, Richard E
 Severe disabilities.

 (American lecture series, publication No. 921. A publication in the Bannerstone division of American lectures in social and rehabilitation psychology)

 1. Physically handicapped—Rehabilitation.
I. Cull, John G., joint author. II. Title.
[DNLM: 1. Counseling. 2. Handicapped. 3. Rehabilitation.
HD7255 H271s 1973]
RD795.H37   362.1'0425   73-10077
ISBN 0-398-02943-1

CONTRIBUTORS

RICHARD E. ACCIAVATTI, Ed.D.: Professor and Director of Rehabilitation Counselor Education, Seton Hall University, South Orange, New Jersey. Formerly, Director of Rehabilitation in the Pennsylvania Department of Health, Flick State Hospital, Cresson, Pennsylvania. Dr. Acciavatti is licensed to practice psychology and marriage counseling, and holds a license to practice marriage, family and child counseling in the state of California. He is a psychological consultant for the Veterans' Administration, New Jersey Division of Vocational Rehabilitation, New Jersey Department of Labor and Industry and the Pennsylvania Bureau of Vocational Rehabilitation.

GUSTAV O. ALEXANDER, Ph.D.: Assistant Professor of Speech and Theatre, Wright State University, Dayton, Ohio. Previously served as Assistant Professor of Communication Theory and Research at Ithaca College, Ithaca, New York. Doctor Alexander's publications and papers presented at professional conferences include: *Teaching Innovations in Speech Communication: An Exploratory Study; Instructional Metacommunication and Self-Directed Learning*, published by the ERIC Clearinghouse on Higher Education.

GLORIA BIDWELL, Ph.D.: Assistant Professor for the Rehabilitation Counseling Program at the University of Connecticut. Earned doctorate at Columbia University, 1967. Previously a counseling psychologist at the Veterans Administration Hospital in West Haven, Connecticut for two years. Research activities and publication have been in the areas of vocational planning of emotionally disturbed patients, vocational training of institutionalized youthful public offenders and ancillary service needs for chronic disability post-hospital clients.

JAMES T. BOWMAN, Ed.D.: Assistant Professor of Student

v

Personnel and Counselor Education, Mississippi State University. B.A.–English, M.A., Rehabilitation Counseling, Ed.D. Special Education and Rehabilitation, University of Northern Colorado. Formerly Rehabilitation Counselor, Oregon Department of Vocational Rehabilitation, Secondary Teacher in Colorado.

JAMES A. CHANEY: Assistant Professor of Education and Psychology and Assistant Coordinator, Rehabilitation Counselor Training Program, Arkansas State University. Doctor Chaney was formerly Director, Social and Rehabilitation Services Program, Arkansas Polytechnic College.

JOHN G. CULL, Ph.D.: Professor and Director, Regional Counselor Training Program, Department of Rehabilitation Counseling, Virginia Commonwealth University, Fishersville, Virginia; Adjunct Professor of Psychology and Education, School of General Studies, University of Virginia, Charlottesville, Virginia; Technical Consultant, Rehabilitation Services Administration, United States Department of Health, Education and Welfare, Washington, D.C.; Editor, American Lecture Series in Social and Rehabilitation Psychology, Charles C Thomas, Publisher; Lecturer Medical Department, Woodrow Wilson Rehabilitation Center; Formerly, Rehabilitation Counselor, Texas State Commission for the Blind; Rehabilitation Counselor, Texas Rehabilitation Commission; Director, Division of Research and Program Development, Virginia State Department of Vocational Rehabilitation. The following are some of the books which Dr. Cull has co-authored and co-edited: *Drug Dependence and Rehabilitation Approaches, Fundamentals of Criminal Behavior and Correctional Systems, Rehabilitation of the Drug Abuser With Delinquent Behavior,* and *Therapeutic Needs of the Family.* Dr. Cull has contributed more than fifty publications to the professional literature in psychology and rehabilitation.

A. G. GARRIS: Rehabilitation Consultant, California Department of Rehabilitation. Formerly owned and operated a private vocational school and was a business analyst–consultant. He has developed extensive devices for use by handicapped individuals such as foot driving device, wheelchair ramps and loaders, special desks, remote controlled recorders, holding clamps for wheelchairs, wheelchair scale adaptation, work area devices, copy holder design for visually handicapped, etc.

ALAYNE K. GRAND: Earned a B.A. degree in English at SUNY at Albany and a M.S. degree in Rehabilitation Counseling at SUNY at Albany. She has clinical experience with the full range of disability groups at agencies such as a comprehensive rehabilitation center, a sheltered workshop and in a Physical Therapy and Rehabilitation Department within a general hospital.

SHELDON A. GRAND, Ph.D.: Associate Professor and Director of the Rehabilitation Counseling Program, Department of Counseling and Personnel Services, State University of New York at Albany. He earned a B.A. degree in Psychology at Brooklyn College, a M.A. degree in Clinical Psychology at Roosevelt University, and a Ph.D. degree in Counseling Psychology at the University of Buffalo. Previous full time clinical positions include staff counseling psychologist and chief counseling psychologist at the Albany Veterans' Administration Hospital. Consulting and part-time positions have been held with agencies such as A.R.C., O.V.R., New York State Department of Mental Hygiene, New York State Department of Corrections, and the Albany Veterans' Administration Hospital. Previous teaching positions (part-time) were at University of Buffalo, Union College (Schenectady), Albany Medical Center (Physical Therapy Training Program), and Russell Sage College. He has publications in the American Journal of Correction, Rehabilitation Counseling Bulletin, Journal of Counseling Psychology, and has contributed book reviews to the Personnel and Guidance Journal.

WILLIAM H. GRAVES, Ed.D.: Director of Rehabilitation Counselor Training and Associate Professor of Student Personnel and Counselor Education, Mississippi State University. B.A.—Psychology, Wake Forest University; M.R.C.—University of Florida, Ed.D.—University of Florida. Chairman, Region IV Rehabilitation Educators Council. Formerly, Counselor, South Carolina Department of Vocational Rehabilitation.

PERRY L. HALL: Assistant Professor, Coordinator, Rehabilitation Education, Wright State University, Dayton, Ohio. Previously worked with Ohio Bureau of Vocational Rehabilitation as University Liaison—Staff Development; Assistant Supervisor—Field Services; Rehabilitation Research Consultant to the Ohio State University and as a Field Counselor with a general caseload. Mr. Hall has publications in rehabilitation related journals.

RICHARD E. HARDY, Ed.D.: Professor and Chairman, Department of Rehabilitation Counseling, Virginia Commonwealth University, Richmond, Virginia; Technical Consultant, United States Department of Health, Education and Welfare, Rehabilitation Services Administration, Washington, D.C.; Editor, American Lecture Series in Social and Rehabilitation Psychology, Charles C Thomas, Publisher; and Associate Editor, *Journal of Voluntary Action Research,* formerly Rehabilitation Counselor in Virginia, Rehabilitation Advisor, Rehabilitation Services Administration, United States Department of Health, Education and Welfare, Washington, D.C., former Chief Psychologist and Supervisor of Professional Training, South Carolina Department of Rehabilitation and member of the South Carolina State Board of Examiners in Psychology. The following are some of the books which Dr. Hardy has co-authored and co-edited: *Drug Dependence and Rehabilitation Approaches, Fundamentals of Criminal Behavior and Correctional Systems, Rehabilitation of the Drug Abuser with Delinquent Behavior,* and *Therapeutic Needs of the Family.* Dr. Hardy has contributed more than fifty publications to the professional literature in psychology and rehabilitation.

RICHARD K. JOHNSON, Ed.D.: Director, Counseling and Placement Center, Gallaudet College, Washington, D.C.; Associate Professor in Counseling, Gallaudet College; Editorial Advisory Board, *Deafness Annual;* Consulting Editor, *Journal of Rehabilitation of the Deaf;* Board of Directors, Professional Rehabilitation Workers with the Adult Deaf Association. Formerly teacher of the deaf; Research Assistant, Michigan Department of Mental Health and Office of Vocational Rehabilitation project RD 8005; Program Administrator, Michigan statewide program for institutionalized retarded deaf people. Doctor Johnson has contributed extensively to the professional literature in rehabilitation, deafness and mental retardation.

EVAN THOMAS JONES, B.A.: Psychologist, Fairfax School Unit. Training Coordinator for Northern Virginia Hotline. Formerly, Draft Counselor at Ohio University.

ROBERT A. MacGUFFIE, Ph.D.: Associate Professor and Director of Rehabilitation Counseling at Bowling Green State University, Bowling Green, Ohio. He is also consultant to the Ohio Department of Mental Hygiene and Retardation, the Division of Forensic Psychiatry and the Lima State Hospital for the Criminally Insane. Formerly, Research Associate at the Regional Rehabilitation Research Institute at the University of Utah and engaged in social work and rehabilitation in the state of Idaho. He received his Ph.D. in Educational Psychology from the University of Utah.

CLEYLON L. McLARTY, Ed.D.: Professor of Education and Coordinator, Rehabilitation Counselor Training Program, Arkansas State University. Formerly, public school teacher and counselor, Mississippi; Assistant Dean of Students, The University of Georgia; Visiting Assistant Professor, The University of Mississippi; Associate Professor and Director, Program to Strengthen Developing Institutions, Delta State College, Cleveland, Mississippi. Doctor McLarty is a disability consultant for several law firms, and he has contributed to the literature of rehabilitation counselor training and educational technology.

MARY MARSHALL ROBERTS, Ed.D.: Associate Professor of Rehabilitation Education, Eastern Kentucky University. Doctor Roberts has held various teaching and counseling positions and has served as consultant to Rocky Mountain Rehabilitation Association and was Director of Research Project for Juvenile Delinquent Boys. Doctor Roberts is quite active in professional associations and counselor consultative activities.

AMOS SALES, Ed.D.: Assistant Professor, Department of Rehabilitation, University of Arizona. Formerly, Associate Professor, Rehabilitation Counselor Education, Kansas State Teachers College, and School Psychologist. Dr. Sales is active in consulting activities and has published in rehabilitation related publications.

CECIL O. SAMUELSON, Ph.D.: Professor of Educational Psychology, University of Utah. Dr. Samuelson has been a High School Counselor, Assistant State Director of Vocational Rehabilitation and State Director of Guidance Services in Utah. He has published numerous articles in rehabilitation and educational journals.

KENT MITCHELL SAMUELSON, M.D.: Doctor Samuelson received his degree from the University of Utah, interned in surgery at the Orange County Medical Center in California and completed his residency in orthopedic surgery at the University of Utah Affiliated Hospitals. Doctor Samuelson is licensed to practice medicine and surgery in the state of Utah. He has several publications in medical journals.

SENA SWORD: Instructor in Rehabilitation at Eastern Kentucky University. Formerly, Home Economics Teacher and Rehabilitation Counselor at Eastern State Mental Hospital. She received her Master's Degree from Eastern Kentucky University.

EDWARD A. WICAS, Ed.D.: Associate Professor of Educational Psychology and Director of the Rehabilitation Counselor Training Program, University of Connecticut. Earned doctorate in Counseling and Educational Psychology from Boston University, 1955. Formerly, counselor in public schools, university and community agency settings as well as consultant in counseling and school psychology to public schools, Veterans' Administration and community rehabilitation agencies. Research interests have primarily focused upon the counselor as a person and the screening, selection and training of counselors.

The following books have appeared thus far in the Social and Rehabilitation Psychology Series:

SOCIAL AND REHABILITATION SERVICES FOR THE BLIND—Richard E. Hardy and John G. Cull

MENTAL RETARDATION AND PHYSICAL DISABILITY—Richard E. Hardy and John G. Cull

UNDERSTANDING DISABILITY FOR SOCIAL AND REHABILITATION SERVICES—John G. Cull and Richard E. Hardy

VOLUNTEERISM: AN EMERGING PROFESSION—John G. Cull and Richard E. Hardy

REHABILITATION OF THE URBAN DISADVANTAGED—John G. Cull and Richard E. Hardy

THE NEGLECTED OLDER AMERICAN—SOCIAL AND REHABILITATION SERVICES—John G. Cull and Richard E. Hardy

FUNDAMENTALS OF CRIMINAL BEHAVIOR AND CORRECTIONAL SYSTEMS—John G. Cull and Richard E. Hardy

THE BIG WELFARE MESS—PUBLIC ASSISTANCE AND REHABILITATION APPROACHES—John G. Cull and Richard E. Hardy

ADJUSTMENT TO WORK—John G. Cull and Richard E. Hardy

VOCATIONAL EVALUATION FOR REHABILITATION SERVICES—Richard E. Hardy and John G. Cull

REHABILITATION OF THE DRUG ABUSER WITH DELINQUENT BEHAVIOR—Richard E. Hardy and John G. Cull

APPLIED PSYCHOLOGY IN LAW ENFORCEMENT AND CORRECTIONS—Richard E. Hardy and John G. Cull

INTRODUCTION TO CORRECTIONAL REHABILITATION—Richard E. Hardy and John G. Cull

DRUG DEPENDENCE AND REHABILITATION APPROACHES—Richard E. Hardy and John G. Cull

CLIMBING GHETTO WALLS—Richard E. Hardy and John G. Cull

APPLIED VOLUNTEERISM IN COMMUNITY DEVELOPMENT—Richard E. Hardy and John G. Cull

CONTEMPORARY FIELD WORK PRACTICES IN REHABILITATION—John G. Cull and Craig R. Colvin

VOCATIONAL REHABILITATION: PROFESSION AND PROCESS—John G. Cull and Richard E. Hardy

MEDICAL AND PSYCHOLOGICAL ASPECTS OF DISABILITY—A. Beatrix Cobb

SPECIAL PROBLEMS IN REHABILITATION—A. Beatrix Cobb

LAW ENFORCEMENT AND CORRECTIONAL REHABILITATION—John G. Cull and Richard E. Hardy

EVALUATION FOR REHABILITATION SERVICES—Richard E. Hardy and John G. Cull

COUNSELING HIGH SCHOOL STUDENTS—John G. Cull and Richard E. Hardy

This book is dedicated to a concerned
leader in the field of rehabilitation:

Dr. Raymond A. Ehrle

CONTENTS

SEVERE DISABILITIES

CHAPTER I

REHABILITATION COUNSELING AND THE MENTALLY RETARDED CLIENT

EDWARD WICAS AND GLORIA BIDWELL

Difference Represented by Retarded Clients
Counseling Needs
Rehabilitation Goals: Community Living and
Job Placement
Preparing for Work
Preparing for Community Living
Some Additional Considerations and Needs

T HE GOALS OF rehabilitation or habilitation of retarded individuals is no different than for those for any other group of individuals. Stated simply, it is to assist the individual to attain the optimum utilization of his potential. With this group the focus is primarily preparation for independent, or as nearly independent, living as they are able to assume. The final level of independence which can be expected of each individual varies according to the degree of intellectual competence, other compounding disabilities, motor coordination, speech, emotional stability, and psychological independence. It is not unrealistic to expect that most educable retarded can achieve a state of independence in earning a living and managing their own affairs.

Differences Represented by Retarded Clients

There are two general groups of retarded individuals being considered in discussing rehabilitation from the point of view of experiences; that is, those who have experienced institutional living and those who have remained with their families in the community. They present quite different problems in planning for independent living.

Retarded children are far from being a homogeneous group. Although the basis of designation as retarded is based upon a test score or level of general mental ability, even in this respect it is extremely difficult to determine whether limited intellectual functioning is due to a low level of mental ability, another problem, or compounding problems. When children are adjudged *retarded* who are really presenting a complex picture of problems, they are frequently not given optimal help. For example, if a delinquent scores within the retarded range on a standard intelligence test, he may be committed to an institution for the mentally retarded; he may actually be a *deprived* or an emotionally disturbed individual who, because of these other factors impinging upon him, is functioning in that range. Given a more stimulating environment or therapy to resolve some of the emotional involvement, he might function on a higher level. There is, in fact, a whole group of youngsters found in special education classes for the educable retarded and in training schools who, because of unfavorable family backgrounds, such as low economic means, broken homes, large families, and other compounding social factors are declared retarded. Not infrequently these youngsters are potentially average or near average in general mental ability.

The child or youth who is emotionally disturbed and tests within the retarded range tends *not* to be served well by either the training school for the retarded or the hospital for the emotionally disturbed, especially if he is disruptive. Neither institution is eager to accept him; the hospital for the emotionally disturbed saying they cannot work effectively with him because of his low intelligence, while the training school claims insufficient psychiatric help to meet his needs.

Counseling Needs

Counseling approaches to individual retardates differ according to various factors; among them other handicaps, length of time the individual will be available for counseling, and his life situation. For example, the approach to a retarded emotionally disturbed youth may differ from that used with a deaf retardate. The time available for counseling may be crucial. Sometimes young people involved in delinquent behavior are committed to an institution for retardates for a short period of time. This necessitates working with them in a short time span as opposed to the usual inmate whose release from the institution has not been specified and is generally dependent upon readiness for community placement.

Another factor is the life situation of the retarded individual. An institutionalized youth may require much more intensive counseling to prepare him for independent living than an individual who has never been separated from the community. The degree of protection imposed upon the home-based child is still another factor involved in both counseling and preparation for work. If parents over-protect these children it becomes more difficult to ready them for employment since they may not have learned simple self-care tasks.

All kinds of counseling assistance are needed by retarded persons living within institutions and those that are community based, whether living in hostels or at home. Whether counseling is group or individually oriented, it must be on a level of comprehension within the client's intellectual capabilities. Frequently, insight therapy is unrealistic because it is predicated on the idea that the individual is capable of intellectual growth which is, by definition, limited. These young people do have many concerns. Among these are how to relate to other people, male-female relations, anxiety aroused by fears of non-acceptance by the community, and uncertainty of what to do in certain situations outside the institution.

Usually retarded individuals have developed very negative self attitudes including such self references as *stupid* which also may be translated to mean *bad*. Positive reinforcement in the institutions and in special classes in the public school systems has almost never been sufficient to allay the retarded youth's fear of rejection by the community. They do possess negative attitudes; they are often failure oriented, and perceive themselves as having been beaten down by parents, schools, and community negative attitudes. An important goal of rehabilitation counselors and other helpers in this area is changing these attitudes so the retarded can see themselves as able to do things and even aspiring to goals once thought of as unattainable. Some positive attitudes can be developed best through group interaction while others need individual counseling. Counseling in groups permits opportunity for retardates to experience some degree of social intimacy not otherwise experienced as well as opportunity to focus on the therapeutic tasks of clarifying and understanding feelings and attitudes. Individual counseling permits opportunity, through behavior modification procedures, to target and work and to alter or modify specific behaviors of a particular retarded client.

Family group counseling has an essential role in helping parents and other family members deal with their attitudes toward retardation, to know and recognize the strengths and limitations of retarded individuals so they can help them grow into as independent adults as their limitations will allow. Many parents have found that meeting with other parents in group counseling sessions to be helpful in understanding mutual problems and discussing better ways of handling troublesome situations. At the other end of the scale another type of family counseling, pre-marital counseling, can help when retarded individuals prepare themselves to marry, establish independent homes and raise their own families. They frequently need very specific help in learning how to care for a home and children, how to budget money, and how to use community resources.

Another area for counseling focus is with the youths and their families who have not resorted to institutional placement and occurs when the public schools are no longer responsible for their education and training after they reach statuatory ages established by law. Many parents need someone to help them seek out help so their child can live as normal a life as possible. Parents are frequently unaware of services and facilities available after the retarded is no longer attending school.

Rehabilitation Goals: Community Living and Job Placement

When possible, the goal of rehabilitation should be community living and job placement. If job placement is not feasible but social placement a possibility, that is, semi-independent community living, that should be the direction chosen. Vocational placement must be carefully worked out to assure success for the client. If a placement is appropriate and the client has participated in his rehabilitation so that the goals are clear to him then he should be able to function adequately with or without supportive services. Supportive services must be arranged where they are important to the client for adequate functioning. Areas of frequent failure in the placement of clients are agency quotas which stress quantity rather than selective or quality placements, and community limitations. The community can help assure success in many ways through educating for better attitudes toward all special groups so that social activities will be available to everyone. Educational and supportive services should be available to retarded adults to help them learn how to care for the home, shop for family and home needs and care for children. Supportive services are necessary to enable them to cope with the attitudes and behavior of the community toward the retarded. Until the attitudes of the community changes, some social activities have to be provided separately.

Retarded individuals want the same rewards from the community that everyone else wants; that is, a feeling of belonging, a job and money. Adjustment to the community of institutionalized retardates varies with the length of time spent in the institution. The longer the institutional time the more difficult community placement becomes. Institutionalization has actually *trained-in* habitual behaviors which serve the institution but are inappropriate for community living. Many have accepted a *laissez-faire* attitude and expect that life should be simple and place no demands upon them; it is easier to be cared for. Training and experience must be provided to help the retardate learn to live and develop behavior patterns appropriate for family and independent styles of living.

Those aspects of community living perceived as rewarding

are money and sometimes a family. House parents in a rehabilitation home or half-way house may be seen as the parents and
family retardates have missed by placement in an institution.
As for money, $15 to $20 is a great deal of money for many of
these young adults and the hope of a job good motivating factor.

Preparing for Work

Training for work should begin in the classroom, whether the
school is within the institution or a special education class in the
regular public school. They must learn good work behaviors
early as do their peers. Putting away materials, hanging up their
coats, being punctual and dependable are behaviors that are
initiated in the early school years. During the formal classroom
experience the individuals should gradually learn about the community to help them begin the process that may eventuate in
their taking a position in the work world. They should see other
people at work and especially some of those jobs which might
be within their capability. Part of this can be accomplished
through field trips which might include the behind-the-scenes
activities in a supermarket, a laundry, a small manufacturing
plant, and other places the retardates can understand.

Actual job training can begin while still in school on a work-
study arrangement or, for the institutionalized retardate, in a
part-time work program in the institution or workshop setting.
They can progress through work assignments which may increase
in complexity, require more independence and demand greater
dependability. It is crucial that the young retardate learn good
work habits early. A workshop within the institution can have a
variety of jobs for skill training. The trainees can progress
through a series of tasks and, when feasible, to skills that can
be directly transferred to jobs in the community.

To the degree that training programs for the retarded are
coordinated with actual available community jobs, the needs of
these employable young people are being met. Workshop jobs
or classroom training that prepares for non-existent jobs in the
youth's community may lead to discouragement and ultimate
failure in the work area of life. More and more effort has been

made to work out contracts with local industry for assured jobs after a successful training period. These training programs may involve several steps. The first could be a machine or assembly line set up at the institution or workshop for the retarded where they would learn the skills involved, as well as good work habits. Following this initial training, the length of which would be individually determined, a similar training period could be initiated at the actual plant where they would be employed so they could transfer their skills to the actual work setting but have an opportunity to become accustomed to plant hours, rules and practices before they were expected to produce at a competitive rate. During this additional training period an institutional trainer could work directly with the trainees. When they are ready, they could then be introduced to the actual job station with full pay and all the responsibilities inherent in the particular work. An institutional counselor would still be readily available to help out with any problems, but the client would be a bona fide company employee.

Preparing for Community Living

Just as the retarded youth's needs and industry needs are best met through a gradual introduction into the job, so is the retarded's involvement in community activities best served through gradual entry. A method currently being explored and used is the establishment of satellite centers for the retarded individuals of that area.

Half-way houses or rehabilitation homes have been available on a limited basis for many years. As generally operated now, when the trainee from the institution is considered ready to go into the community he is introduced to the home and helped to adjust to life at the home and on the job by a counselor from the institution. House parents take charge of the home and excepting for what help these people can offer, the residents have little else. There are generally no planned entertainment and recreational activities or educational programs. They work, take care of their rooms and clothes, and watch television.

One thrust which might be made in the establishment of

the satellite centers would be toward offering the residents a more complete life. A treatment team could come out to the center from the institution on a frequent and regular basis as well as responding to emergencies. Individual and group counseling, recreation, educational, and social needs would be met, in part, through a staff from the institution. Additionally, community volunteers and part-time paid personnel could teach the residents simple and essential things such as how and where to shop, where to go to the barber shop or beauty parlor and where to go for various kinds of entertainment and professional services. The residents may melled into the activities the general population enjoys.

A social director who takes charge of entertainment for several rehabilitation homes could arrange for short trips, occasional dining out, theater, bowling and other sports ventures; in brief, all the kinds of things other people do for enjoyment. Many of these people do not have a family willing or able to take them for a drive in the country or for a day in the city. It becomes a community responsibility to oversee living, plus programs.

When a satellite rehabilitation home is available for the retardate's transition from the institution, the necessary services can be provided which will help him acquire behaviors appropriate to a small nucleus of individuals similar to a family constellation. He must learn such things as sharing, dependability, and cooperation to degree never necessary in an institution. Instead of responding to institutional rules and regulations which have an impersonal quality, he must upon entering the rehabilitation home relate to a few individuals who are mutually dependent upon each other for personal satisfactions as well as essential daily necessities in such activities as food preparation and care of the home. There is a vast difference between knowing only that the rules are that a bed must be made before breakfast and realizing that unless each person's share of work is integrated with all the others in the group to assure the purchase of food and preparation of meals, there will be no breakfast. It is the difference between isolation and group activity; each becomes a valuable person contributing to his own and the group's welfare.

Each rehabilitation home could consist of about eight to fifteen individuals. Since there are various degrees of independent functioning in the groups of retardates who may be placed in rehabilitation homes, it should be possible to establish homes catering to different needs. It is envisioned that some homes may need more supervision and more programs within the center than others.

Those composed of all residents employed in the community or attending a vocational training program need more help in participating in activities outside the home than a unit having terminal work-shop residents. A home catering to employed workers might, however, also include as part of their family one or two whose job would be that of homemaker. In a center that has several homes in fairly close proximity this could be accomplished easily by having a skeleton house parent staff on duty during normal working hours to simply supervise employed homemakers. One houseparent could supervise several homes. If there were two homemakers in each home, for example, a houseparent would only have to stop in at each house occasionally during the day to make certain no problems have developed. By using two instead of one person the loneliness experienced by a former institutional resident can be avoided. This is a frequent problem in placing retarded persons in community jobs, sometimes because they are physically isolated as they might be in a private home and other times because they are excluded by fellow employees from the normal social on-the-job contacts.

Some Additional Considerations and Needs

For those who will never enter competitive employment, they might live in hostels close to a sheltered workshop. In fact, there could be a cluster of homes with a workshop as an integral part of the community. Local community residents living with families or with foster parents could also work at the shop and participate in social functions. The workshop could be part of a multi-purpose community center with the rest of the building being used for recreational, educational, medical and other functions.

An arrangement could be made with a local physician and nurse to hold scheduled clinic hours in the center if there is no community health clinic easily available to the resident. The satellite community could enter into a partnership agreement in an area needing clinic services to provide physical and mental health care for all the residents of a given section of the city with, of course, a pay-scale arrangement.

For some youths and adults who have been institutionalized the break from the institution to the community may be too sudden even when they have been well trained and are familiar with the job they are to perform. It may be necessary to have still another transitional stage of working outside the institution on a daily basis with a return to the familiar training school at night. Gradually the youth can spend one night in the hostel and increase the time away from the parent institution. The feasibility of that procedure may, of course, be somewhat dependent upon the distance from the institution to the hostel and job setting. Individual as well as group needs should be considered. If one person in the home needs help learning to read certain words essential to his job or life in the community, then a tutor should be provided to help him achieve the desired knowledge. Some of the activities desirable for the residents in terms of leisure-time planning, community orientation, and educational assistance could be contributed by voluntary action groups of concerned citizens. An aware community has many people who gladly contribute their time and talents to help others. It can and should be a mutually beneficial relationship between the rehabilitation home youth and adults and the general community residents. Participation and sharing will help break down barriers which set the retardates apart as different and of lesser value.

Those retardates who have never been institutionalized may at some time need the services of the rehabilitation home. This would especially be true if the family were no longer able to provide a home for their retarded member, whether permanently or temporarily.

There should be provisions made to accommodate these young people temporarily if a parent is ill or on vacation. All too often parents of retarded children are never able to go away alone. Even more critical is the problem of where a retarded person who has always lived at home and who is able to assume partial responsibility for himself goes when the parents can no longer provide for him. The hostels should be operated in such a manner that these people may also be served.

Those retardates who have never been institutionalized have different problems depending upon their acceptance by their families, and neighbors, the training they have received in school and community, the socioeconomic conditions in which they have lived, and their particular intellectual, physical and emotional state. Optimal conditions would, of course, provide the young retarded individual with an educational background commensurate with his ability and appropriate vocational training. Work study programs and rehabilitation workshop evaluation and training would prepare the individual for the employment situation best suited to him. Counselors from the school, Division of Vocational Rehabilitation, or the workshop would place these trainees in industry or business when feasible or terminal workshops, if that is their level of functioning. Unfortunately, not all community based retardates have experienced favorable development conditions. They may reach adulthood having experienced little practical training in either independent living or prevocational skills.

A satellite center could offer a good vocational evaluation service that would be helpful to anyone needing it. It could, in fact, make contractual arrangements with other agencies to help them with their vocational planning. Other groups which might need such services would be those with cerebral palsy and other severe physical disabilities.

One of the problems frequently encountered in a community is intra-agency rivalry and exclusiveness. It is the thesis of this paper that everyone needing community services can best be served if the impermeable walls between agencies be broken down and cooperative units established. If a blind or deaf intellectually limited youth can be served better at a school for the sensory deprived than at a facility for the retarded, his needs should be the only determining consideration, not artificial agency rules. It is conceivable that the satellite community could become a catalyst in services for all disabilities.

CHAPTER II

EPILEPSY

SHELDON A. GRAND AND ALAYNE K. GRAND

~~~~~~

~~~~~~

Social Attitudes Toward Epilepsy

Misinformation, fear, and therefore prejudice, have character-ized attitudes toward epilepsy from ancient times to the present. These attitudes have been prevalent in primitive society as well as in industrial society, among the highly educated (including physicians) as well as the masses and the laymen, and such attitudes have resisted significant change in the absence of sup-portive evidence and even in the presence of contradictory data. The greatest obstacle to the rehabilitation of the epileptic is, therefore, prejudicial social attitudes.

The earliest thoughts on the epileptic view him with spiritual possession of either a demonic or sacred and holy nature (Temkin, 1971). More often, he was not treated with reverence, and attempts at managing his condition ranged from operating on his skull to release evil spirits to various forms of social banishment. Hippocrates (fifth century, BC), suggesting that epilepsy is like other diseases in that it has natural causes, such

14

as some dysfunction of the brain, is credited with being the first investigator to offer a systematic and objective statement on seizures. While his observations were generally confirmed by interested physicians over the course of the next two thousand years, societal attitudes and misconceptions hardly changed. Primitive and simplistic treatments were used until the discovery of anti-convulsive types of drugs in the latter part of the 19th century. In 1870 John Hughlings Jackson (Taylor, 1952) made significant advancements toward understanding seizures, but there was almost no other progress in this field for another sixty years. Kram (Cruickshank, 1963) suggests that the absence of further exploration was not due to society's disinterest in epilepsy but rather to its fear. Thus, during the 19th century, efforts best characterized as attempts to protect society from the epileptic such as construction of isolated state institutions and implementation of restrictive legislation assumed precidence over further investigation of means to aid the epileptic with management of his disability. Kram (1963) further states "The impressions, social attitudes, and customs which developed and were strengthened throughout this period were accorded sufficient initial support and impetus to maintain them to an appreciable extent right up to the present (p. 373)." Commenting on the progress of psychiatry in the beginning of the 20th century, Szasz (1966) states:

In the initial decades of this century much was learned about epilepsy. As a result physicians gained better control of the epileptic process (which sometimes results in seizures). The desire to control the disease, however, seems to go hand in hand with a desire to control the diseased person. Thus epileptics were both helped and harmed: they were benefited insofar as their illness was more accurately diagnosed and better treated; they were injured insofar as they as persons, were stigmatized and socially segregated.

Was the placement of epileptics in *colonies* in their best interest? Or their exclusion from jobs, from driving automobiles, and from entering the United States as immigrants? It has taken decades of work, much of it still unfinished, to undo some of the oppressive social effects of *medical progress* in epilepsy, and to restore the epileptic to the social status he enjoyed before his disease became so well undestood (p. 448).

Some recent studies demonstrate the survival of primitive

attitudes toward epilepsy. In a study of Africans in South Rhodesia, Levy *et al.* (1964) reported that children with epilepsy are ridiculed and that adults tended to be unemployed and socially rejected. Giel (1968) found similar attitudes in Ethiopia. In a study of the Wapogora Tribe in Tanganyika, Aall-Jilek (1965) found that there was a 1.5 percent incidence of epilepsy, and that the epileptic was considered untouchable both during and after an attack. He was required to live alone and separated from the village and generally received poor care.

Studies of public attitudes toward epilepsy in western cultures indicate some improvement, but the presence of prejudice remains. Caveness *et al.* (1969) reports national random samples of attitudes in America between 1949 and 1969. In 1949, 47 percent of the respondents objected to their children associating with epileptic children, while twenty years later only 19 percent felt this way. In 1949, 45 percent of the sample agreed that epileptics should be employed in the regular job market, while 76 percent held this view in 1969. Prejudice against epilepsy was even stronger in West Germany where a study by Hauck (1968) reported that 27 percent of Germans and 4 percent of Americans surveyed believed that epilepsy was a form of insanity; and 37 percent of Germans and 13 percent of Americans objected to their child associating with an epileptic child. Investigators in Spain (Moya & Julian-Ramo, 1968) concluded that public opinion there reflects apathy and ignorance and seems to associate epilepsy with insanity, unemployability, and exclusion from normal education.

Several studies reflecting prejudice toward epileptics by employers in America will be discussed later in this chapter. But perhaps the most dramatic portrayal of society's prejudice toward epileptics is manifested by physicians who are trained in scientific thinking and identified with a helping and humanistic role. Bagley (1971) cites several examples of unwarranted medical opinion on epilepsy and further states:

> There is evidence, then, that in other areas besides epilepsy physicians have been capable of irrationality and prejudice. The writer has gained the strong impression in reviewing the literature on the connections between organic brain injury and psychosis

that studies in this field, including those carried out in the early part of the century, have been carried out with much greater scientific rigor and sophistication than those in the field of epilepsy in the same period. It seems that physicians are most likely to adopt irrational attitudes (like other members of the community) in areas which arose the passions deeply, such as the problems of sexual conduct and behavior. Epilepsy appears to be one of these areas (p. 109).

In an attempt to explain the extreme and widespread prejudice against epilepsy, Bagley hypothesizes a common but unconscious fear of a sudden loss of physical and emotional control. The epileptic is feared and in turn rejected, because he evokes our own fears of loss of control over forbidden impulses. A similar process has been hypothesized as the basis of prejudice toward homosexuality and incest.

Our society's widespread ignorance about epilepsy is tragically exemplified by legislation aimed at preventing them from marrying, reproducing, and driving automobiles. Eugenic marriage and sterilization statutes are based on the belief that epilepsy is primarily a hereditary condition, and, furthermore, that it is a form of feeblemindedness or may lead to mental deterioration. Today, of course, we know that both premises are fallacious. The first eugenic marriage law was enacted in Connecticut in 1895 and as recently as the mid-fifties a total of seventeen states had laws prohibiting marriage of epileptics (Barrow & Fabing, 1966). Finally in 1969 the last state having a law of this nature, West Virginia, amended the statute completely freeing the United States of eugenic marriage laws applicable to epileptics.

The first eugenic sterilization law was enacted in Indiana in 1907 and in 1969 there were still eleven states with eugenic statutes applying to epileptics: Arizona, Delaware, Indiana, Mississippi, Montana, New Hampshire, Oklahoma, South Carolina, Utah, Virginia and West Virginia (Livingston, 1972). Barrow and Fabing (1966) pointed out that although sterilization has not been practised in many years, the existence of the law reinforces the continuation of the stigma associated with epilepsy. These authors also note that the actual number of epileptics who have been sterilized is not known, but that more than sixty thousand persons have been sterilized under these statutes; the majority of these persons were probably mentally ill but mental defectives were also a target of the legislation.

The other type of restrictive legislation which affects the adjustment of the epileptic is drivers' license laws. A 1965 survey of all fifty states concerning their practices in respect to issuance of drivers' licenses to epileptics indicated favorable changes in comparison with the study done ten years earlier (Barrow & Fabing, 1966). All states now grant licenses to epileptics who can provide evidence of reasonable seizure control. While most states require a seizure free period of one year, some require a two year free period, and only two states require a three year period. Another difference among states pertains to the role of anti-convulsive drugs, with twenty-two states requiring that seizure control be achieved through medication and twenty-one states having no such requirement. In all states medical confirmation of the seizure free period is required. Some states require two medical statements while a few states rely on their own medical boards for final adjudication of an epileptic's license application.

Medical Aspects

A simple and also comprehensive definition of epilepsy is not available, but most physicians use the term to imply a brain disorder resulting in a tendency toward recurring seizures which are frequently characterized by loss of consciousness (Schmidt & Wilder, 1968). There is less than total understanding of the relationship between brain function and seizures, resulting in disagreement over an acceptable classification system of epilepsy (Livingston, 1972). However, the most frequently used systems are two fold, first, classifying the disorder in terms of its etiology, and then, according to a clinical description of the seizure pattern.

Classifying seizures according to their causes usually results in differentiating between *symptomatic* or *organic* seizures and *idiopathic* seizures. Symptomatic seizures are produced by definite alterations in the brain tissue or its blood vessels caused by conditions such as congenital defects, tumors, abscesses, blood clots, head trauma, infections, cerebral vascular accidents and metabolic disorders. When seizures develop and no cerebral lesion or alteration can be demonstrated, they are classified as idiopathic seizures. These seizures of undetermined etiology are also known as *cryptogenic, essential, pure, primary, true* and *genetic* seizures (Livingston, 1972). Approximately 75 percent of all cases of epilepsy are considered to be idiopathic.

The total incidence of epilepsy in our population is estimated at 1 percent (Merck Manual, 1961). Accurate figures are not available primarily because a diagnosis of epilepsy is not a reportable disorder in most states. As recently as 1969 only the states of Connecticut, Delaware, Indiana, Nevada, New Jersey and Oregon reported diagnosis of epilepsy by name, while in other states epilepsy disorders were indistinguishable from the general category of disorders characterized by lapses of consciousness.

The incidence of epilepsy has been increasing due to the following factors: (1) improved obstetric and pediatric care which results in survival of infants who previously would have died; (2) improved treatment of conditions such as brain tumors, head injuries, meningitis and encephalitis also results in greater survival rates; (3) decreased stigma associated with the disease which has resulted in people having less fear of revealing their disorder; (4) improved diagnostic skill due to the electroencephalagram (EEG).

The classification system of epilepsy based on the seizure patterns has the greatest acceptance among clinicians and investigators. Four types of seizures are usually delineated: Grand mal, petit mal, psychomotor, and focal. Grand mal seizures are usually (in over 50 percent of the cases) preceded by an aura or period of warning which lasts less than a minute and may include a variety of sensations, feelings, and muscle movements. While the patient often cannot describe the episode, reports of bright lights, unpleasant odors, strange sounds, tingling sensations, twitching or muscle jerks, restlessness, anxiety, and mental confusion have been cited. Following the aura, the patient may cry out, and then lose consciousness. A rigid stiffening of the body (tonic phase) quickly changes to generalized jerking movements (clonic phase). During these phases there may be tongue biting and bowel or bladder incontinence, as well as irregular breathing and changes in skin color. If the seizure is brief, the patient may be able to resume normal activity. However, following a long seizure, the patient usually drifts into a state of sleep, or he may become conscious and seem confused before going to sleep. Upon waking he generally complains of fatigue, muscular aches, and other ill feelings. In most cases the tonic and clonic phases last up to a few minutes, and recurrence varies from several times a day to once every few years. This type of epilepsy may occur at any age.

Petit mal seizures consist of periodic lapses of consciousness which usually last from five to thirty seconds. The most common symptom is a sudden staring into space with occasional rolling of the eyes back into the head. Other petit mal symptoms may include mild jerking movements of the head or upper extremities and automatisms consisting of repetitive chewing and swallowing movements, smacking of lips, and sometimes mumbling speech. These automatisms are also found in psychomotor epilepsy patients. The petit mal spell terminates abruptly, and the patient can usually resume his normal activity. These spells are usually daily occurrences, and some patients experience as many as one hundred a day. Petit mal seizures usually occur between four and eight years of age and rarely before three or after fifteen years of age.

Psychomotor seizures are the most complex and may include staring, followed by automatisms such as chewing, drooling, lip smacking and muttering, as well as more complex automatisms such as walking around, touching and searching for objects. Sometimes this behavior appears to be quite purposeful, but following any of these attacks, the patient is almost always unaware of what transpired. Other psychomotor patterns are pulling of the body and head to one side and what are referred to as psychic seizures or the display of a range of extreme emotional reactions such as delusions, hallucinations, laughing, crying, and changes in perception and thought. Psychomotor seizures are found in older children and adults and may last several minutes or longer. In many patients these seizures are daily occurrences.

Focal seizures may be motor or sensory attacks which begin in one part of the body and may spread to other parts and even result in a grand mal seizure. However, the attack may be limited to one part of the body. Frequently, they occur without loss of consciousness, and the attacks may take the form of muscle twitchings or numbness of some body part. Jacksonian seizures which are limited to one side of the body are a type of focal motor seizure. These types of seizures are rarely found among children.

Epilepsy involves a malfunctioning of the brain which sometimes can be specified (symptomatic) and usually is associated with an abnormal EEG measurement. However, it must be noted that there are cases of abnormal EEGs and specific brain defects similar to those found in symptomatic epilepsy which do not result in seizures. These exceptions as well as other data have led many investigators to conclude that individuals possess varying seizure thresholds, which, in conjunction with other physiological and psychological stress factors, may result in epilepsy. Similarly, the role of heredity in causing epilepsy is also complex, and the most definitive statement is probably that heredity can be a partial or sole cause of epilepsy. It has been suggested that a convulsive predisposition is inherited rather than epilepsy itself (Gastaut *et al.*, 1969). However, most present day medical opinion holds that the majority of the epilepsies are not inheritable. Treatment of epilepsy is primarily by drugs such as Dilantin and barbituates with a high rate of successful seizure control now possible. It is estimated that complete seizure control is obtained in 50 percent of the cases, with reduced frequency or severity of seizures in another 30 percent, so that vocational rehabilitation is feasible for a large majority of epileptics. Selection of the appropriate drug or combination of drugs, however, is a highly individualized matter and may involve a long period of time before the effective prescription can be determined for a given patient.

Personality and Epilepsy

It has been commonly held for many centuries that epileptics have abnormal personalities (Temkin, 1971). During the past century the progression of beliefs and professional statements concerning the behavioral or psychological correlates of epilepsy paralleled the evolution of social attitudes toward the condition. Guerrant *et al.* (1962) observes specific trends of thinking about the personality of epileptics and divides the last one hundred years into four periods. *The Period of Epileptic Deterioration* (late 19th century) is characterized by the following views: The majority of epileptics show intellectual impairments; intellectual impairment is more common in personality deterioration marked by irritability, apathy, and social withdrawal; insanity is not a frequent occurrence, but the incidence is higher among epileptics than among non-epileptics; intellectual limitations in idiopathic epilepsy are due to seizures but may be reversed when seizure control is achieved; although heredity is a major cause of epilepsy, intellectual and personality deficiencies are related to the seizures rather than to heredity. *The Period of the Epileptic Character* (1900-1930) includes the following character-istics: Epileptics experience disorders of mood and attitude which usually are followed by intellectual deterioration; the epileptic is a constitutionally or congenitally inferior organism which accounts for his intellectual impairment; most common in per-sonality traits are egocentricity, supersensitiveness, eccentricity, rigidity, impulsiveness and apathy. *The Period of Normality* (1930-present) reflected the view that there is no epileptic personality, and that the majority of epileptics are of normal intelligence and personality. Limitations in either of these spheres were attributed to brain damage, uncontrolled seizures, drugs, and social rejection. *The Period of Psychomotor Peculiarity* (1948-present) supports the views of the Period of Normality except in the case of psychomotor epileptics, the majority of whom are observed to have a variety of psychiatric disturbances. This view is commonly held today and the etiology of the personality disorder is generally ascribed to organic factors (temporal lobe lesions), rather than to the patient's reactions to his social environment.

Another comprehensive discussion of the varying views toward the epileptic's personality is presented by Tizard (1962) who describes five different theories or belief systems. The oldest notion holds that there is an epileptic personality characterized by emotional explosiveness, perseveration, viscosity in emotional and intellectual spheres, impulsivity, selfishness, and sexual and criminal deviance. In addition, epilepsy and these personality disturbances were considered to be of genetic origin. A second major theory states that there is no epileptic personality, and that the incidence of personality abnormality is the same for epileptics and non-epileptics. A third theory is that there is no epileptic personality, but the incidence of personality problems is higher among epileptics than among non-epileptics. A fourth belief is in agreement that an epileptic personality doesn't exist, but states that epileptics demonstrate personality traits similar to those of patients with brain damage. The fifth theory suggests that while there is no universal epileptic personality, each type of epilepsy is associated with a different personality pattern.

Bagley (1971) does an exhaustive review of the literature in this area of personality disorders in epilepsy and stresses that the methodology of many research studies was extremely poor, resulting in contradictory findings and all too frequently unsubstantiated conclusions. He offers the following hypothesis to explain psychological disturbances among epileptics:

> Personality disorder in epilepsy is the result of the complex interaction of the personality existing before the onset of epilepsy, the effect of the epilepsy itself, brain damage underlying the epilepsy, the parental reactions, the environmental reactions to the epileptic child and perhaps the effect of anti-convulsants (p. 50).

In his analysis of the data concerning the associations between epilepsy and psychosis, temporal lobe epilepsy and personality disturbance, epilepsy and criminal behavior, and epilepsy and intellectual functioning, he repeatedly states that no firm conculsions can be drawn until more adequate research is conducted. His cautions against inferring simple conclusions on the basis of limited experimentation in such a complex area of investigation is well taken. He does seem to imply, however, increasing evidence for interpreting many of the above mentioned relationships in terms of some underlying brain damage as a likely causal factor of both the epilepsy and the abnormal behavior.

The World of Work and the Epileptic

Vocational attainment is one of the means by which most individuals secure a degree of self esteem, but for the epileptic, nowhere does the destructive prejudice towards epilepsy find greater expression than on the job market. Public health sources estimate that between 15 percent and 20 percent of the epileptic population of employable ages are involuntarily unemployed (Frank, 1969). Furthermore, in the last twenty years only 2 percent of the total population of successful rehabilitants have been epileptics (Goldin *et al.*, 1971).

One study documenting the degree of prejudice toward epileptics was conducted by Rickard, Triandis & Patterson (1963). The authors surveyed the attitudes of personnel directors and school administrators in respect to hiring practices with several disabled groups. Both were asked to determine whether or not they would recommend hiring individuals representing various disability classes for the positions of accountant or third grade teacher. Their responses indicated the greatest prejudice toward epileptics, ex-prisoners, and ex-psychiatric patients, in that order. Factors found to mitigate the employers' attitudes were degree of competence and sociability; sex was not a determinant of hirability except in respect to ex-prisoners and ex-mental patients, where greater prejudice was directed toward women.

Another survey of personnel officers in industrial areas was conducted in New York City by the Federation Employment and Guidance Service (1969). The officers were interviewed in respect to their hiring practices with the following groups: Cardiac, epileptic, orthopedic, cerebral palsied, and visually impaired. The percentage of firms reporting experience with each of the above classes was as follows: Orthopedic, 88 percent; cardiac, 72 percent; epileptic, 44 percent; visually impaired, 12 percent; cerebral palsied, 6 percent. The percentages of firms in the sample excluding the handicapped from employment were: Visual, 93 percent; epilepsy, 81 percent; cerebral palsied, 69 percent; cardiac, 41 percent; orthopedic, 10 percent. The statistics illustrate again that in comparison with other handicapped groups, epileptics are classed among the least desirable employees and among the most functionally handicapped.

In yet another survey on employers' attitudes toward the epileptic (Risch, 1962), 314 companies engaged in a variety of activities (food processing, printing and publishing, etc.) were questioned. It was determined that less than .1 percent of the companies' employees were epileptic, that is only fifty-nine of the total 64,811 people employed by the 314 companies. Only twelve, or 4 percent, of the companies currently employed epileptics, while eleven had employed thirty-five during the past ten years but presently did not employ any. Twelve reported that they had no hiring restrictions, while thirty-six would hire only those with controlled seizures for non-dangerous work, and 73 percent would not knowingly hire an epileptic. In response to the question of why they wouldn't hire a person with this condition, 58 percent stated that they feared the epileptic might injure himself, and 23 percent feared he might injure others. Another 4 percent were concerned that the epileptic would lose excessive time from work due to the condition. Of those who had had experience with epileptics, only one reported dissatisfaction, complaining that the one person whom he had hired drank excessively, while twenty-two respondents stated that in regard to quality, production, safety, absenteeism, advancement, acceptance by fellow workers, and participation in company activities, the epileptic performed as well or better than fellow co-workers. Those who had never hired an epileptic had a more negative attitude toward them. Of the group of epileptics currently employed in this sample, most of the industrial respondents reported that they were employed in lower status, unskilled occupations.

More discouraging still are the results of a study by Sands (1970) in which he determined that a public education campaign directed toward policy making executives did not alter their attitudes toward hiring epileptics. Furthermore, Sands found that the general impression of executives in respect to epileptics was that they were able and not handicapped, even though the administrators wouldn't hire them. The executives also asserted that their attitudes were fixed, had not changed in the last ten years, and were not likely to change in the next few years.

However, contradicting employers' attitudes toward epileptics is evidence indicating that the epileptic's performance is comparable to, or better than his fellow employees. A study by L. J. Goldwater (1968) on epilepsy and cerebral vascular disease in an industrial population revealed that 72 percent had job performance ratings equal to, or better than co-workers, lower accident rates, and no significant differences in absenteeism. This is further supported by a Department of Labor study (#923) in which it was found that no significant differences existed in respect to the accident experience of epileptics and unimpaired workers, and that work attendance records were as good among epileptics as among the non-disabled. Although employers express fears that hiring the epileptic will increase their Workmen's Compensation, the truth of the matter is that in only highly unusual circumstances might this occur. In a study conducted by Sands (1966) of closed compensation cases in New York State for a thirteen year period, it was found that the number of cases due to epileptic seizures averaged 8.1 a year with an average award of $1,261.60. For a comparable period covering claims resulting from coughing and sneezing, the cases averaged 20.2 a year with an average award of $300.40.

In respect to Workmen's Compensation laws certain facts should be kept in mind and relayed to employers. The compensation premium is based on degree of hazard in the industry and the total accident experience of the employees. The premium is not affected by the presence of handicapped workers, and as studies have indicated, the epileptic is no greater risk than any other employee as long as he is employed in a situation appropriate to his disability and is not placed in hazardous circumstances such as working at great heights, or driving heavy machinery.

Due to the prejudice toward epileptics evidenced among employers, the question arises of whether or not the prospective employer should be told about the disability. Some would agree that concealment is the only means of successfully obtaining a job, but on the other hand, this course also is fraught with unpleasant results. As Patterson (1962) states, "With the ever present danger of discovery, the client is always haunted by the fear of being discovered. This is not a good state of mind for anyone to be in. It is particularly of potential danger for the epileptic since the increased tension may make effective control of the seizures more difficult (p. 158)."

Unfortunately, the epileptic is forced to choose between the proverbial lesser of two evils. However, some material indicates that although the epileptic will face greater difficulty in finding employment after disclosing the existence of his condition, his chances of remaining on the job afterward are greater than those of the individual who passes. In the latter group the hobgoblin of tension and resulting seizures often destroys their pose. Forest of OVR Atlanta (1962) documents an experiment with two groups of epileptics. One group was instructed to tell the employer about the disability and the other group was instructed to conceal the condition. It was found that those who told the employer stayed on the job longer, although they initially had more difficulty finding a job, while those who did not tell the employer "sometimes developed a considerable amount of tension and had seizures as a result (p. 14)."

The problem of disclosure raises other considerations as well. First of all, the epileptic client who elects to deal with his disability openly provides the employer and those around him with a greater understanding of the condition. On the other hand, those who pass, although their desire to do so is understandable, may create resistance on the part of the employer if the fact of the disability becomes known. Then, too, the client's decision to pass or not to pass has ethical implications for the counselor as well. As Patterson (1962) states:

> The counselor has a responsibility which requires that he be open and honest about his client. It seems to me that the counselor must be free to tell the employer the nature of the disability. On the other hand, the counselor should not tell the employer without the consent of the client. The client should reach the decision freely

and without coercion. He may decide to attempt to find employment himself without telling employers about his disability. The handling of this problem, assisting the client to reach his own decision, is one of the functions of the counselor in preparing the client for employment (p. 159).

A Successful Employment Program for Epileptics

One successful model for a comprehensive approach to aiding the epileptic in his quest for employment is The Three Cities Job Clinic and Services System (Frank, 1969), a demonstration project under the auspices of the Department of Labor. The program supplemented services of existing agencies with intensive vocational group counseling and placement services of its own.

This program could not be replicated easily by existing agencies, but some of the program practices could inform current agency procedures. For instance, the recruitment policy used resulted in inclusion of individuals, like minority group members or culturally deprived epileptics, who frequently do not avail themselves of services. In contacting this group as well as other participants, project field workers reached out to them (by mail, telephone, or personal contacts), rather than waiting for them to ask for aid. Liberal intake procedures allowed for the acceptance of almost everyone contacted. Neither multiple disability nor inadequate seizure control were basis for rejection. Once accepted, the clients participated in a structured group counseling program where their disabilities and vocational prospects were discussed and their assets as job seekers emphasized. Groups were often led by epileptics who had faced and overcome similar problems. Sessions also included discussion and rehearsal of the various skills needed for the employment quest. Job interviews were role played and practiced, tests taken, and applications filled out. Concurrent with the group process, project workers publicized the program in the community and contacted prospective employers. If an employer demonstrated interest, he immediately received possible future prospects. In other words, rather than selling the general group of unemployed epileptics, project representatives offered specific clients for specific jobs, thus avoiding oversell and vagueness. At a point when the client had reached a level of job readiness, employers were re-contacted in order to insure their continued interest, and the client sent out for an interview. In this manner, participants were shielded from facing another rejection on the basis of disability alone. After the client had been placed, follow-up services provided for continued support in dealing with on-the-job problems. It was found that contacts in the first few days after the client started a job aided the person in dealing with the seizure provoking anxiety that a new situation often causes.

However, some of these procedures are suited primarily for a city where a concentrated group of individuals is within easy access of programs and employers. The problems of the epileptic living in a rural or small city region are multiplied as transportation often becomes the major detriment to his participation in a rehabilitation program. At this time, few agencies, private or public, provide transportation for individuals out of reach of public transportation, and the epileptic's problems in obtaining a driver's license are many. Consequently, effective rehabilitation programming for the rural epileptic, as well as other groups, is dependent on resolution of this one basic logistical problem.

The Family and the Epileptic

Like any disabled individual, the epileptic's adjustment to his disability is predicated to a large extent on his family's handling of the feelings which the child's condition may evoke. The presence of a handicapped child often elicits guilt and shame in the parents and raises questions of who is to blame for the condition. Given the alleged hereditary basis of epilepsy, parents may fear that they are tainted with *bad blood* which may doom their children to disablement. If religion is an informing component in their lives, they may perceive the birth of an epileptic as God's punishment for sin and the child himself as proof of their wrongdoing. Unfortunately, the myths surrounding epilepsy which were discussed earlier reinforce such misconceptions. If the family is not aided in working through their negative feelings, then guilt and shame can become translated into overprotection or rejection, both of which have regrettable psychological consequences for the child. A study conducted by Grunberg & Pond

(1957) on conduct disorders in epileptic children compared fifty-three epileptic chilren with conduct disorders and fifty-three psychologically normal epileptic children. The results showed that the greatest difference between the two groups was in the realm of social environment, the children with conduct disorders having more disturbed family relationships. The authors found that the most significant environmental factors were disturbed maternal feelings toward the child and experiences by the child of breaks and alterations in the environment.

By implication, then, the professional's attempts to aid the epileptic will necessarily include the family. Research evidence supports this approach and although most of the existing material focuses on the epileptic child, the studies have certain validity for older individuals as well. In one such study conducted by Defries & Browder (1952), two groups of children, a boy's group and a girl's group, and two groups of mothers met for an hour at weekly intervals. The therapist working with the mothers' group assumed a non-directive approach responding only to issues raised by them. At first, the women used the sessions for a general discussion of epilepsy but gradually they raised more pressing problems surrounding the mother-child relationship. A similar format was used in the children's groups where the therapists introduced the topic of epilepsy in early sessions but otherwise were also non-directive. The results of the therapy program were positive. Of the six girls, two demonstrated improved behavior at home and two improved in school work. In the boy's group the boys became more accepting of their own disability as they learned to accept the conditions of others. Here, too, behavior improved and aggression became better controlled. Members of the mothers' group evidenced greater acceptance of their child's condition, and mothers who had previously been over protective now became more permissive with their children. The mothers as a whole also displayed less anxiety over their children's seizures.

In another group program conducted by Baus, Letson, & Russell (1958), the sessions were aimed at informing parents on the topic of epilepsy. Different professionals—pediatricians, social workers, and psychologists—addressed the parents in five weekly sessions of an hour to an hour and a half each. Medical, social, and psychological issues surrounding epilepsy were discussed as well as the parents' attitudes and conflicts surrounding the condition. The clinical results revealed that sessions aided the parents in venting their frustrations and dealing with previously denied feelings. Thus, they were able to correct some of their misconceptions and prejudices in respect to epilepsy.

An accurate understanding of epilepsy is a vital factor in helping both the epileptic and his family to assume a constructive attitude toward the condition. Although the counselor will usually have to assume the role of informant, whenever possible the aid of a neurologist or physician experienced in the handling of epileptics should be obtained, since a medical person has more validity than a counselor in the realm of physiological issues. Setting up a group situation for information giving is the most advisable approach from a practical standpoint and, as was illustrated in the studies, from a therapeutic standpoint, for parents discover that they are not alone with their problems.

Of course, many of the clients whom the counselor encounters are older and neither the client nor his family have ever received the type of therapeutic intervention described. By dint of social difficulties and/or overprotection from the family resulting in increased dependency, the client may still be living with his parents, having become locked into a dependency role mutually satisfying to all involved. Rehabilitation efforts in the direction of independence and self sufficiency frequently disrupt well-established patterns, and the family may undermine the client's positive strivings. In cases of this nature, the counselor's best efforts are likely to have little effect in resolving long standing problems, and the best approach is likely to be one of involving the client in a program which necessitates independent living away from the home. However, this doesn't necessarily preclude continued counseling contacts with the family, for the client will probably need familial approval for his new endeavors. In achieving the goal of family acceptance the counselor, then, should utilize the physician, family group approach, or any positive force in the environment to aid the family in its adjustment.

Counseling Considerations

Since epilepsy is an unobservable condition, the epileptic can easily conceal his disabiilty in most situations. Although passing is an excellent means of avoiding rejection or ostracism, the psychological consequences are usually less than beneficial. Tension and anxiety are maintained at high levels with the incumbent possibility of increased seizures. Basic feelings of guilt, shame, and inadequacy are perpetuated, for the person never risks testing out the reality of his felt unworthiness. With seizures an unpredictable threat to the pose, the only guaranteed means of concealment becomes social isolation or distance.

Kleck (1968) reports on a study of disclosure patterns among epileptics in which subjects were urged to disclose to others outside the family. The results were as follows "The sense of stigmatization began to break down when a person risked exposure outside of the family and discovered that the reactions of others were not strongly negative (p. 17)." However, he also found that the subjects tended to disclose only to one or two carefully chosen people. Often the person was a close friend. Consequently, the "subjects tended to view positive reactions as exceptions to the norm, i.e., they continued to expect rejecting responses from most people (Kleck, 1968, p. 20)."

It would appear, then, that although resolution of disability related feelings rests partially in social openness, openness alone is not the total answer. For the fact remains that epilepsy is a stigmatizing disorder and some people would reject the epileptic. From the counselor's standpoint, the issue of disclosure will have relevance if the counselee is a person who is suffering extensively from feelings related to the disability and is maintaining an extreme degree of social isolation. Aiding the client to perceive the necessity of openness with a few trusted others may be helpful in at least minimizing negative feelings. On the other hand, the counselor should use discretion and never impose on the client a demand that may be unrealistic or could be destructive. Even though passing can be psychologically debilitating, there are instances where it is advisable, for example, superficial social situations, or instances where revelation might result in rejection which the client is not strong enough to handle. Ideally, the counselor will discuss with the client the relevant meanings and implications of passing for that client. After the client has gained understanding and awareness of his own behavior, he will be better able to choose the course of action best suited for him.

Other issues that arise in counseling with the epileptic may center upon the client's denial of the disability. The person who fails to adhere to his medication schedule, or ignores the cautions in respect to alcohol intake, is probably an individual who is attempting to deny the existence of his epilepsy. Further evidence of denial can become manifested in the person's pursuit of a vocation or activity that is physically hazardous due to seizures. In the event that the client reports any of the above, the counselor should bear in mind the possible emotional meaning of the client's behavior, and aid him in dealing with the basic feelings that have given rise to his actions.

Although no special therapeutic bag of tricks exists for epileptics or any other group, certain aspects of the therapeutic process may assume more importance in dealing with the epileptic client. If the client has experienced a good deal of rejection due to the disability, the counselor's acceptance will be of paramount concern. Therefore, if the counselor is to be of aid and give the client full acceptance, the counselor himself must become aware of his own feelings about all aspects of the disability and his own attitudes toward epilepsy.

Due also to disability related experiences, the client may have difficulty in trusting a counselor and forming a relationship in which disability issues or any painful issues can be dealt with openly. The only approach available to the counselor is a non-directive one in which the client has latitude to test out the counselor and gradually develop enough trust in him to reveal those feelings which are troublesome. The worst thing that a counselor can do with an individual like this is to bludgeon him with a series of confrontations aimed at *opening him up.*

Another highly possible circumstance in counseling a person with epilepsy is overt dependency on the counselor, especially if the person has been over-protected. The counselor shouldn't become unduly concerned in the event that this occurs, for a necessary phase of dependency has to be present before an individual feels secure enough to reach out for those experiences which will ultimately result in independence. As with the issue of trust, the counselor can't push a client toward freedom, or expect him to suddenly learn to live without a sizeable anchor in his life. The counselor has to be willing to accept the role that parents have played, the difference being that rather than placing restrictions, the counselor aids the client in removing restrictions.

Undoubtedly, the number of tools available to the counselor in aiding the client are many and varied. However, the group approach for either vocational or personal counseling seems to be quite fruitful. As Bradley (1947) points out, groups are particularly beneficial with epileptics since they provide vehicles of interaction to the often socially isolated individual. Given this and the epileptic's other needs, the formation of a homogeneous group of epileptics could be beneficial, bearing in mind, of course, several other alternatives. For example, consideration must be given to the extent of withdrawal which the client may display. An individual who has avoided close relationships most of his or her life would be threatened by a group situation, and probably would require the experiences of trust and acceptance which individual counseling offers prior to entrance into a group. On the other hand, an individual who displays only minor maladjustment with respect to his disability could easily stagnate in *an epileptics only* group. For someone of this ilk, group counseling with people representing other disability groups may be the advisable approach, thus giving the person an opportunity to perceive that he is not unique due to his disability.

Many of the studies in which group counseling was successfully employed with epileptic clients were conducted with children or adolescents. Certainly this particular group faces the most disability related set of problems, for the youthful peer group is critical and likely to have little understanding of epilepsy. The epileptic child or adolescent, like all of his or her age group, is eager to win the approval of his peers, a necessary element to the formation of an independent adult personality. Yet, the epileptic child is burdened with the knowledge of his disability and of the real or imagined social value of epilepsy. Superficial relationships are obviously an excellent means of avoiding rejection, although a lonely course for the young epileptic. Groups, then, of others with the same disability provide a necessary outlet to the young person who has either been denied or has denied himself an important means of achieving adulthood.

However, an adult with epilepsy or any other disability faces an entirely different set of life situations. The social ramifications of disability remain but not with the same critical impact as during adolescence when one is in continual contact with his peer group. The problems now are those of a vocational nature, problems surrounding a marital or family situation or problems of finding a mate, etc., all of which may or may not relate to the existence of a handicap. The extent to which an individual's life situation or problems of daily living are the result of the disability will have to determine the usefulness of exposing him or her to a group of other individuals with the same disability.

It would seem, then, that group counseling with an homogenous group of epileptics will probably be most functional with younger epileptics for whom social, parental, and vocational problems may be directly related to epilepsy. However, caution should be used in assigning an older person to a primarily therapeutic group with other epileptics. While the younger epileptic may find social acceptance for the first time in his life in a group of this nature, the older epileptic may be falsely encouraged to perceive all of his life problems as disability related when they are not.

Although the ideal outcome in counseling with any disabled client is a state of disability acceptance, certain realistic considerations should be kept in mind. First of all, epilepsy is a socially stigmatizing disability. The client probably has and always will experience a degree of social rejection that may prevent him from achieving the ideal. Secondly, years of negative experiences related to the disability, such as over-protection or rejection by family or peers, may have resulted in a myriad of problems that only psychotherapy could resolve. Then, too, the issue of epilepsy may not even become a significant concern in counseling sessions, especially if the client faces a variety of problems of more immediate import. In this instance, the counselor should deal with those things of importance to the client and direct the session toward the issue of the disability only if the presenting problem is directly related to feelings associated with the disability, or if the client is engaging in self-destructive behavior in respect to the disability. In most cases, then, the more realistic objective is one in which the client can be aided in at least minimizing the number of areas affected by the existence of epilepsy.

REFERENCES

Aall-Jilek, L.: Epilepsy in the Wapagora Tribe in Tanganyika. *Acta Psychiat. Scand.*, 61:57-86, 1965. Cited by C. Bagley, *The Social Psychology of the Child with Epilepsy.* London, Routledge & Kegan Paul, 1971, p. 98.

Bagley, C.: *The Social Psychology of the Child with Epilepsy.* London, Routledge & Kegan Paul, 1971.

Barkemeyer, L. E.: Selling of the employer. In *Total Rehabilitation of the Epileptic—Gateway to Employment.* Washington, D.C., U.S. Department of Health, Education, and Welfare, 1962.

Barrow, L., and Fabing, D.: *Epilepsy and the Law* (2nd ed.) New York, Harper & Row, 1966.

Baus, G. J.; Letson, L. L., and Russell, E.: Group sessions for parents of children with epilepsy. *Journal of Pediatrics,* 52:270-273, 1958.

Bradley, C.: Treatment of the convulsive child in a children's psychiatric hospital. *Nervous Child,* 6:81, 1947.

Caveness, W. J.; Merrit, W. H., and Gallup, G. H.: A survey of public attitudes toward epilepsy in 1969 with an indication in trends over the past twenty years. *Epilepsia, 10:*429-440, 1969.

Defries, Z., and Browder, S.: Group therapy with epileptic children and their mothers. *Bulletin of the New York Academy of Medicine,* 28:235-240, 1952.

Federation Employment and Guidance Service: Survey of employer's practices and policies in hiring of physically impaired workers. Cited by J. W. McDaniel, *Physical Disability and Human Behavior.* New York, Pergamon Press, 1969, p. 34.

Forrest, J. W.: Vocational rehabilitation. In *Total Rehabilitation of the Epileptic—Gateway to Employment.* Washington, D.C., U.S. Department of Health, Education, and Welfare, 1962.

Frank, D. S.: *The Multi-troubled Jobseeker: The Case of the Jobless Worker with a Convulsive Disorder.* Washington, D.C., The Epilepsy Foundation, 1967.

Frank, D. S.: *Three Cities Job Clinic and Services System Manual.* Washington, D.C., The Epilepsy Foundation, 1969.

Gastaut, H., *et al.*: Epilepsy and heredity. *Epilepsia, 10*:3-96, 1969.

Giel, R.: The epileptic outcast. *East African Med. J., 45*:27-31, 1968. Cited by C. Bagley, *The Social Psychology of the Child with Epilepsy.* London, Routledge & Kegan Paul, 1971, p. 98.

Goldin, G. J.; Perry, S. L.; Margolin, K. L.; Stotsky, B. A., and Foster, J. C.: *The Rehabilitation of the Young Epileptic.* Lexington, Mass., D. C. Heath, 1971.

Goldwater, L. J.: *The Investigation of Epilepsy and Cerebral Vascular Diseases in an Industrial Population.* Cited by G. N. Wright and A. B. Trotter, *Rehabilitation Research.* Madison, University of Wisconsin, 1968.

Grunberg, S., and Pond, D. A.: Conduct disorders in epileptic children. *Journal of Neurology, Neurosurgery and Psychiatry, 20*:65-68, 1957.

Guerrant, J. J.; Anderson, W.; Fisher, A.; Weinstein, M. R.; Jaros, R. M., and Deskins, A.: *Personality in Epilepsy.* Springfield, Charles C Thomas, Publisher, 1962.

Kleck, R.: *Self Disclosure Patterns Among Epileptics.* Hanover, Dartmouth College, 1968.

Kram, C.: Epilepsy in children and youth. In W. M. Cruickshank Ed.), *Psychology of Exceptional Children and Youth* (2nd ed.). Englewood Cliffs, Prentice-Hall, 1963.

Levy, L.; Forbes, J., and Parirenyatwa, T.: Epilepsy in Africans. *Cent. African Journal of Medicine. 10,* 1964. Cited by C. Bagley, *The Social Psychology of the Child with Epilepsy.* London, Routledge & Kegan Paul, 1971, p. 98.

Livingston, S.: *Comprehensive Management of Epilepsy in Infancy, Childhood and Adolescence.* Springfield, Charles C Thomas, 1972.

Merck Manual (10th ed). New York, Merck & Co., 1961.

Morgan, M.: Feelings of the epileptic. In G. N. Wright, F. A. Gibbs and S. M. Linde (Eds.): *Total Rehabilitation of the Epileptic—Gateway to Employment.* Washington, D.C., U.S. Department of Health, Education, and Welfare, 1962.

Moya, G.; Julian-Ramo, S., and Grandas, I.: Spanish public opinion on the subject of epilepsy. *Rev. Sanid. Hig. Publ., 42*:203-76. Cited by C. Bagley, *The Social Psychology of the Child with Epilepsy.* London, Routledge & Kegan Paul, 1971, p. 100.

Patterson, C. H.: Preparing the epileptic to work. In *Total Rehabilitation of the Epileptic—Gateway to Employment.* Washington, D.C., U.S. Department of Health, Education, and Welfare, 1962.

Performance of Physically Impaired Workers in Manufacturing Industries. U.S. Department of Labor, Bulletin No. 923.

Rickard, T.; Triandis, H., and Patterson, C.: Indices of employer prejudice toward disabled applicants. *Journal of Applied Psychology,* 47:52-55, 1963.

Risch, F.: Attitudes and practices in industry. In *Total Rehabilitation of Epileptics—Gateway to Employment.* Washington, D.C., U.S. Department of Health, Education, and Welfare, 1962.

Sands, H.: Study undertaken for the committee on neurological disorders in industry, Council on Industrial Health, American Medical Association. Cited by R. L. Barrow, and H. D. Fabing, *Epilepsy and the Law* (2nd ed.). New York, Harper & Row, 1966.

Sands, H.: *Changing Employment Policies and Attitudes Towards Persons with Epilepsy.* Washington, D.C., Epilepsy Association of America, 1970.

Schmidt, R. P., and Wilder, B. J.: *Epilepsy.* Philadelphia, F. A. Davis Company, 1968.

Szasz, T.: Whither psychiatry? *Social Research.* 1966, pp. 439-462.

Taylor, J.; Holmes, G., and Walsh, F. M. R. (Eds.): *Selected Writings of John Hughlings Jackson,* Vol. 1, New York, Basic Books Inc., 1958.

Temkin, O.: *The Falling Sickness* (2nd ed). Baltimore, Johns Hopkins Press, 1971.

Tizard, B.: The personality of epileptics: A discussion of the evidence. *Psychology Bulletin,* 59:196-210, 1962.

CHAPTER III

THE CEREBRAL PALSIED

CLEYLON L. MCLARTY AND JAMES A. CHANEY

Introduction and Definition
Incidence and Etiology
Symptomatology
Rehabilitation
Summary

Introduction and Definition

REHABILITATION OF THE individual with cerebral palsy is a story with a short history. Though writers believe that cerebral palsy existed in the earliest of ancient societies, the earliest recorded medical recognition of this problem was by the English physician, W. J. Little, in 1843 (Wolfe and Reid, 1958). His book, *On Deformities*, which followed in 1853, described deformities such as being unable to walk, unable to speak, drooling, and low intelligence. He believed that these deformities were due to disorders of the nervous system and seemed to follow first pregnancies and premature births. The syndrome which he described came to be known as Little's Disease, subsequently named Cerebral Palsy.

Since the days of Little, the clinical nature of the syndrome has been further described by numerous authors. However, it was not until the 1930's that a concentrated research effort was directed toward the treatment and care of persons with cerebral palsy (Wolfe and Reid, 1958).

This research has generated a number of concepts concerning the nature of cerebral palsy, and, consequently, the manner in which cerebral palsy is defined. Though the pros and cons of many definitions have been widely debated, the definitions essentially incorporate the view that cerebral palsy is a neurologic dysfunction, rather than a disease, manifested in physical impairment and often accompanied by intellectual and sensory impairment. The various manifestations of cerebral palsy result from lesions in certain areas of the brain, and since, at the present, the lost brain cells cannot be regenerated, the anatomical defects have been considered permanent. However, recent advances in medical research have demonstrated that the physical impairments may be corrected in some cases. Dr. Irving Cooper (1972) reported that freezing a small portion of the thalamus had produced restoration of motor functioning in approximately 60 percent of the seventy-five patients on whom this operation has been performed. If such surgical techniques prove effective and become widely used, the role of the rehabilitation counselor should become increasingly important as abberant motor behaviors are removed.

Incidence and Etiology

Many surveys have attempted to determine the incidence of cerebral palsy, but estimates have varied widely. Phelps (1950) estimated that seven children per 100,000 were born with cerebral palsy. On the other hand, Wolfe and Reid (1958) found 308 cases per 100,000. A study by Cruickshank and Raus (1955) noted 152 cases of cerebral palsy per 100,000 of the population. In 1956, United Cerebral Palsy estimated that there were 550,000 CP's in the United States. Regardless of the estimates taken, however, cerebral palsy remains a major crippler of children in the United States. As such it is a disability which deserves the careful attention of professionals in the field of rehabilitation.

A plethora of explanations have been advanced as etiological agents of cerebral palsy. These have been generally classified into three categories: (1) prenatal factors, which occur at any point from conception until onset of labor, (2) paranatal factors, which occur during the birth process, and (3) postnatal factors, which occur after birth. Prenatal and paranatal factors are generally believed to account for 90 percent of the cases. The remaining 10 percent are caused by postnatal factors.

Concerning prenatal causes of cerebral palsy, Keats (1965) reported several studies which indicated that various anomalies of cerebral palsy occurred within families, though the frequency of these occurrences was estimated to be three percent or less of the subjects studied. Maternal infection and physical problems during pregnancy were cited by Wolfe and Reid (1958) to be present in one-third of the mothers of cerebral palsied children. Among those conditions noted to be present were anemia, high or low blood pressure, toxemia, bleeding, vaginal discharges, high fever, German measles, and convulsions. Another prenatal factor often related to cerebral palsy is prematurity of the infant. Originally noted by Little (1853), prematurity has been cited in research by various authors (Wolfe and Reid, 1958; Ford, 1946; Illingworth, 1958). Illingworth (1958) reported that approximately one-third of all cases of cerebral palsy were the result of prematurity. Among other prenatal factors less frequently cited are therapeutic x-ray treatment of the abdominal area during the first trimester of pregnancy (Keats, 1965), kernicterus (a blood disease of the newborn), and metabolic disturbances such as diabetes during pregnancy.

Paranatal difficulties have been described as major causes of cerebral palsy. Delivery of infants with the use of instruments has been noted as the most important of these factors. Wolfe and Reid (1958) reported that 32 percent of the CP's they studied were delivered with instruments. Anoxia (deficiency of oxygen) due to the umbilical cord being wrapped around the neck of the neonate was present in 16 percent of the cases they studied. Anoxia resulting in cerebral palsy may also be caused by pneumonia, improper use of anesthetics and pain-killing drugs, non-expansion of the infant's lungs at birth, reduced hemoglobin in the blood, or formation of a thin membrane in the lung which interferes with the flow of oxygen (Russ and Soboloff, 1958).

The principle postnatal cause of cerebral palsy is disease. Wolfe and Reid (1958) estimated that approximately six percent of the cerebral palsy cases they studied were due to diseases following birth. The most common infections which resulted in cerebral palsy were meningitis, encephalitis, and abscess of the brain. Additionally, infections such as scarlet fever, rheumatic heart disease, tumors, toxic factors, and brain injuries have been suggested to infrequently result in cerebral palsy (Keats, 1965). Other postnatal causes of CP include tumors and poisons.

Symptomatology

While the cause of cerebral palsy is widely varied, the symptomatology of the dysfunction is also legion. Methods of classifying cerebral palsy have been traditionally based on the predominant physical symptoms which are present. Robinault (in press) and others have described five characteristic forms, the first two of which constitute approximately 80 percent of the cases. The first and most predominant form is the spastic, characterized by loss of voluntary control of muscles, mass-reflex movements, and abnormal postures. The second form is the athetoid individual, wherein there are slow, worm-like movements in the limbs of the body. The third form is the ataxic individual, who has deficiencies in balance and muscle tone. The fourth is the individual with tremors; that is, rapid and repetitive movement of the body. The final form is rigidity, wherein there is a resistance to almost all movement.

While persons with cerebral palsy are classified according to physical impairment, there are numerous other handicaps which may appear in conjunction with these difficulties. One of the most prominent of these is intellectual impairment. Various studies have indicated that approximately 50 to 60 percent of those with cerebral palsy have IQ's below 90 (Asher and Schonell, 1950; Burgemeister and Blum, 1949). Robinault (in press) estimates that the mean IQ for the cerebral palsied is 70 to 75. She estimates that approximately 50 percent are retarded, 25 percent score within the dull-normal range, and the remaining 25 percent are distributed between the average, bright-normal, and superior ranges.

Other handicaps which are associated with cerebral palsy include seizures, visual defects, speech defects, and hearing defects. These difficulties result from neurological abnormalities, as do the physical and intellectual impairments previously discussed. Concerning the incidence of visual defects in the cerebral palsied, Perlstein (1955) estimated that 50 percent of the CP population have visual defects. Most of these problems are related to difficulties in eye movement, field of vision, impaired visual acuity, and blindness. Keats (1965) reviewed several studies related to incidence of seizures in cerebral palsy. Estimates ranged from 50 to 86 percent in patient categories. Speech defects in persons with cerebral palsy have been estimated to occur at a rate of 76 percent (Dunsdon, 1952 and Lehrhoff, 1958). Among the speech defects noted by Denhoff and Robinault (1960) were delayed speech, articulation problems, aphasia, stuttering, and voice disorders.

Thus cerebral palsied persons may be quite different in the type and degree of impairment. One may have severe physical, intellectual, and sensory impairment, while another may be impaired minimally in these areas. However, the vast majority lies somewhere in between these extremes, presenting varying degrees of impairments in each of these areas. As the types and degrees of impairment are increased in each person, the rehabilitation counselor will find increased challenge and increased possibility that some must be considered unfeasible for vocational rehabilitation.

Rehabilitation

Until the last quarter-century, cerebral palsy was considered to be an almost untreatable disability (Robinault, in press). Until that time cerebral palsy was essentially treated only by physicians and only to a limited extent. Orthopedic specialists attempted to correct the physical deformities, but the emotional and social adjustment of such persons was rarely given much attention by other professionals.

Modern treatment methods have incorporated the skills of other professionals to deal with the physical, emotional, and social needs of cerebral palsied individuals. Comprehensive delineation of various approaches is beyond the scope of this chapter but may be reviewed in Denhoff and Robinault (1960), Keats (1965), Illingworth (1958), Cruickshank (1966), as well as others.

Rehabilitation has been defined in many ways. However, from the view of the rehabilitation counselor it is the process of helping his client evolve from a position of dependency to a state in which his fullest capacities in the physical, mental, social, and economic areas are realized. Since the cerebral palsied individual is often multiply handicapped with varying degrees of disability, the extent of services which can be provided will vary considerably from client to client.

As with persons of any disability, the interpersonal skills of the rehabilitation counselor may have great effect on the process of his rehabilitation. However, barriers to the establishment of effective interpersonal relationships by the counselor may stem from a number of factors, as indicated by Garrett (1966). He states that counseling with the cerebral palsied individual may be a difficult job because of factors such as unattractive appearance, unintelligible speech, inability to coordinate movement, and grimacing. The unprepared counselor confronting such an individual may be overwhelmed by the disability, while consideration of the person's abilities may be completely overlooked. Add to this the possibility of drooling and the fact that the potential client is likely to be under considerable stress when he first meets the counselor, it is not surprising that counselors encounter difficulty in dealing effectively with this group.

The process of counseling and vocational exploration with cerebral palsied individuals has been indicated by several authors to be identical to that used in counseling with persons of other disabilities. However, Garrett (1966) has discussed several factors which the counselor may wish to consider when working specifically with cerebral palsied persons. It usually takes a greater number of sessions to counsel with cerebral palsied clients, generally because they are often multiply handicapped with many factors to be considered in vocational exploration and selection of a vocational objective. Coupled with an increased number of sessions is the suggestion that the length of the session should be shorter than the length for most other clients. The reason for shorter length is due to the tendency of many CP's to tire easily. Additionally, Garrett suggests that, because many CP's have perceptual difficulties, the counseling room should be kept as simple as possible in order to minimize undue distractions.

Among the many factors which are relevant to successful rehabilitation of the cerebral palsied patient are evaluations of his strengths and weaknesses. Failure to consider strength and weakness has resulted in many errors that could have been avoided. A common error resulting from inadequate consideration of the client's strengths is the misconception that CP's with unintelligible speech are retarded. The individual with almost unintelligible speech may actually be quite brilliant. While failure to consider the client's strengths is important, failure to consider his weaknesses may be equally important. A common problem resulting from failure to consider the client's weaknesses is the heartbreak faced by many cerebral palsied persons as they graduate from college and find that they are unable to find employment at a level commensurate with their college education. A study by Glick and Donnell (1953) indicated that of thirty-three persons who had attended college, only two persons following graduation had jobs for which they were trained. The authors pointed out that 75 percent of these persons were unable to obtain such jobs because of physical impairments. These results would seem to indicate that decisions regarding their education were essentially unrelated to knowledge concerning their weaknesses. Adequate evaluation of the individual's strengths and weaknesses may help to prevent occurrences such as these.

The best time to begin vocational evaluation of the CP, however, is not when he presents himself to the rehabilitation counselor upon completion of high school, but, rather, before the beginning of high school. As soon as possible, the individual with cerebral palsy should be placed in prevocational evaluation designed to encourage work habits, work tolerance, social skills, a sense of responsibility, and realistic assessment of his own abilities. Robinault (in press) reviewed Moed's (1956) suggestions regarding the schedule of prevocational activities. Moed believes that by six years of age, the individual should be evaluated intellectually to determine the range of his abilities and gain some prognosis of the helpfulness of future intellectual training. In addition, realistic goals should be discussed with his parents in view of precautions from physicians, appearance, and indicated potential. Robinault notes that such an age may seem to be a premature stage at which to begin such an evaluation. Certainly vocational theories would indicate that the individual is many years away from crystallization of vocational choice. However, early guidance and counseling were noted by Moed to help in the prevention of the unrealistic self assessment and future goals that CP's often make. By the time they are ready for graduation from high school, many CP's have been so treated as to have little awareness of the world of work, how they would get into it, and their place in it. Moed pointed out that many wanted to begin at the top of the organization, and Garrett (1966) noted that CP's often bring their parents with them when they apply for a job.

At the elementary school level, the CP child should have an opportunity to explore his environment and to begin to adjust socially. He should also enter a program of education adapted to his abilities and needs. Cruickshank (1966) believes that a complete educational program must be envisioned at this time, including the secondary level and the possibility of a college education, as well as vocational, technical, or trade school programs. The programs recommended for each child depends on the degree of his handicap. The cerebral palsied child who is severely retarded and severely handicapped physically will need an educational program that is markedly different from the individual who has at least average intelligence and minimal motor handicaps.

In junior high and high school, the individual's social development and sense of responsibility are important areas to be emphasized. His attitudes in these areas will crucially affect the possibility of vocational success in later years. Field trips can be taken to factories, lectures can be arranged by persons in various vocations and the youngster can have the opportunity to test his motor abilities in various types of situations. A more innovative program developed by Kramer (1962) and reviewed by Robinault (in press) placed a group of disabled persons between nine and sixteen years of age in a summer prevocational program for two and one-half hours each day, three times per week. They attended a workshop program, worked on an assembly line, punched time cards, took regularly scheduled coffee breaks, and worked toward production goals. Such experiences in simulated work environments provide immeasurable opportunity for the person to learn about his work tolerance and work habits, as well as his ability to get along with fellow workers and to accept responsibility.

While prevocational programs beginning at the age of six years can be crucial in the development of proper attitudes for work, the rehabilitation counselor does not usually have clients who have gone through prevocational evaluation programs. To a counselor confronted with such an individual, the task of rehabilitation is easier. However, if a client has not gone through such a program, the counselor has several sources of information to help in determining his client's job readiness.

The first important source of information to the counselor is the required medical evaluation. This evaluation will provide information regarding the physical limitations of the client, including the sensory handicaps which will limit choices of vocation. Garrett (1966) pointed out that two of the most important areas requiring evaluation are speaking effectiveness and use of hands. He notes that severe impairment in both of these areas makes placement in competitive employment unlikely. As mentioned previously, other impairments also decrease vocational alternatives. The individual with severe athetosis and impaired vision will not be able to successfully enter occupations requiring fine motor coordination. The individual with an articulation difficulty is not likely to become a successful announcer, in spite of the fact that he may have little limitation of physical movement.

A second important factor which needs consideration by the rehabilitation counselor is the physical appearance of the client. Many cerebral palsied individuals have a rather untoward appearance, which, in reality, may constitute a substantial barrier to employment, regardless of his intelligence or degree of training. Many employers will not hire such persons in positions where appearance is likely to make customers uncomfortable. Though this is a limiting factor in placement of the cerebral palsied, due consideration may prevent the countless heartbreaks from educating persons with severe physical impairments for professional level positions in which they are unable to find jobs because of their appearance.

Another area needing prime consideration by the counselor is how well the client has mastered, or is capable of mastering, the activities of daily living. An individual is not likely to remain in competitive employment if he has not learned to dress himself, feed himself, and use toilet facilities independently. In addition, the counselor must determine whether the individual's physical, intellectual, or sensory impairments prevent him from performing other daily activities such as independent travel to and from a place of employment.

The fourth area to be considered in vocational planning is the extent to which an individual is capable of satisfying the physical demands of work. While the individual may have a suitable appearance and is able to take care of the activities of daily living, he may not have the endurance to engage in physical activities over a period of several hours. Additionally, some individuals are restricted from almost all effective use of their limbs. Prognosis for vocational rehabilitation of these individuals is usually poor.

The fifth factor which may expand or limit the vocational choices available to the client is the level of his intellectual functioning. Clients who are severely limited physically and have barely intelligible speech are often mistaken to be retarded. To prevent this error it is important to have a complete psychological evaluation, including an evaluation of his intellectual status.

Other areas that should be included in the psychological evaluation are personal adjustment and interpersonal skills. In the normal population, poor interpersonal skills are the most frequent cause of termination from jobs (Garrett, 1966). It is especially important to evaluate personal adjustment and interpersonal skills in the cerebral palsied, because they are often subjected to experiences that impair their vocational functioning. For example, Garrett (1966) and Crickmay (1966) pointed out that cerebral palsied individuals seem to be particularly over-protected by parents and thus may expect that an employer is willing to give them all of the attention that a parent would give a child. Thus the cerebral palsied employee who had been overprotected might feel that he is being treated unfairly in a work situation if his employer does not provide continuous super-vision and support. He may then react in ways which would minimize the likelihood of his continued employment. The extent of over-protection may also determine the quality of his perform-ance in other areas necessary to employment. Many persons with cerebral palsy have been accompanied on job interviews by parents. Thus the employer who is looking for an individual capable of independent functioning is not likely to be encouraged.

Additional emotional difficulties which may limit vocational success in cerebral palsied individuals are intense feelings of insecurity and fear, brought on by years of failure in various areas (Garrett, 1966). Thus in a work situation the fear of failure may prevent his attempting unfamiliar tasks with the result that he appears to be unmotivated.

In spite of these findings regarding similarities of emotional difficulties in the cerebral palsied, it is important to note that each individual is different and that personality characteristics in cerebral palsy may differ widely. Personality factors that limit success in one individual with CP may not be limiting factors in another person.

Vocational evaluation of the cerebral palsied client may also be performed in rehabilitation facilities. Many programs have developed across the country, based on the TOWER (Testing, Orientation, and Work Evaluation in Rehabilitation) program, developed at the Institute for the Crippled and Disabled in New York City. While enrolled in such a program, the individual is evaluated by physicians, psychologists, social workers, physical therapists, and occupational therapists among others to help determine realistic vocational objectives. Perhaps the most im-portant aspects of the evaluation is done by assessing his performance in miniature job situations based on job analysis of thirteen occupational areas. Such job tests assess the individual's abilities in clerical, semiskilled, and skilled areas, such as jewelry, clerical work, bookkeeping, welding, drafing, bench assembly, delivering messages, and leather work, among others.

When all of these areas have been evaluated and considered, the counselor should have some degree of knowledge concerning the ability of his client to take care of his daily personal needs, to get to and from work, to handle the physical and intellectual demands of work, to get along with his supervisor and fellow workers, and to accept vocational alternatives where appearances would likely prevent his employment. Considering an individual's strengths and weaknesses in these areas, vocational evaluation and vocational choices can then be made more appropriately, as well as the choices which will satisfy the monetary and personality needs of the client.

The vocational objectives of the cerebral palsied would, at first glance, appear to be quite limited as a result of multiple impairments. This is quite true in many cases. However, the jobs in which cerebral palsied clients are presently working are varied. Though the percentage of CP's who are employed is not known, the most recent national statistics on cerebral palsied workers are essentially the same as those reported by Garrett (1966). They are listed below:

38%—clerical, sales, and kindred
23%—skilled and semiskilled
11%—professional, semiprofessional and managerial
11%—service
 8%—unskilled
 5%—agricultural and kindred
 4%—family workers and homemakers

From these statistics it can be seen that CP's are represented in all levels of socioeconomic strata. The degree of physical impairment, intellectual impairment, personality impairment, and education affect the vocational alternatives which are open to the CP. Thus the counselor need not be restricted in his conception that the cerebral palsied individual is limited to unskilled jobs.

Another important area to be considered is that of the potentially college-bound individual with cerebral palsy. Those persons with severe physical problems and retardation are often unable to take care of their activities of daily living and thus would be limited from profiting from an extensive program of formal education. Whether the individual with slight physical impairment should attend college has been debated. As noted previously, many cerebral palsied individuals with severe physical limitations have been unable to find employment in professional level positions. Glick and Donnell (1953) have proposed that counselors may avoid such difficulties by considering whether the client possesses the following characteristics:

(1) sufficient intellectual ability
(2) self sufficiency in the activities-of-daily living
(3) ability to communicate
(4) a college major oriented toward training for a vocation
(5) motivation to attain his degree.

Absence of any of these factors will increase the probability of failure of the CP client to complete college and become employed in a vocation allowing him to utilize his formal education. Research by Muthard and Hutchison (1968) emphasized the importance of the fourth characteristic. They found that when the college-bound CP student chose a college major that provided training for a specific vocation, the probability of his being hired was increased. In a follow-up study of college students who received this type of counseling, four percent of the CP's were unemployed. Additionally, 36 percent had professional job titles, as compared with 18 percent of a group who had no impairments. While the authors stated that the study could not be offered as definitive proof that the college-bound CP should choose a college major that is oriented toward a specific vocation, those who did so were more likely to be hired, had fewer adjustment problems, higher salaries, and found more satisfaction in their work than those who had chosen a general curriculum.

SUMMARY

In summary, cerebral palsy is a major crippler of children, resulting from lesions in the brain which primarily occur prior to or during birth, leaving the affected person with permanent motor impairment. In addition to motor dysfunction, there is usually one or more co-existing conditions such as mental retardation, sensory loss, convulsions or residual emotional disturbances. Most cerebral palsied individuals are multiply handicapped, and, as such, will require intricate and extensive counseling, evaluation, and training, followed by individualized vocational placement.

REFERENCES

Asher, P., and Schonell, F. E.: A survey of 400 cases of cerebral palsy in childhood. *Archives of Diseases in Childhood*, 25s360-369, 1950.

Burgemeister, B. B., and Blum. L. H.: Intellectual evaluation of a group of cerebral palsied children. *Nervous Child*, 8:177-180, 1949.

Cooper, I.: As reported in *Hope for Stroke Victims. Newsweek*, 80:81, 1972.

Crickmay, M. C.: *Speech Therapy and the Bobath Approach to Cerebral Palsy*. Springfield, Charles C Thomas, Pub., 1966.

Cruickshank, W. M.: *Cerebral Palsy: Its Individual and Community Problems*. Syracuse, Syracuse University Press, 1955.

Cruickshank, W. M., and Raus, G. M. (Eds.): *Cerebral Palsy: Its Individual and Community Problems*. Syracuse, Syracuse University Press, 1955.

Denhoff, E., and Robinault, I. P.: *Cerebral Palsy and Related Disorders*. New York, McGraw-Hill Book Company, 1960.

Dunsdon, M. I.: *The Educability of Cerebral Palsied Children*. London, Newnes Education Co., 1952.

Ford, F. R.: *Diseases of the Nervous System*. Springfield, Charles C Thomas, Pub., 1946.

Garrett, J. F.: Realistic vocational guidance. In W. M. Cruickshank (Ed.), *Cerebral Palsy: Its Individual and Community Problems*. Syracuse, Syracuse University Press, 1966, 606-632.

Glick, S. J., and Donnell, C.: Non-medical problems of the adult with cerebral palsy. *Nursing Outlook, 1*:277-279, 1953.

Illingworth, R. S.: *Recent Advances in Cerebral Palsy*. Boston, Little, Brown and Company, 1958.

Keats, S.: *Cerebral Palsy*. Springfield, Charles C Thomas, Pub., 1965.

Kramer, J.: Work experience for the teenager. In *Work Adjustment as a Function of Occupational Therapy*, Study Course No. 5, World Federation of Occupational Therapy, 1962.

Lehrhoff, I.: Speech problems in children. *Journal of Pediatrics,* 52:94, 1958.

Little, W. T.: *On Deformities.* London, Fongman's, 1853.

Moed, M.: Reports of teachers' conference at University of Georgia and University of Kentucky. *Cerebral Palsy Review,* 1956.

Perlstein, M. A.: Infantile cerebral palsy. *Advances in Pediatrics,* 7:209, 1955.

Phelps, W. M.: Etiology and diagnostic classification of cerebral palsy. In *Proceedings of the Cerebral Palsy Institute.* New York, Association for Aid of Crippled Children, 1950.

Robinault, I. P.: *The Multiple Dysfunctions Called Cerebral Palsy.* (Advanced mimeograph form.)

Russ, J. D., and Soboloff, H. R.: *A Primer of Cerebral Palsy.* Springfield, Charles C Thomas, Pub., 1958.

Wolfe, W. G., and Reid, L. L.: *A Survey of Cerebral Palsy in Texas.* Austin, United Cerebral Palsy of Texas, 1958.

CHAPTER IV

HANDICAPPING SPEECH DISORDERS

PERRY HALL AND GUS ALEXANDER

Principles of Speech
Common Speech Disorders
Speech Defects and Mental Retardation
Diagnosis and Treatment
Rehabilitation Resources
Counseling and Adjustment
Conclusions

Principles of Speech

NEVER BEFORE IN human history has the ability to comprehend, organize and communicate information been so critical as it is in today's society in which man's interpersonal and social interdependence increases daily. It is critical because the discovery and dissemination of new information is increasing at a phenomenal rate and because every aspect of life in a scientific, technological society is affected by this information explosion. At home, work and play man is continually bombarded with potentially vital information about all of his activities, interests and concerns. To determine whether and/or how data may have relevance, value and applicability to his own situation, the individual requires interpersonal communication skills to process this information by discussing it with other persons. Thus speech disorders which limit effective verbal interaction may significantly impair an individual's ability to meaningfully participate in our modern, complex society.

54

Speech disorders are disabilities which impose limitations upon a person's ability to function in oral communication. The degree of severity ranges from slight speech distortion to speech which is unintelligible to all but highly skilled speech pathologists. A slight speech distortion is a deviation of speech which is outside the range of acceptable variation in a given social environment. In the United States, for example, there are differences in speech by geographical location such as *southern drawl* and *Brooklynese*. These speech differences, while interfering with communication, would not constitute a speech handicap because after a short period of adjustment oral communication is established at an acceptable level. Severe speech impairment, on the other hand, is so limiting and poses so many problems for the individual that he is extremely handicapped in many of the major areas of life activity such as psychological/social adjustment and educational/vocational achievement.

Speech disorders often stem from problems concerning the mechanics and anatomical mechanisms of speech itself. The physical mechanics of speech are based upon simple, easy to understand principles. Air is drawn into the lungs and expelled up the trachea through the vocal bands. The force of the air—which is regulated by voluntary muscle functions of the diaphram and stomach and by actual lung capacity—causes the vocal bands to vibrate, creating sound waves. The sound waves are then shaped by the anatomical structures of the mouth and face (i.e., the lips, teeth, nasal cavity, sinuses, hard palate, soft palate (velum), uvula, pharynx, epiglottis, tongue, and the muscles of the jaw and face) to form sounds according to the desires of the speaker.

The nervous system is a major anatomical area which affects the mechanics of speech. The brain is responsible for two important functions in the process. The most important is the storage of the symbols of communication that are essential in providing meaning for the sounds and noises articulated by the vocal anatomy of the mouth and face. The second important function is the voluntary motor control which coordinates all the mechanics and mechanisms of speech.

There is another anatomical-physiological factor associated

with speech problems. Since human sound reproduction is based upon recalling or imitating sounds as perceived, the quality of speech is no better than the sounds received. Speech involves auditory perception of the stimulus input, interpretation and storage. The hearing mechanism, consisting of the outer ear, middle ear, and inner ear along with the auditory nerves, is totally responsible for the quality of sound stored in the memory cells. If there is dysfunction with the mechanism of audition, then the quality of sound which is stored is defective; and the resulting imitation will reflect the auditory deficiency.

The auditory mechanism is also responsible for monitoring speech along with the kinesthetic feedback from the muscles of the jaw and throat that provides the speaker with instant knowledge of his rate of speech, volume and pitch. In this sense, the hearing becomes the quality control inspector of speech production. If hearing is defective, the speaker must rely totally on the less dependable kinesthetic feedback for the quality control factor.

A common method of classifying speech disorders is based upon sound or symbol distortion. This method of classification generally includes disorders of phonation, articulation, fluency and symbolization or a combination. Phonation disorders involve distortions of pitch or intensity of speech. Disorders of articulation refer to sound production problems. Problems of fluency involve the rate or flow of speech. Symbolization disorders result from central nervous system dysfunction which creates associative difficulties in the sensory motor areas of speech.

Common Speech Disorders

The following will be an examination of some of the most prevalent speech disorders. The discussion will be two part: first, a description of the disorder; and second, a short statement on treatment. The disorders of aphasia, cerebral palsy, cleft-palate, stuttering, deaf speech and other numerous problems will be included.

Aphasia

Aphasia is the loss of ability to speak or comprehend the spoken word either totally or partially. This condition results from damage to the cerebral cortex of the brain. The most common causes are stroke (cerebrovascular accidents), tumors or traumatic injury to the brain. The essential process of translating thoughts into proper symbols for verbalization is disrupted. This disability is not clearly understood and arguments still persist among neuro-physiologists as to whether the areas of association involved in the process are localized or general. It is generally agreed that the left hemisphere is most often involved. In aphasia, since there is a lesion in the brain, the motor areas are also often affected. Coordination of the tongue, lips and fine muscles of the larynx are a part of the overall speech problem.

Aphasia is divided into three types: expressive aphasia, receptive aphasia, and associative aphasia. Expressive aphasia is characterized by the inability to speak coherently, even though the individual can still produce the basic speech sounds to some degree. In receptive aphasia, the individual can hear what is said to him, but the sounds he hears are scrambled and unintelligible. The expressive aphasic can communicate by simple signal devices of nodding his head or waving his hand, but the receptive aphasic cannot communicate in any way since the sounds he hears are distorted. The most severely disabled are those with a combination.

After onset the initial response of the patient is immediate panic upon discovering that he cannot communicate. After a period of time goes by without substantial change, the aphasic patient becomes highly frustrated. Later he becomes very depressed if no significant gains are made. Even after some communication is restored, the patient may react emotionally to communication problems and have temper outbursts or crying episodes when the frustration of not being understood becomes too much for him. For example, a patient at a rehabilitation center was being tested by a resident physician who felt that the patient was capable of better communication than he actually was. The physician asked him to count backwards from one hundred. The patient attempted to do so with great difficulty several times. Finally the physician accused him of not trying. As a result the patient became very angry and checked out of the hospital. In a matter of a few hours he returned with his huge German shepherd dog to *get the s.o.b.*

There is considerable difference of opinion as to when the speech restoration process should begin. Some physicians prefer to wait for the hoped for spontaneous recovery of speech which may or may not occur. The general consensus is to wait about six to eight weeks. This waiting period may use up valuable treatment time and should be avoided for a number of reasons. In the early stages of recovery, motivation to communicate is high in the patient. This motivation can be used to great advantage by the speech therapist in both diagnosis and treatment. In later stages of recovery, much of the patient's energy is directed toward physical recovery and considerable energy is required for good participation in speech therapy. Finally the actual depression and retirement of the patient will set in so that there is acceptance of defeat and poor motivation. It would be indicated from this that early intervention by speech therapy is essential.

The treatment process should begin with a speech diagnosis. The diagnosis involves several different tests to determine areas of damage and areas that may remain intact. The speech therapist then initiates the speech restoration program best suited to the client's needs. Recovery is slow and may require from six months to several years of treatment. Employment or return to work may be hastened if the client can utilize secondary communication devices such as reading and writing.

Inability to read in aphasia is referred to as alexia and difficulty in writing is called agraphia. In receptive aphasia the individual may have difficulty in reading and in expressive difficulty, in writing. The motor and associative processes involved in reading and writing, however, differ to some extent from those involved in hearing and speaking. Therefore, the ability to read and write may be more easily made functional than speech alone. Treatment must include efforts in both of these areas.

In summary, the treatment process should begin at the earliest possible time. The treatment should be a team effort with the goal of effective communication. The therapists, physicians and rehabilitation counselor should define the level of skill needed for return to employment. Potential employers may, upon request of the counselor, redefine job duties so that required speech can be replaced by written communication. For instance, an attorney who has had a stroke may have other attorneys appear in court for him after he has done all of the research and prepared the case for presentation.

Cerebral Palsy Speech Patterns

Cerebral palsy refers to a wide variety of neurological conditions affecting the central nervous system. (The total effects of this disorder are discussed more thoroughly elsewhere in this text.) The characteristic symptoms are loss of motor control of the voluntary muscle functions of the face, mouth, lips and tongue. This loss of motor control prevents proper articulation of speech sounds.

There are three types of neuromuscular involvement associated with cerebral palsy. These are classified as spastic, athetoid and ataxic. In cases of spasticity, the individual has lost the ability to inhibit the contraction of muscles. Thus, he lacks the selectivity essential to speech. In athetosis, there is a more or less continuous uncontrolled contracting and relaxing of the muscles of the diaphram and larynx, causing meaningless inflections in the voice. The speech of those who have ataxia is complicated because the person has no feedback from muscles to let him know that the proper contractions have occurred. There is also no coordination between the different muscles which are involved.

Treatment is directed toward improvement in muscle control and coordination. Particular emphasis is placed on control of the muscles involved in breath control to eliminate the problems of phonation. The muscles of the throat and face must be conditioned for maximum voluntary control. The speech therapist, physical therapist and other specialists must continually work as a unit to produce the best results.

The rehabilitation counselor in working with persons who have cerebral palsy may initially be so overcome by the generalized symptoms of the condition that he fails to take notice of the ability of the individual to communicate. The counselor should pay particular attention to this area, since the key to successful adjustment of the individual may be primarily dependent upon ability to communicate. In a recent rehabilitation course requiring group participation, a moderately involved student was excluded from the group after attempting to communicate with them. If the group had not been so hasty, they would have found that she could communicate effectively after they adjusted to her speech.

Cleft Palate

This disorder is considered primarily a problem of articulation. Cleft palate is a fissure in the roof of the mouth which opens into the nasal cavity. The condition exists from birth. In the most severe forms the cleft or fissure extends from the lips all the way back through the soft palate (velum). When it is this serious, it also is a problem of phonation; because the soft palate is used to close the naso-pharynx and direct sounds through the mouth. The speech defects involved are severe and complex. The hard palate serves as a sounding board for the voice quality and provides a natural resting place for the tongue essential to production of many sounds used in language production.

In addition to the speech defects, this disability also affects the individual cosmetically. The upper lip is divided along with the front teeth, and in the most severe cases, the nose is even split. Since food and other matter has easy access to the nasal cavity, the individual is plagued with infections and breathing problems.

Treatment is as involved and complex as the problem. The exterior cosmetic problems are corrected by procedures of plastic surgery. Oral surgery could possibly correct the cleft in the roof of the mouth in less serious cases. Orthodontic treatment to realign the teeth is often required. The manufacture of a prosthesis called an obturator to replace the hard palate is required in instances where surgery cannot close the cleft. Speech therapy or training is always a part of the program of rehabilitation and emphasizes adjustment to the result of surgery or the prosthesis. If treatment is instituted at the appropriate critical stages of development, the individual can achieve very satisfactory adjustment.

The rehabilitation counselor will generally receive the referral of the cleft palate client from the crippled children's agencies at age eighteen or twenty-one. The major portion of the surgical repair and speech therapy will have been completed unless there was considerable neglect on the part of parents or other responsible persons. The counselor will need to assess the vocational quality of the voice prior to entering the client into training or placing him in employment.

Stuttering

Stuttering is defined as disturbances of rhythm. The fluency or flow of speech is disrupted by repeated sounds or words, prolonged sounds, pauses or blockages. This disorder is differentiated from other types of speech defects with similar configurations on the basis of a lack of an organic cause for the disturbance. It is generally agreed that stuttering is a functional disorder which is either a conditioned response pattern with emotional overlay or an emotional state with a high degree of tension and anxiety.

The person who stutters may exhibit a number of behaviors that are related to the stuttering. These may be exhibited in tensing of the muscles of specific areas of the body or as general tenseness. The individual will appear to exert overall effort to overcome the pause. Spasms of the muscles used in phonation and articulation may be evident. The individual may have tics such as blinking the eyes, nodding the head, squeezing the hand into a fist or other behavioral traits that develop as a result of the individual's attempt to offset or overcome the communication blocking.

Many studies indicate that stuttering constitutes the largest single category of speech defects. The disorder is largely confined to the male population. It is estimated that three of four stutterers will be male. Onset of the disability is generally prior to age thirteen.

There appears to be little correlation between stuttering and intelligence. Some studies done with groups of stutterers have found that their intelligence is generally higher than average, while other studies indicate slightly lower than average intelligence for stutterers.

Treatment is generally psychiatric or psychological in nature. The psychiatric approach has as its objective the reduction of the anxiety which is believed responsible for the erratic behavior. The psychological approach stresses operant or classical conditioning in behavior modification of the speech patterns.

The family should be counseled in proper acceptance of the individual. In many instances, the family will attempt to provide therapy which just exaggerates the problem because of the additional demands made upon the individual. The personality pattern of the person who stutters serves to indicate that there is a concerted effort on the part of the individual to conform to rigid standards of behavior and morality. Family acceptance and support in a relaxed home would do much to relieve the individual of much of this internal pressure.

The objective of the speech therapist in treating this disorder is to increase the confidence of the individual in his ability to carry on a meaningful dialogue. This is done primarily by having conversations with the client in a very patient and relaxed atmosphere. The level of conversation is kept simple and is designed to avoid stress-producing topics or topics which are threatening to the client.

The rehabilitation counselor working with the therapists in providing realistic objectives and assuring the services necessary for the training, education and employment of the client, should coordinate such services in a nondirective self-determining manner. The counselor should provide for medical diagnostic services with particular emphasis on medical problems of a psycho-physiologic nature such as ulcers.

Hearing Loss and Defective Speech

The organs of hearing have been described earlier as the quality control mechanism for speech production. The person with hearing constantly monitors his speech for loudness, pitch and clarity of articulation. The quality of speech decreases at a rapid rate in conjunction with a hearing loss. The speech problems, however, differ in each individual in accordance with a number of different circumstances.

The problems of a person who is born without hearing

capability are much different than those of a person who has learned speech prior to sustaining a severe hearing loss. This individual must learn to produce speech by having his vocalization monitored and directed by others. If he is to produce speech with any degree of success, he must depend solely upon kinesthetic feedback from the sensory mechanisms of the larynx and musculature of the face, mouth and tongue. It is rare, however, for a congenitally deaf person to learn to produce speech in which there is present variance in pitch and intensity.

The individual who has learned speech prior to loss of hearing has already developed the kinesthetic feedback as well as a repertoire of symbols. If the individual has a partial loss of hearing, he will probably adjust his speech so that it becomes unnecessarily loud in his attempt to continue monitoring control. The quality of speech in the person who becomes totally deaf degenerates in proportion to the amount of practice he maintains.

Treatment of deaf persons should begin at the earliest possible time. The parents of a congenitally deaf child should be instructed to reward the child for making sounds. They should talk to the child making sure that the child can see the mouth. Early referral to a speech therapist is essential. Treatment for persons who lose their hearing after learning speech should be directed toward helping the individual utilize kinesthetic feedback to maintain good speech. All persons should have periodic retraining to prevent deterioration.

It should be emphasized that all persons concerned with the treatment and education of deaf persons must work toward the same objectives. These objectives should include the production of meaningful speech if at all possible.

The rehabilitation of the person who is deaf must include a complete audiological examination. In many instances, the provision of a hearing aid will supply enough hearing so that the kinesthetic process is given some assistance with the result that there is considerable improvement in the quality of speech.

Nodules and Other Problems of the Vocal Bands

Nodules are lumps or knots which form on the vocal bands. The nodules cause a distortion in the quality of sound produced by the vibration of the bands. The voice of the person who has this problem will be very hoarse or rough. The nodules may form as the result of prolonged abuse of the vocal cords.

The vocal bands may become deformed in other ways such as stretching abnormally causing the voice to become low in pitch. The problem of stretching of the vocal bands can be caused by straining the cords while they are in the process of developing. Unusually tight vocal bands will cause the voice to be high in pitch. This condition results from improper development of the vocal cords.

The conditions outlined are handicapping only to the extent that they detract from the individual's effectiveness in the process of communicating. For instance, it may be very handicapping for a man to have a high, feminine voice, while to have a low, masculine voice could be equally troublesome for a woman. The individual could be forced to make undesirable vocational choices as a result of such deformities. Thus, a man with a high pitched voice might decide not to become a courtroom lawyer because he lacks the quality of voice required for the oration that demands respect in this profession.

The rehabilitation counselor in planning a program of treatment for persons with nodule and other vocal band problems should give prime consideration to physical restoration procedures. The nodules on the vocal bands can often be surgically removed restoring the individual to normal sound production. The vocal cords may also be surgically lengthened or shortened. Atfer these surgical procedures have been performed, speech therapy may be utilized to provide the individual with exercises which will enable him to improve the quality of his sound production.

Dental Malformations

Since the teeth serve an articulatory function, severe dental malformations can create defective speech. There are two major types of dental malformations: oversized teeth and improper spacing. Oversized teeth are a condition in which the teeth are too large for the bone structure. This condition leads to overcrowding, which prevents the tongue and lips from functioning properly in the articulatory process. Oral surgery combined with orthodontal intervention to remove and realign the teeth is the first consideration. Speech therapy to retrain the individual in good speech habits is essential because the speech defect will have been exaggerated during the period of compensation for the dental malformation. For instance, the individual may have learned to avoid words which have sounds that are difficult for him to articulate.

Improper spacing is a condition in which there are wide spaces between some of the teeth. The speech defect which is most notable in this condition is the whistling that accompanies words with *s* sounds. Othodontic realignment of the teeth is again the first consideration. Speech therapy may also be utilized to provide some compensation for this condition.

Extreme overbite is another malformation which is even more severe than either oversized teeth or improper spacing. Extreme overbite results from an elongated or shortened mandibular or maxillary process. This condition causes defective articulation and may also be a cosmetic problem for the individual. In mild to moderate cases, speech therapy to compensate for defective articulation may be sufficient. In severe cases consideration should be given to the provision of maxofacial surgery. The surgeon can realign the bone structure by lengthening or shortening the mandibula or maxilla. This is an expensive and time-consuming operation, but the end result is often remarkable for both the speech articulation and cosmetic appearance of the client.

Laryngectomy

A laryngectomy is the complete surgical removal of the larynx. This surgical procedure also requires that a tracheotomy be performed. Thus, there is no possibility for the normal phonation required for speech. A laryngectomy is the most widely used treatment procedure for cancer of the throat.

After a laryngectomy has been performed, there are three treatment alternatives which may be employed to provide the individual with the ability to speak: a mechanical larynx, an electric larynx, and esophageal speech. The method utilized must be selected by applying some established criteria.

The most important selection criterion is acceptance by the client. A second criterion concerns the ability of the client to learn to use the device. Of importance as well is the occupation of the individual.

The use of esophageal speech is probably the most desirable, since it requires no appliances. In esophageal speech the client swallows air and then expells it, causing loose tissue in the throat to vibrate producing sound. After proper training by a speech therapist, the client can learn to control the sound and is capable of speaking with considerable clarity even though there is no ability to control pitch. Training in esophageal speech requires a highly skilled speech therapist.

The mechanical larynx consists of a box containing a vibrator. The box is attached to the outside of the throat and is connected to the tracheotomy by a tube. When air is expelled from the lungs, it causes the vibrator to function producing sound which is directed through the mouth. There is a bypass which is manually opearted that allows the vibrator to be silenced when the individual is not speaking. The electrical larynx functions in much the same manner as the mechanical larynx. The electrical larynx is a battery operated vibrator which is held against the throat by the client. It produces sounds which are directed upward into the mouth, permitting articulation of fair quality. The resulting speech in both instances has a mechanical, almost robot sound, without variation in pitch.

The rehabilitation counselor should help his client to select an occupation in which the quality of the air in the working environment is good. Working in air which is dust laden or which contains noxious substances should be avoided.

Other Defects

Loss of lung capacity is another condition which results in defective speech. Inadequate lung capacity may be defined as lung capacity which does not provide the volume of air essential for primary speech function. Inadequate lung capacity is caused by many different conditions which interfere with the functioning of the lungs. Pneumonectomy to eradicate cancer, emphysema, enlarged heart or loss of function of the diaphram from a phrenic nerve lesion are examples of these conditions. In some instances, the degree of loss is such that the individual's voice is reduced to the level of a whisper.

In treatment the speech therapist may train the individual to use stomach muscles to increase the force of air expelled. In other instances the individual may be taught to gulp in small amounts of air which is stored in the esophagus and released in a similar manner as in esophageal speech.

There are many other problems which result in defective speech such as paralyzed lips due to nerve injury, loss of use of the fine muscles in the face and so on.

Each condition should be evaluated and attention given to correction whenever possible in order to increase each client's self-esteem if for no other reason.

Speech Defects and Mental Retardation

Defective speech is a common complication of mental retardation. There are several explanations for this high occurrence. First, mental deficiency does not permit the individual to function at a high level in processes requiring ability to abstract. Language consists of symbols which are highly abstract.

Mental retardation results from many causes of which brain damage is central. Throughout this chapter we have discussed several different types of speech defect, many of which are definitely related to organic brain damage, particularly to the cerebral cortex. The relationship between organic brain damage, speech defect and mental retardation is evident.

Functional speech disorders also are of higher incidence in the mentally retarded population than the non-impaired. High expectations, pressure to conform and feelings of inadequacy may combine to create anxiety at the level necessary to cause functional disturbance.

Diagnosis and Treatment

The diagnosis and treatment of speech defects requires a well organized team approach that deals with the individual as a total person. The treatment may include any combination of the following:

1. Surgery: Surgical intervention has been mentioned in connection with many of the specific disorders. Surgery may include oral surgery, neuro-surgery, maxo-facial surgery, otolaryngeal surgery, plastic surgery and orthopedic surgery.

2. Family Counseling: Family counseling should be utilized for several different purposes. It should have the following five objectives: the interpretation of the condition, the provision of full understanding of the disability within the family, the gaining of cooperation for the rehabilitation process, the education of the family in terms of the treatment which it may provide, and the contribution of financial support for the program.

3. Special education: Considerable attention should be given to the educational needs of the child who has speech problems. The school speech therapist should work with the individual teachers in order to encourage the child to participate in all verbal activities of the classroom. The teacher should also be aware of techniques to assist the child in developing the highest quality of speech possible.

4. Vocational Counseling: The vocational counseling objectives for the speech handicapped are the same as for any other disability. The counselor should be aware of the defect and be in a position to advise the client as to the efficacy of considering occupations in which a high degree of verbal communication is a primary component.

5. Psychotherapy: The objectives of psychotherapy are either primary or secondary. A primary objective would be to provide for the removal of the symptoms in a functional speech disorder. A secondary objective for psychotherapy would be to assist the individual in overcoming emotional

problems ancillary to a non-functional speech defect. The therapy may be provided by a psychiatrist, clinical or counseling psychologist or a psychologist who specializes in behavior modification techniques in treating defective speech behaviors.

6. Speech training and therapy: The objectives of speech training and therapy are to assist the individual in improving the quality of speech to as high a level as the individual is capable. The speech therapist and pathologist are specially trained in diagnosing and treating all speech disorders. In all cases the rehabilitation must include the speech therapist.

7. Artificial appliances: Artificial appliances that are commonly used in the treatment of speech defects are the obturator in cleft palate, the mechanical larynx and electrical larynx in laryngectomies, dentures in some instances and hearing aids for persons with defective speech due to a hearing loss.

8. Audiology: The objectives of audiology are to diagnose the extent of the loss of hearing. Hearing may be restored through use of artificial appliances or surgery. It is also important to determine if the loss is receptive or conductive. Surgery and diagnosis would also utilize the skills of the otologist.

The rehabilitation process for the speech handicapped person must be concerned with the objectives of the rehabilitation program depending upon the progress of the client and the point in time that the objectives are specified. In the case of those who are congenitally disabled, the preoccupation with the primary disease process may be such that medical and other professional persons involved overlook the communicative aspects of the disorder with the exception of cleft lips, palate, and deafness. When this occurs, the pathology in later life is more severe because the individual will have formed habits and communication compensation devices that hamper therapy.

The objectives for the process are as diverse as the treatments which were outlined. For instances, if the objective is vocational placement, then the rehabilitation process will be geared toward remediation suitable to meet job reqiurements and would focus primarily upon the vocational rehabilitation aspects. If the objective is speech oriented, the program would focus upon the speech therapy and so on. The process should always include all of these objectives with emphasis on each aspect at the critical time.

The treatment program which involves reduction of the limitations imposed begins with focus on the alteration of the anatomical and physiological structures to increase function. When the problems are functional in nature, the initial step would be psychotherapeutic intervention to deal with the cause. The second step would be to provide speech therapy or training to further reduce the limitations imposed. The third stage would be vocational counseling to select the occupation best suited to the client's abilities and aptitudes, with the final occupational goal one in which the residual speech limitations would not be handicapping.

Rehabilitation Resources

The resources essential for full treatment of the individual with defective speech exist within almost any community. Almost every school system has a speech therapist who can be utilized not only for children still in school, but may provide valuable assistance to adults in the community on a private consultation basis.

Most communities of any size will have one or more speech and hearing center which provides a wide range of services in speech training and therapy as well as audiology. These centers are often located in children's hospitals or general hospitals. All comprehensive rehabilitation centers should have speech therapy services available on an inpatient or outpatient basis. Most major universities have academic programs to train speech pathologists with all of the required treatment facilities. Treatment may be provided by students under supervision of the faculty. This is generally a low cost method of obtaining the required treatment.

The American Speech and Hearing Association should supply a complete registry of qualified speech pathologists located in any area of the nation. The state and local chapters of the National Rehabilitation Association should also be a source of information as to the location of qualified therapists as well as clinical facilities.

Physicians who specialize in ear, nose and throat problems can be located by contacting the local affiliation of the American Medical Association. All physicians who specialize in the treatment of any disorder must be certified by the appropriate board. They provide complete lists of certified physicians upon request.

Financial support for treatment services may be obtained from many difference sources. The most notable of these agencies are the State-Federal Vocational Rehabilitation Programs, State Services for Crippled Children or the more local county chapters of the Society for Crippled Children and Adults supported by the Easter Seal campaigns.

Counseling and Adjustment

Counseling for the speech handicapped should focus on four areas of client adjustment: psychological, social, educational and vocational. The psychological problems resulting from speech disorders are generally an internalized negative self-concept, low frustration tolerance, and high anxiety level along with personality trait disturbances which may be either acute or chronic. The psychological problems associated with a speech defect may diminish with improvement in speech ability or they may be so severe as to require intensive psychotherapy as a part of the training process.

The social problems of the individual resulting from a severe speech defect are based upon the reaction of others to the speech rather than the person. The social responses most commonly associated with speech defects are exclusion from desired social interactions, such as dating; peer group rejection; forced social isolation; pity and sympathy; and excessive difficulty in conduct of normal, routine activities of daily living. In order to overcome these limitations, the individual will need counseling as well as support and acceptance from significant others.

The educational and vocational implications of severe speech defects may in and of themselves cause the individual to achieve maximum adjustment at a level far beneath his actual capacity. The overall educational development may be greatly retarded since much of the process depends upon the ability to express one's self orally in classrooms. Teachers, parents and classmates can have an adverse effect upon the individual's development by establishing low level expectations. The vocational aspirations of the individual must include only occupations which do not include as a primary requirement useful oral communication. Vocations such as sales, acting and teaching are examples of occupations which may be contra-indicated for those with severe speech defects. Rehabilitation should focus on assuring that those persons who are unemployed or underemployed have opportunity through training or retraining to achieve maximum vocational success.

In seeking to facilitate the client's psychological, social, educational and vocational adjustment, the counselor should provide a therapeutic climate characterized by strong support, encouragement and acceptance to help the individual through the entire rehabilitation process. In attempting to do this, the counselor should be aware of the fact that it may be difficult for him to provide unconditional positive regard for the speech handicapped. It is usually more emotionally upsetting, threatening, and time-consuming for a counselor to relate to the speech handicapped than to many other types of disabled persons.

Even if the counselor succeeds in masking his verbal messages, it may not be possible for him to hide his true attitudes and feelings as these are expressed through his nonverbal communication behavior. For example, if the rehabilitation counselor continually turns his head and looks out the window when the speech handicapped person is speaking, this is a clue to the client that the counselor is not paying attention to his conversation and that the counselor is rather anxious (which will make the client, in turn, feel even more uneasy). The nonverbal messages which are intentionally sent or unintentionally *given off* in a counseling situation are of considerable importance. The research evidence indicates that whenever a contradiction is perceived between the verbal and nonverbal messages, the information conveyed through the nonverbal band is regarded as having higher validity by receivers. It is believed rather than the verbal message.

In regard to the possibility of discrepant verbal and nonverbal messages, two methods are suggested to make communication between rehabilitation counselors and speech handicapped persons more effective: videotape training and interactional metacommunication. Workshops may be held in which rehabilitation counselors role-play videotaped interview sessions with selected speech handicapped persons. In critiquing the tape an observer can help the rehabilitation counselor to spot the points were he exhibits nonverbal rejecting behavior.

Interactional metacommunication is communication about communication as the counselor and client are interacting during the course of a counseling session. Here the rehabilitation counselor might say to the speech handicapped client, "I have been attempting to be warm and supportive during our session today. Have you perceived my communication behavior in this way?" Interactional metacommunication is perhaps the most effective device for gaining immediate feedback from clients. However, it is only rarely used because it requires considerable risk-taking behavior on the part of the counselor.

Conclusions

This discussion has in no way attempted to provide a complete coverage of all speech defects with all of their ramifications. It is hoped, however, that the reader has been led to the following conclusions:

1. That most speech defects have considerable significance in all of the major areas of the life of the individual.
2. That the treatment of any individual with a speech defect will require a team approach.
3. That speech therapy is important in the treatment of all types of speech and hearing disorders.
4. That the individual client will need assistance in selecting suitable objectives and that support while attempting to reach these objectives is essential.
5. That all of the professional and significant others must

provide an accepting, patient and non-threatening atmosphere for the client at the social level.

SUGGESTED READINGS

1. *A Survey of Medicine and Medical Practice for the Rehabilitation Counselor.* U.S. Department of Health, Education and Welfare, Social and Rehabilitation Services, Washington, D.C., 1969.
2. Barbara, Dominick A., M.D., Ed.: *Psychological and Psychiatric Aspects of Speech and Hearing.* Springfield, Charles C Thomas, Pub., 1960.
3. Beech and Fransella: *Research and Experiment in Stuttering.* New York, Pegamon Press, 1968.
4. Martin: *Communicative Aids for the Adult Aphasic.* Springfield, Charles C Thomas, Pub., 1962.
5. Travis, Lee Edward, Ed.: *Handbook of Speech Pathology.* New York, Appleton Century Croft, 1957.
6. West, Ansberry and Carr: *The Rehabilitation of Speech,* 3rd Ed., New York, Harper & Row Publishers, 1957.

CHAPTER V

VOCATIONAL REHABILITATION OF THE BLIND AND SEVERELY VISUALLY IMPAIRED

RICHARD E. HARDY AND JOHN G. CULL

Psychological Adjustment to Blindness
Providing Counseling Services
Vocational Placement and Blindness

Psychological Adjustment to Blindness

IT IS TRUE THAT our clients are much more like us than unlike us, but they differ in one major respect. They have suffered the psychological impact of disability and have adjusted or are in the process of adjusting to this impact. In this chapter we shall discuss the factors which affect the psychological adjustment to blindness and the mechanism by which an individual adjusts to his blindness.

During the first and second world wars, behavioral scientists noticed an increased incidence in conversion reactions. Conversion reactions are (APA, 1965) a type of psychoneurotic disorder in which the impulse causing anxiety is *converted* into functional symptoms in parts of the body rather than the anxiety being experienced consciously. Examples of conversion reactions include such functional disabilities as anesthesias (blindness, deafness), paralyses (aphonia, monoplegia, or hemiplegia), dyskineses (tic, tremor, catalepsy).

75

The study of these conditions along with other studies led to the development of a discipline known as psychosomatic medicine. Psychosomatic medicine is concerned with the study of the effects of the personality and emotional stresses upon the body and its function. This psychological interaction with physiology can be observed in any of the body systems.

After the establishment of psychosomatic medicine, behavioral scientists (psychiatrists, psychologists, social workers, etc.) began observing the converse of this new field. Instead of studying the effects of emotional stress on bodily functioning, they studied the effects of physical stress on emotional functioning. Their concern was directed toward answering the question, "What are the emotional and personality changes which result from physical stress or a change in body function or physical configuration?"

Role of Body-image in Adjustment to Blindness

This new area of study became known as somatopsychology. The basis for this study is the body-image concept. The body-image is a complex conceptualization which we use to describe ourselves. It is one of the basic parts of the total personality and as such determines our reaction to our environment. According to English and English (1966) the body-image is the mental representation one has of his own body.

There are two aspects of the body-image concept—the ideal body-image (the desired body-image) and the actual body-image. The greater the congruity between these two images the better the psychological adjustment of the individual, and conversely, the greater the discrepancy between these two parts of the self-concept, the poorer an individual's psychological adjustment. This is very understandable. If an individual is quite short and views himself as such but has a strong ideal body-image of a tall person, he is less well adjusted than he would be if his desired image were that of a short person. This is a simplistic example, but it portrays the crux of the psychological adjustment to blindness.

In order to adjust to the psychological impact of blindness, the body-image has to change from the image of a sighted person to the body-image of a blind person. Early in the adjustment process the actual body-image will change from that of a sighted person to the actual body-image of a blind person; however, for adequate psychological adjustment to the blindness the ideal body-image must make the corresponding adaptation. Therefore, in essence, psychological adjustment to a disability is the acceptance of an altered body-image which is more in harmony with reality.

Factors Associated With Adjustment

There are three groups of factors which determine the speed or facility with which an individual will adjust to his disability. They help an individual understand the degree of psychological impact a particular disability is having on a client and the significance of his adjustment.

The first of these three groups of factors are those directly associated with the disability. Psychological effects of disabilities may arise from direct insult or damage to the central nervous system. These psychological effects are called brain syndromes and may be either acute or chronic. In this instance there are a variety of behavioral patterns which may result directly from the disability. In disabilities involving no damage to brain tissue the physical limitations imposed by the disability may cause excessive frustration and in turn result in behavioral disorders. For example, an active outdoorsman and nature lover may experience a greater psychological impact upon becoming blind than an individual who leads a more restricted and physically limited life since the restrictions imposed by the disability demand a greater change in the basic life style of the first person. Therefore, factors directly associated with the disability have an important bearing upon an individual's reaction to disability.

The second group consists of those factors arising from the individual's attitude toward his disability. An individual's adjustment to his disability is dependent upon the attitudes he had prior to his disability. If his attitudes toward the blind were quite negative and strong he will naturally have a greater adjustment problem than an individual with a neutral or positive attitude toward disabiilty and the disabled, or specifically, the blind and blindness. A part of this attitude formation prior to blindness is dependent upon the experiences the client had with other blind individuals and the stereotypes he developed.

The amount of fear a client experiences or the emotion he expends during the onset and duration of the illness or accident leading up to the disability will determine the psychological impact of the disability. Generally, the greater the amount of emotion expended during onset the better the psychological adjustment to the disability. If an individual goes to sleep a sighted person and awakens a blinded person, his psychological reaction to the disabiilty is much greater than if a great deal of emotion is expended during a process of becoming blinded.

The more information an individual has relating to his disability the less impact the disabiilty will have. If the newly blinded individual is told about his blindness in a simple, straight-forward, mechanistic manner, it is much easier to accept and adjust to the disability than if it remains shrouded in a cloak of ignorance and mystery. Any strangeness or unpredictable aspect of our body associated with its function immediately creates anxiety and if not clarified rapidly can result in totally debilitating anxiety. Therefore, it is important for psychological adjustment to a disability that the individual have communicated to him, in terms he can understand, the medical aspects of his disability as soon after onset of disability as possible.

When we are in strange or uncomfortable surroundings, our social perceptiveness becomes keener. Social cues which are below threshold or are not noticed in comfortable surroundings become highly significant to us in new, strange or uncomfortable surroundings. Upon the onset of blindness, the client will develop a heightened perceptiveness relative to how he is being treated by family, friends, and professionals. If others start treating him in a condescending fashion and relegate him to a position of less importance, his reaction to the psychological impact of the blindness will be poor. Professionals can react to the client from an anatomical orientation (what is missing) or a functional orientation (what is left). The anatomical orientation is efficient for classification purposes but is completely dehumanizing. The functional orientation is completely individualistic and, as such, enhances a client's adjustment to his disability.

Perhaps a key concept in the adjustment to blindness is the evaluation of the future and the individual's role in the future. In many physical medicine rehabilitation centers, a rehabilitation counselor is one of the first professionals to see the patient after the medical crisis has passed. The purpose of this approach is to facilitate the patient's psychological adjustment. If he feels there is a potential for his regaining his independence and security the psychological impact of the blindness will be lessened. While the counselor cannot engage in specific vocational counseling with the patient, he can discuss the depth of the vocational rehabilitation program and through these preliminary counseling sessions the counselor can help the newly blinded person evaluate the roles he might play in the future.

The last factor which determines the adjustment process is based upon the individual's view of the purpose of his body and the relationship this view has with the type and extent of disability. The views individuals have of their body may be characterized as falling somewhere on a continuum. At one end of the continuum is the view that the body is a tool to accomplish work; it is a productive machine. At the other end is the view that the body is an esthetic stimulus to be enjoyed and provide pleasure for others. This latter concept is much the same as we have for sculpture and harks back to the philosophy of the ancient Greeks. Everyone falls somewhere on this continuum. To adequately predict the impact of a disability upon an individual, one has to locate the placement of the individual upon this continuum and then evaluate the disability in light of the individual's view of the function of this body.

As an example of the above principle, consider the case in which a day laborer and film actress sustain the same disabling injury—a deep gash across the face. Obviously, when considering the disability in conjunction with the assumed placements of these two upon the functional continuum, the psychological impact will be greater for the actress; since we have assumed the day laborer views his body almost completely as a tool to accomplish work and the disability has not impaired that function; the psychological impact of the disability upon him will be minimal. However, if the disability were changed (they both sustained severe injury to the abdomen resulting in the destruction of the musculature of the abdominal wall) the psychological impact would be reversed. In this case the actress would view her disability as minimal since it did not interfer with the esthetic value of her body, while the day laboror's disability would be over-powering since it had substantial effects upon the productive capacity of his body.

The most obvious conclusion to be drawn from the above three factors is that the degree of psychological impact is not correlated with the degree of disability. This statement is contrary to popular opinion; however, disability and its psychological impact constitute a highly personalized event. Many counselors fall into the trap of equating degree of disability with degree of psychological impact. If the psychological impact suffered by a client is much greater than that considered *normal,* the counselor will oftentimes become impatient with the client. It should be remembered that relatively superficial disabilities may have devastating psychological effects. The psychological impact of total blindness is not necessarily greater than partial blindness or, for that matter, more anatomically superficial physical disabilities.

Role of Defense Mechanisms in Adjustment

While the three groups of factors discussed above determine the length of time required for adjustment to blindness, the path to adjustment is best described by defense mechanisms. Defense mechanisms are psychological devices used by all to distort reality. Often reality is so harsh it is unacceptable to us. Therefore, we distort the situation to make it more acceptable. Defense mechanisms are used to satisfy motives which cannot be met in reality; they reduce tensions in personal interactions; and they are used to resolve conflicts. To be effective they must be unconscious. They are not acquired consciously or deliberately. If they become conscious they become ineffective as defenses and others must replace them. For the major part of the remainder of this chapter we will look at the defenses most often employed by the disabled in the general order of their use.

Denial

Denial is an unconscious rejection of an obvious fact which is too disruptive of the personality or too emotionally painful to accept. Therefore, in order to soften reality the obvious fact is denied. Immediately upon onset of disability the individual denies it happened. Then, as the fact of the disability becomes so overwhelming its existence can no longer be denied, there is a denial of the permanency of the disability. The newly blinded individual, while utilizing the defense of denial, will adamantly maintain that he shall see again. There will be a miraculous cure or a new surgical technique will be discovered.

While there are few steadfast rules in human behavior, one is that rehabilitation, at best, can be only marginally successful at this point. Rehabilitation cannot procede adequately until the client accepts the permanency of the disability and is ready to cope with the condition. This is what is meant by many professionals when they say a client must accept his blindness. Most clients will never accept their blindness, but they should and will accept the permanence of the blindness. Denial is the front line of psychological defense but it may outlast all other defenses.

Withdrawal

Withdrawal is a mechanism which is used to reduce tension by reducing the requirements for interaction with others within the individual's environment. There are two dynamics which result from withdrawal. In order to keep from being forced to face the acceptance of the newly acquired blindness, the individual withdraws. As a result of the client's changed physical condition—blindness—his social interaction is quite naturally reduced. His circle of interest as determined by friends, business, social responsibilities, church, civic responsibilities and family is drastically reduced. Thus, the client becomes egocentrically oriented until finally his entire world revolves around himself. Rather than functioning interdependently with his environment to mutually fulfill needs as our culture demands, he is concerned exclusively with his environment fulfilling his needs. As his world becomes more narrowed, his thoughts and pre- occupations become more somatic. Physiological processes here- tofore unconscious now become conscious. At this point he begins using another defense mechanism—regression.

Regression

Regression is the defense mechanism which reduces stress by avoiding it. The individual psychologically returns to an earlier age that was more satisfying. He adopts the type of behavior that was effective at that age but now has been outgrown and substituted by more mature behavior—behavior which is more effective in coping with stressful situations.

As the newly blinded individual withdraws, becomes ego- centric, and hypochrondriacal, he will regress to an earlier age which was more satisfactory. This regression may be mani- fested in two manners. First he may, in his regression, adopt the dress, mannerisms, speech, etc. of contemporaries at the age level to which he is regressing. Secondly, he may adopt the outmoded dress, mannerisms, speech, etc. of the age to which he regressed. This second manifestation of regression is con- siderably more maladaptive since it holds the individual out to more ridicule which, at this point in his adjustment to his blind- ness, quite possibly will result in more emphasis on the defense mechanism of withdrawal.

While utilizing the first three defense mechanisms, if reality is being harshly pushed on him and his defenses are not working, he may, as a last resort, become highly negative of those around him and negative in general. This negativism is demonstrated as an active refusal, stubbornness, contradictory attitudes and rebellion against external demands. He may become abusive of those around and may become destructive in an effort to act out the thwarting he is experiencing. This negativisic behavior is an indication that the defense mechanisms he is employing are not distorting reality enough to allow him to adjust to his newly acquired disabled status. If, however, he is able to adjust and the defense mechanisms are effective to this point, he will employ the next defense.

Repression

Repression is selective forgetting. It is contrasted with suppression which is a conscious, voluntary forgetting. Repression is unconscious. Events are repressed because they are psychologically traumatic. As mentioned above the attitudes the client had relative to blindness and the blinded has a major bearing upon his adjustment. If these attitudes are highly negative the client will have to repress them at this point if his adjustment is to progress. Until he represses them he will be unable to accept the required new body-image.

Reaction Formation

When an individual has an attitude which creates a great deal of guilt, tension, or anxiety and he unconsciously adopts the opposite of this attitude, he has developed a reaction formation. In order to inhibit a tendency to flee in terror a boy will express his nonchalance by whistling in the dark. Some timid persons, who feel anxious in relating with others, hide behind a facade of gruffness and assume an attitude of hostility to protect themselves from fear. A third and last example is that of a mother who, feeling guilty about her rejection of a newborn child, may adopt an attitude of extreme overprotectiveness to reduce the anxiety produced by this guilt of rejection. This example is seen more often in cases of parents with handicapped children.

In this new, dependent role the blinded individual will feel a varying degree of hostility and resentment toward those upon whom he is so dependent—wife, relatives, etc. Since these feelings are unacceptable he will develop a reaction formation. The manifest behavior will be marked by concern, love, affection, closeness—all to an excessive degree.

Fantasy

Fantasy is daydreaming. It is the imaginary representative of satisfactions that are not attained in real experience. This defense mechanism quite often accompanies withdrawal. As the client starts to adjust to a new body-image and a new role in life, he will develop a rich, overactive fantasy life. In this dreamworld he will place himself into many different situations to see how well he fits.

Rationalization

Rationalization is giving socially acceptable reasons for behavior and decisions. There are four generally accepted types of rationalization. The first is called blaming an incidental cause: the child who stumbles blames the stool by kicking it; the poor or sloppy workman blames his tools. Sour grapes rationalization is called into play when an individual is thwarted. A goal to which the individual aspires is blocked to him; therefore, he devalues the goal by saying he did not really want it so much. The opposite type of rationalization is called sweet lemons. When something the individual does not want is forced upon him, he will modify his attitude by saying it was really a very desirable goal and he feels quite positive about the new condition. The fourth and last type of rationalization is called the doctrine of balances. In this type of rationalization we balance positive attributes in others with perceived negative qualities. And conversely, we balance negative attributes with positive qualities. For example, beautiful women are assumed to be dumb, bright young boys are assumed to be weak and asthenic and the poor are happier than the rich.

The blinded individual will have to rationalize his disability in order to assist himself in accepting the permanence of the blindness. One rationalization may be that he had nothing to do with his current condition, but that something over which he had no control caused the blindness. Another dynamic which might be observed is the adherence to the belief on the part of the client that as a result of the blindness there will be compensating factors. He will develop in other areas such as additional senses or aptitudes and talents he previously did not possess, e.g. an aptitude for music.

We once had a client whose rationalization of his disability ran something like this: All of the men in his family had been highly active outdoors types. They all had died prematurely with coronaries. He, the client, was a highly active outdoors type; however, now that he was severely disabled he would be considerably restricted in his activities. Therefore, he would not die prematurely. This logic resulted in the conclusion that the disability was positive and he was pleased he had become disabled. Granted, rationalization is seldom carried to this extreme in the adjustment to blindness, but this case is illustrative of a type of thinking which must occur for good adjustment.

Projection

A person who perceives traits or qualities in himself which are unacceptable may deny these traits and project them to others. In doing so he is using the defense mechanism of projection. A person who is quite stingy sees others as being essentially more stingy. A person who is basically dishonest sees others as trying to steal from him. A person who feels inferior rejects this idea and instead projects it to others; i.e. he is capable but others will not give him a chance because they doubt his ability. These are examples of projection. With the blinded person many of the feelings he has of himself are unacceptable. Therefore, in order to adjust adequately, he projects these feelings to society in general. *They* feel he is inadequate. *They* feel he is not capable. *They* feel he is inferior and is to be devalued. This type of thinking, normally, leads directly into identification and compensation which are in reality the natural exits to this maze in which he has been wandering around.

Identification

The defense mechanism of identification is used to reduce an individual's conflicts through the achievement of another person or a group of people. Identification can be with material possessions as well as people. A person may derive his social adequacy and psychological adequacy through his clothes (*The clothes make the man*), his sports car, his hi-fi stereo paraphernalia, etc. People identify with larger groups in order to take on the power, prestige, and respect attributed to that organization (*our team won*). This larger group may be a club, lodge, garden club, college, professional group, etc.

In adjustment to his blindness, the client will identify with a larger group. It may be a group of other blind persons, an occupational group, a men's lodge, a veterans' group, etc. But at this point in the adjustment process, he will identify with some group in order to offset some of the feelings he has as a result of the projection he is engaging in. If successful, the identification obviates the need to employ the mechanisms of denial, withdrawal, and regression.

Compensation

If an individual's path to a set of goals is blocked and he finds other routes to achieve that set of goals, he is using the defense mechanism of compensation. A teenager is seeking recognition and acceptance from his peers. He decides to gain this recognition through sports. However, when he fails to make the team he decides to become a scholar. This is an example of compensation. Compensation brings success; therefore, it diverts attentions from shortcomings and defects, thereby eliminating expressed or implied criticism. This defense mechanism is most often used to reduce self-criticism rather than external criticism. As the individual experiences successes he will become less preoccupied with anxieties relating to his disability and his lack of productivity.

Identification and compensation usually go together in the adjustment process. When the client starts using these two defenses he is at a point at which he may adequately adjust to the new body-image and his new role in life.

Implications for Professionals Working With Blind Persons

Almost everyone in our society views handicapping and disabling conditions from an anatomical point of view rather than functionally. It is imperative that the newly blinded be helped to view their disability functionally rather than anatomically. The client should gain an appreciation for the abilities he has left rather than classifying himself with a group based solely upon an anatomical loss.

The worker with the blind should make sure the information which the client has is factual, concise, and clear. He should be sure the client's perception of his disability is correct and the cause is completely understood. This understanding greatly enhances the adjustment of the client to his blindness.

The client should be helped in exploring his feelings regarding the manner in which he is currently being treated by family and friends. Help him to understand the natural emotional reactions he will have resulting from his newly acquired blindness; and help him to understand that the feelings of family and friends are going to be different for a period of time while they adjust to his disability.

Do not fall into the trap of thinking that the degree of blindness is correlated with the degree of psychological impact. Realize that each individual's disability is unique unto that individual and his reaction to his disability will be unique.

Lastly, in summary, the most important role anyone can play in assisting a client in the adjustment to blindness is to be a warm, emphatic, accepting individual who is positive in his regard toward the client and who is pragmatic in counseling and planning efforts with the client.

Providing Counseling Services

What is Counseling

Counseling has been defined in various terms and by many experts. Gustad (1953) has written that "counseling is a learning oriented process, carried on in a simple, one-to-one social environment in which a counselor, professionally competent in relative psychological skills and knowledge, seeks to assist the client to learn more about himself, to know how to put understanding into effect in relation to clearly perceived, realistically defined goals to the end that the client may become a happier and more productive member of his society."

While definitions vary according to the orientation of the counselor, certain truisms have resulted from the enormous amount of research concerning the effectiveness of counseling. These will be explained in the following paragraphs.

No matter what particular school or theory of counseling is accepted by the practitioner, the most important factor determining the outcome of counseling effectiveness is the *personality* of the counselor himself. In other words, whether he counts himself as Rogerian, Ellisonian, or eclectic, the personality of the counselor will come through in counseling sessions and affect the outcome to a degree which will determine whether or not the counseling session is effective. Just as teachers can bring about enormous growth and changes in students by modifying their attitudes toward various subject matter, the counselor can bring about substantial changes in his client for better or worse.

Effective counseling requires certain basic ingredients. As the strength or weakness of these ingredients vary so does the ability of the counselor to help the client. There are three basic prerequisites to effective counseling. First, the counselor must accept the client without imposing conditions for this acceptance. He must be willing to work with the client and become actively involved with him as an individual no matter what the counselee's race, attitudes, or mode of life may be. This is necessary in order for the counselee to gain the knowledge that the counselor as a person wishes to help him with his problems and is not prejudging.

The counselor must be *genuine* in that he must function in a way which indicates to the client that he is being true to his own feelings and to himself. To be otherwise is to present a facade to the client—a false image which will act as a deterrant to a successful relationship. Counselors must avoid artificiality in their relationships. If the counselor hides behind a professional mystique, he may find that the counselee is better at *fooling* him than he is at deceiving the client. The professional worker cannot expect his client to be open, sincere, and genuine if he himself does not represent these characteristics well.

In addition, the counselor must have an empathetic understanding and feeling *vis-à-vis* the client. He must make a sincere effort to see the client's problem through the *client's eyes* and he must be able to communicate the depth of his understanding.

Counseling can be considered a relationship between two persons which is conducive to good mental health. Inherent in an effective counseling relationship is the absence of threat. The counselor must remove threat if the client is to grow and be able to solve his problems in an uninhibited manner. Counseling as a relationship is also typified by the types of feelings that many of us have for our closest friends. True close friendships are characterized by honest caring, genuine interest, and a high level of concern about helping in a time of need. Real friendships often require one person to put aside his own selfish needs in order to listen long enough and with enough empathy so that a friend's problem may begin to work itself out in a natural and constructive manner.

There are a number of adjectives which apply to various types of counseling (religious, marital, rehabilitation, educational, personal, vocational, and others). Counseling services vary according to the needs of the client, not the counselor. A counselee who comes to the counselor for help will often, at first, outline a concern which is not the real problem. The counselor must have considerable flexibility and insight to know what is required in each individual situation.

Rehabilitation Counseling

Rehabilitation counselors are concerned mainly with individuals who have vocational handicaps. These handicaps may result from physical disability, emotional and mental illness, social or cultural deprivation. In each individual case, the counselor must be able to decide what remedy is required in order to move the counselee toward successful personal adjustment in his family, community, and on the job.

Rehabilitation counseling requires the ingredients mentioned earlier for effective counselor-client relationships; however, much of rehabilitation counseling consists of advice-giving and coordination of services to the client. In a sense, *rehabilitation counseling* can be considered a misnomer when the term is applied across the board. A substantial number of clients need considerable advice and information which the counselor has to offer concerning social and rehabilitation services from which they can profit. When the counselee needs advice and information, the rehabilitation counselor must be able to recognize this need and provide what is required. There also will be many instances in which the client and counselor must enter into a number of counseling sessions in depth. The counselor must make the judgment concerning what type of help is needed for the client to solve his particular problems. Rehabilitation counselors need appropriate training that will enable them to decide whether or not they are qualified to do the kind of counseling which is necessary.

Many counselors fall into the trap of wanting to play the role of *junior therapist* and involve high percentages of their clients in in-depth counseling sessions. This is particularly true of the graduates of many rehabilitation counselor training programs. Some workers hide behind *counseling* (as synonymous with quality) in terms of their justifying low numbers of rehabilitated clients. There is much talk of quality services and in-depth counseling which require considerable time. The rehabilitation counselor who is an effective manager of his caseload can *rehabilitate* the number of persons required by his agency administrator and while doing so can provide counseling services as needed to his clients.

Rehabilitation work requires a broad definition of counseling which includes the offering of some, and coordination of other professional services to clients. Generally, agency administrators —especially those trained in counseling—do not accept the explanation of *the time required and quality services* for a low client rehabilitation rate. Any agency administrator or supervisor knows that some cases require much involved counseling, and that these cases, in many instances, are the most difficult ones. They are time-consuming, and they can test the fiber of the rehabilitation counselor. Untrained counselors generally cannot handle such cases without help from someone who had had some advanced orientation in counseling. However, counselors who play the role of *junior therapist* in trying to become deeply involved with all of their clients—whether or not this type of service is called for— will be ineffective and probably will not remain long in rehabilitation work.

The rehabilitation counselor will find his coordinating and facilitating role highly rewarding when it is done well and gets needed services. One of the greatest satisfactions that the counselor can have is the assurance that he knows when certain types of services are required and whether these should be more therapeutically oriented or more oriented toward advice, information, and coordination of community resources and professional services.

Rehabilitation counselors should not rank-order their clients in a psychological need hierarchy which places the individual with severe psychological problems at the top of the counselor's list for services. Certainly, these persons should be served immediately upon the counselor's realization that severe psychological problems exist. They should be referred to the appropriate psychologist or psychiatrist if problems are so severe that the counselor cannot handle them alone, or they should be served by rehabilitation counselors who are competent in the type of service required. The point to be made here is that the rehabilitation process is a complicated procedure; the client who may be adjusting normally to a loss and who does not need substantial in-depth therapeutic involvement is as good a case for services as one requiring more therapeutic work. Coordination of services of supportive personnel and professional personnel is a substantial part of the work of the rehabilitation counselor. In many cases, he will have to bring this team together in order that the client can continue to receive effective and necessary rehabilitation services.

The rehabilitation counselor must actively involve himself within the community in order to be fully aware of the many resources which exist that can be of substantial benefit to his clients. Generally, counselors have indicated that so much of their time is taken with counseling and coordination of services that they are unable to put forward enough effort to learn all that the community has to offer. Counselors who utilize community resources effectively are very familiar with the offerings of various agencies and through coordination and cooperation find that their work load is lessened by the support of other social service programs.

The counselor will wish to offer his services to various types of community agencies. For instance, most counselors can give a great deal of useful advice to such programs as the community action and model cities efforts sponsored by the Federal Government. Agencies and organizations such as family service programs and welfare agencies can be of considerable help in getting needed services for the rehabilitation client. The counselor should take a major responsibility in coordinating efforts of agencies and programs that can help in the rehabilitation of clients, and he should volunteer his time and energies to help strengthen other social service programs.

The rehabilitation counselor must keep in mind that he should be moving the client toward end objectives of independence and successful adjustment on the job. Rehabilitation differs from some other social service professions in the regard that a substantial test of the counselor's work is made at the end of the rehabilitation process. That test consists of the appropriateness of the client's behavior in work situation (Hardy, 1972).

Rehabilitation Counseling With the Blind and Severely Visually Impaired

No special counseling theory need be constructed in order for the rehabilitation counselor to serve blind persons. There is, however, a substantial body of knowledge with which the counselor should be thoroughly familiar. Topics include the etiology of diseases related to blindness, problems in adjustment to visual loss including mobility, social adjustment, occupational advice and job placement. The counselor serving blind persons has a real responsibility to undertake considerable study in order to acquaint himself with what Father Carroll (1961) has called in the title of his book, *Blindness: What It Is, What It Does, and How to Live With It.*

The rehabilitation counselor serving blind persons has as much or more of a coordinating function as does the counselor in a general agency setting. A counselor concerned with the blind will work closely with the educational services specialist, the social worker, the ophthalmologist, the placement specialist, the rehabilitation teacher, and the mobility instructor who help in the team effort of moving the blind individual toward adjustment to his visual problem and later to adjustment on the job.

Rehabilitation counselors serving the blind, just as counselors working with any other rehabilitation client, must be certain that their clients are without need of further medical or psychological treatment. In this regard, the counselor helping the partially sighted should make certain that no visual aid or professional service can offer additional help to the client. He should be fully aware of the various problems which go hand in hand with a loss of sight. Persons who are experiencing a severe physical inadequacy lose some ability to be independent. They feel socially inadequate and in some cases may have additional problems which at first might not be apparent to the counselor. Advanced age or other physical incapabilities may add to the blind person's adjustment problems.

The client will be very much interested in the prognosis for his future, and the rehabilitation counselor should make sure that valid information is provided. An effective counselor must be ready to help the blind person understand what his opportunities are for education, employment, and social activities. He should also talk with those persons who give information to the blind client, especially professional individuals such as ophthalmologists, to make certain that they have useful information concerning blindness and the services of the state rehabilitation agency.

Bauman and Yoder (1966) have suggested that the rehabilitation counselor must offer:

> a combination of several qualities: (1) his own emotional acceptance of blindness (he must be the first person to whom the client has spoken who did not immediately show great pity and anxiety— a helping new experience for the client); (2) formal or informal instruction in procedures which make it easier to live as a blind person (the home teacher and also some adjustment on pre-vocational training can help here); (3) realistic planning for the future, including vocational planning if the age and general health of the client make this appropriate. It is true that all of these may be rejected for a time, in which case the counselor must offer (4) understanding, patience, and a gentle persistence which keeps him available until the client and his family are able to reorient themselves to the future instead of clinging to the past.

In counseling with blind persons, the rehabilitation counselor must remember that he is working with individuals who cannot see or whose sight is impaired. The client will differ from fellow blind persons as much as he will differ from sighted persons. Some blind persons are very healthy; others are sickly. Some are well adjusted psychologically; others are poorly adjusted. In many cases, blindness will have caused severe psychological stress which has not been overcome, just as an accident or some other type of tramuatic experience may have caused either a sighted or a blind person severe psychological difficulty.

Often, reaction to partial vision causes as much or more frustration and anxiety than reaction to total blindness. One reason for this seems to be that partially sighted persons are unable to function normally and do not want to accept their loss of sight as a reality. They live in a no-man's-world between blindness and sight.

The rehabilitation counselor serving blind and severely visually impaired persons must be even more planful and thoughtful than the counselor who is concerned with individuals who are sighted. Often it will be necessary to anticipate problems which may arise for the blind client. For instance, simply getting to and from the counselor's office may become a very troublesome and embarrassing task. The blind client may be traveling over unfamiliar terrain with or without the help of relatives or friends. The counselor, in many cases, may want to visit initially in the home and later during the relationship invite the client to the rehabilitation agency.

The counselor must be very much aware that this blind client is *tuned in* to auditory clues (yes's and unhum's may be helpful), since the usual eye contact and other nonverbal communications are not effective with blind persons. For instances, silence over a considerable period of time often takes place in counseling sessions, but when the counselor is working with a blind client, silence may be interpreted at times as disinterest or rejection.

It is respectful and appropriate for the counselor to look directly into the face and eyes of the client just as if the counselee were fully sighted. Blind persons are often aware that sighted persons are not looking at them and they get the impression, which may be true, that the counselor is not listening.

Counselors should be particularly careful about shuffling

papers, tapping a pencil on the desk, or making other sounds that are distracting. They should also be aware that many blind persons, especially the congenitally blind give the counselor little to go by in terms of facial expression. The counselor who is used to reading emotionality in various facial responses may be at a considerable loss with some persons who have been blind for a number of years and who are not nearly as responsive in this respect as sighted people (Jordan, 1962).

A rehabilitation counselor providing professional services to blind persons must avoid fostering unnecessary dependence. Often counselors, unknowingly as well as knowingly, build their own self-esteem by continually allowing clients to rely on them for personal advice and other services. On the other hand, many rehabilitation counselors are afraid to show sufficient interest in the problems of the client because they are concerned about being forced to give a great deal of time and attention to the client. Neither of these extremes will allow the counselor to be effective.

Summary

It has been said that the most important variable for helping people which the counselor brings to the counseling relationship is *himself*. The rehabilitation counselor, whether he is working with blind or sighted clients, must make a substantial effort to maintain genuiness, openness, sincerity, honesty, and respect for the client. While techniques and procedures are important in accomplishing goals in counseling sessions, the real key to successful counseling is whether the counselor genuinely cares for the individual. A rehabilitation counselor provides substantial professional and coordinated services from which the client benefits enormously. Most rehabilitation counselors will have certain quotas to meet and the effective counselor, through proper caseload management, will be able to provide quality and quantity services. He will also realize that his coordinative and facilitative function is as important as his counseling function. He must serve clients according to *their needs* and not his own; when this is done, counselees will not claim that his work lacks quality because he will have been much more concerned with

them as individuals than with whether or not his services were
professional in nature.

VOCATIONAL PLACEMENT AND BLINDNESS

There are many commonalities between approaches to the
placement of the generally handicapped and those persons who
are visually handicapped. Many persons who have visual problems also have a second handicap. One of the purposes of this
section is to provide general information which will be useful in
vocational placement.

One of the most substantial contributions a rehabilitation
counselor can make which affects his client's overall mental and
physical adjustment is the placement of the individual on a job
that is well suited to his abilities and interests. Vocational
placement is underrated by many rehabilitation counselors and
others who do not understand the full effects of its outcome.
Helping the client find employment is often relegated to scanning
newspaper want ads in search of opportunities or responding
to a call from an employer who happens to have a job available.
Certainly, occupational opportunities can be located through
these means; however, the matching of the individual and the
job is a complicated process which requires careful study and
evaluation through interrelating all casework data on the individual with all information that can be secured relating to
job requirements and job settings.

Vocational Placement and Blind Persons

Blindness is a severe disability, and the counselor concerned
with the placement of blind persons must be certain that the
placement program is carefully planned. No magic is involved
in the placement of the blind in competitive employment; however, a great deal of hard work and effective public relations
are necessary.

There are many special considerations and much pertinent
information with which the placement counselor must be very
familiar. For instance, he should have some understanding of
the physiological aspects of loss of sight. Such information can

be obtained through the study of the medical aspects of blindness. The counselor will need to have answers readily available to many questions concerning the client's adjustment, his ability to communicate with others, to get to his work station, and to get to and from work. The better the counselor understands his client, the more effective he will be in vocational placement. One of the most important concepts for the counselor to remember in working with blind persons is that blind persons are people first and blind second. There are varying levels of potential according to the individual's personality and general intelligence.

A very important aspect of the placement of blind persons concerns getting the client psychologically ready for employment. He must believe in his own ability to do the work which is necessary and he must have confidence in the counselor's judgment concerning the types of jobs he can perofrm.

Blind workers have proven themselves over the years to be safe, dedicated, loyal, and low in absenteeism (American Mutual Insurance Alliance). Job opportunities for blind persons cover a very wide range and no list of jobs that blind people can perform is ever appropriate or complete. When he is helping the blind person decide on his vocational future, the counselor should remember that key sources of information for counseling are the client himself and his family. Counselors must move away from stereotyping jobs for blind persons and toward innovative placement. A great deal of information must be acquired about the client through interviews and counseling sessions with him and his family. It can be highly effective in counseling and psychological evaluation of blind persons to ask about the types of job fields they would be most interested in if they were fully sighted. This allows a broad vocational exploration which brings out many possible areas for consideration. Often, jobs in the suggested fields or in closely related ones are feasible.

The counselor concerned with the placement of blind persons will find that many industrial jobs do not require sight. Some of the jobs which do not require sight are the very ones which employers and counselors have thought definitely required sight. Blind persons, according to the legal definition, may have various amounts of vision up to 20/200 in the best eye with best correction or a visual field not exceeding an angle greater than 20 degrees (Jones, 1962). The counselor will have to know his client physically, psychologically, and socially and proceed with the placement plan after all information has been carefully studied and interrelated. Jobs can be evaluated with specific clients in mind or the counselor can approach the evaluation of jobs with various levels of required vision in mind. Again, the key to successful placement is careful planning. The counselor must think of various contingent possibilities. It is most helpful to observe workers performing jobs and to talk with them concerning all aspects of the jobs under observation, including whether they continue to do the job under consideration hour after hour, day after day without modification during all periods and seasons. This approach is often necessary in evaluating the job for a blind worker.

Generally speaking, blind persons continue to need the rehabilitation counselor in a salesmanship capacity. Most blind persons need help in selling their abilities to perspective employers. This is another reason why the work of vocational placement in rehabilitation counseling of blind persons has great importance.

The remaining sections of this chapter will offer various types of information which will be useful to the rehabilitation counselor serving blind individuals.

A Science of Vocational Behavior

Lofquist and Dawis (1969) discussed a *science of vocational behavior* which they see as essentially vocational psychology. Whether one agrees or not that the science of vocational behavior is actually vocational psychology, the necessity for the full development of vocational behavior study as a science cannot be over stressed. The substantial growth during recent years of interest in the Vocational Evaluation and Work Adjustment Division of the National Rehabilitation Association and the subsequent publication of the *Vocational Evaluation and Work Adjustment Bulletin* have done a great deal to stimulate thinking and research on vocational behavior and practical problems of the individual and groups in the world of work. Certainly, in the future, vocational adjustment studies and work evaluation will take an even more prominent place in the rehabilitation counselor's work and in rehabilitation counselor education within university settings.

Above all, the rehabilitation counselor must be able to understand the *work personality* of his client. The *work personality profile* consists of such factors as vocational and avocational interests; abilities, needs, work habits; psychological maturity; and interaction with on-the-job factors including job hierarchies, communication, and health factors.

The rehabilitation counselor interested in developing expertise in placement should become familiar with available research on work adjustment. Studies done in vocational rehabilitation at the University of Minnesota (Lofquist, 1957) since 1957 offer a great deal of useful information.

Client-Centered Placement

Rehabilitationists have heard much about *client-centered counseling* over the years. Because placement is an important part of the rehabilitation process, counselors should think of *client-centered placement.* Job placement is a major client service which has helped rehabilitation agencies in getting substantial amounts of federal and state funds for program operations. The goal of work is one of the unique characteristics of rehabilitation. The placement of individuals on jobs through which they can find methods to maintain themselves is the concept which has allowed rehabilitation counseling to gain in stature as a social service profession with a substantial contribution to make to the individual and to society. In fact, most laymen would probably say that the location of appropriate jobs for clients is the main function of the rehabilitation counselor. It is interesting that rehabilitation counselors downplay the importance of placement in their jobs when they describe their activities to their friends and colleagues. Counselors might reflect more seriously upon their placement responsibilities if clients were thought of as consumers of their services and were given an opportunity to actually evaluate the jobs which they have obtained with the help of the counselor.

In fact, the use of the phrase *PLACE in employment* is one which misleads the rehabilitation counselor trainee and others concerning the method which should be used. The client and counselor must work together in order for the client to reach a decision concerning the type of job he wishes to have. After this decision is made and the rehabilitation counselor helps the client secure information about various jobs that exist in the geographical area where he wants to be employed, the client himself should take some initiative whenever possible to get employment with the assistance of the counselor. Once a feasible job is located, the client should be given the opportunity to evaluate it as the source of his future livelihood.

Quite often, when considering placement, the counselor is confronted with the dilemma of determining to whom he owes basic loyalty, the client or the employer; that is, should he be protective of the client when dealing with an employer or protective of the employer. How much of the client's problems and disability should the counselor relate to the employer? Should he obscure the client's disability in discussion with the employer?

If the professional relationship was bilateral and concerned only the client and counselor, the answer to the dilemma would be immediately obvious; however, the relationship is trilateral.

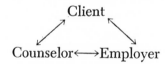

As such, the counselor owes equal professional responsibility to both the client and prospective employer. Therefore, the counselor should communicate with the employer in a basic, forthright manner. The counselor is professionally obligated to be honest in his dealings with the employer.

If the counselor fails to be completely honest and forthright with the employer, he not only jeopardizes his professional relationship with this employer, thereby obviating any possibility of placing clients in this area in the future, but he also takes a great chance of jeopardizing the client-employer relationship later when the employer becomes more aware of the client's attributes which the counselor chose to hide or misrepresent. Consequently, I feel rather strongly that the counselor should discuss with the client what he is planning to relate to the employer. If the client refuses to allow the counselor to discuss his assets, liabilities and disability with the employer, the counselor should modify his role in the placement process. His role should be one of providing placement information to the client, but he should not enter actively into the placement process with the client.

There are two limits to this interchange between the counselor and employer relative to the client and they are the following:

1. The counselor and employer should discuss thoroughly those aspects and only those aspects of the client's background which has a direct relation with the job.
2. The counselor should communicate with the employer on a level at which both are comfortable in the exchange of information.

Quite often a counselor approaches a prospective employer regarding a specific client and as the conversation progresses, the counselor finds himself relating information which, while highly pertinent in the rehabilitation process, has little to do with the client as an employee. In each instance in which the counselor makes an employee contact for placement purposes, the counselor should have previously summarized all material in the case folder which is directly related to the client's proficiency in a particular position—both his assets and liabilities. After reviewing this summary, the counselor should refrain from relating any other information he may have derived from counseling sessions, training evaluations, or diagnostic work-ups. A mark of professionalism is the abiilty to communicate the essential, factors relating to the client and still respect the client's fundamental right to confidentiality of case material.

The second limitation to communication between the counselor and employer requires the counselor to assess the sophistication of the employer and to communicate with him on that level. As a general rule, the counselor should avoid using terminology which, though descriptive, is highly laden with emotional connotations. The most effective approach the counselor can take in discussing the client's assets and liabilities is to describe behavior rather than categorizing behavior with diagnostic labels. It is much more effective to relate to an employer that a client experienced learning difficulties in the academic areas rather early and is slow in learning new procedures, is ineffective in dealing with abstract concepts and carrying out complex, oral instructions and should not be placed in a situation requiring independent judgments in changing conditions but that he is very adept in performing concrete forms of tasks and is capable of making routine, repetitive judgments, than to relate to the employer merely that the client is a mental retardate and assume the employer is sophisticated enough to translate this diagnostic label into behavioristic terms as described above rather than stereotyping the client immediately with a diagnostic label.

Developing an Employment Program

Counselors who are involved with placement should be familiar with information offered in the publication, *Workers Worth Their Hire* (American Mutual Insurance Alliance), which is available through the President's Committee on Employment of the Physically Handicapped. Myths concerning employment of the handicapped are dispelled by information given in this publication. Counselors will find that discussions of the excellent record of handicapped persons in such areas as safety, absenteeism, production, and motivation to work are of considerable help to them in their discussion with employers, union leaders, and work supervisors. The counselor should be certain that he not only talks about these factors with top agency employment officials, but also that he manages, at the appropriate time, to mention these subjects to supervisors within the work area. The degree of acceptance which supervisors give to handicapped clients is often highly influential in not only helping them *get off to a good start* but also in maintaining their work at a level commensurate with the supervisor's expectations.

Some rehabilitation counselors have felt that the counselor

should not have a specific client in mind when talking with an employer, but that he should sell the concept of hiring the handicapped to the employer and later get into the work setting in order to locate the types of jobs which would be available to handicapped individuals. This concept can be extremely useful and can help open many doors to blind employees; however, after convincing the employer of the value of hiring blind persons, the counselor often will be asked to refer a prospective employee immediately if a particular opening exists in the work setting. If a counselor is unable to meet this request, his public relations and sales program can be substantially damaged in terms of future placements with the employer.

Each rehabilitation counselor should constantly evaluate his efforts in placement to make certain that he is moving clients toward jobs in line with their overall adjustment and ability. One of the key sources of learning about job opportunities for any client is often the client's past experiences and previous job responsibilities. In many cases, clients will wish to return to the type of employment held prior to the onset of the employment handicap. In fact, many former employers will feel a responsibility for injured employees and wish again to offer them employment after they have received rehabilitation services. The client will offer many insights about himself to the counselor who then has the responsibility to match abilities, needs, and interests of the client with requirements and offerings of the job. One of the primary sources, then, of information about types of employment for the client is the client himself. This information can be gained by a study of his background and from interest inventories and interviews with him and his family.

The counselor will also wish to use the services of the state employment agency which maintains local offices throughout the United States. Many prospective employers inform the employment service of job openings. This agency also offers counseling, placement, and evaluation services for handicapped job applicants. The Vocational Rehabilitation Act, Public Law 89-565, stipulates that the vocational rehabilitation state plan shall "provide for entering into cooperative agreements with the system of public employment offices in the state and the

maximum utilization of the job placement and employment counseling services and other services and facilities of such offices."

Questions Counselors Must Be Able to Answer

Of course, many different problem areas can arise when the
counselor is discussing hiring handicapped workers with an
employer. Questions range from "How will the person get to
the place of employment?" to "What will he do in case of fire?"
Incidentally, these two questions usually can be answered with
the same responses which any employee would give (in the first
case, "By bus or car," and in the second, "Get the hell out like
everyone else.").

The first basic question which usually arises is that of increased
insurance rates if handicapped workers are employed. This is
most often an honest employer reaction to the question concerning employment of handicapped workers. Insurance rates would
rise if individuals were employed in an agency which tended to
have more accidents; however, handicapped workers have been
proven to be as safe in the performance of their duties as other
workers. In fact, some handicapped persons such as the blind
have actually shown better records of safety than nonhandicapped workers. The counselor should have this information
readily available and indicate to the prospective employer that
indeed, workmen's compensation insurance rates are determined,
in part, according to the relative hazards of the work done by
the industry in question. Yearly rates also are determined according to the industry's record of accidents and insurance claims.
These are good reasons for hiring handicapped workers. If an
employer persists in believing that his insurance rates will
increase, the counselor should ask him to contact his insurance
agent or read again his insurance contract.

A second question which often arises is this: "Why should I
hire a handicapped individual when I can employ normal persons
whom I can count on for employment without difficulty?"

The counselor will have to answer this question according to
his own philosophy and training. Some helpful responses might
include the following:

1. Asking why he should not employ individuals whose em-

ployment records have been proven and who are well known and highly recommended by rehabilitation employment specialists.

2. Describing the medical, social, and psychiatric evaluations completed on all clients (not being specific or violating confidentiality). In other words, why not hire an individual who comes to the employer in a sense *certified* as ready for employment?

3. Reminding him that he is actually supporting what he, as a taxpayer, has already invested some money in—an employment program for the handicapped which has proven to be highly successful.

Another question which frequently is raised in employment interviews concerns the firing or dismissal of the employee and the employer's reluctance to treat the rehabilitant in the same manner as he would treat other employees. The counselor again will have to rely on his own resources; however, an analogy may be helpful here: If a salesman were selling refrigerators and the employer bought one which later malfunctioned, the salesman would stand by his product and attempt to get it in good working order. The counselor could briefly discuss follow-up procedures with the employer at this time. He might also indicate that once the handicapped employee has worked for the employer for a time, the employer will feel that he is a fully functioning, well-adjusted employee who should be treated just as all other employees are. The counselor should assure the employer of his confidence in the client.

A fourth question which counselors must be ready to answer concerns architectural barriers and physical limitations of the work setting. Counselors should be frank in their responses to questions concerning limitations of the client and restrictions imposed by the work testing. The counselor should be the first to indicate that certain jobs are infeasible for many of his clients. He should be certain to get across to the employer the fact that he is not going to place a blind person on an unsafe job or on a job which he cannot handle.

A fifth question which often arises concerning employment of the handicapped is that of the *second injury* which might result in total disabiilty and affect the workmen's compensation

payments made by the employer. In a vast majority of states
and the District of Columbia and Puerto Rico, *second injury*
funds or equivalent arrangements have been established. In
these localities, the employer is responsible only for the last
injury and the employee is compensated for the disability which
results from combined injuries.

Some Guidelines and Tools in Locating Employment Opportunities

The following are some suggestions:

1. The counselor should be aware of industrial developments
   within the area that he serves and in adjacent areas.
2. The three volumes of the *Dictionary of Occupational Titles*
   (1965) offer a wealth of useful information for rehabilitation counselors. Much emphasis is given to descriptions of
   physical and personality requirements for various jobs.
   In addition, these volumes can help expand the counselor's
   concepts about various types of jobs which are related to
   the general interest area of the rehabilitation client.
3. Employers with whom former clients have been placed
   can be important sources of information.
4. Previously rehabilitated clients can offer many sound ideas
   about existing employment opportunities.
5. Local chambers of commerce usually provide an industrial
   index which lists types of work available in their communities. Counselors also should coordinate their efforts
   with those of the state employment service since the
   mutual sharing of job information can be valuable to
   both employment services counselors and rehabilitation
   counselors.
6. When placing persons on jobs in rural areas, the worker
   should consider enlisting the support of local community
   leaders such as doctors, city councilmen, postmasters, and
   religious leaders as well as Rotary, Kiwanis, Ruitan and
   other civic groups.
7. If the counselor is interested in assisting individuals in
   becoming small business managers and operators, he

should get in touch with the Small Business Administration office serving his local area.

Professional Placement

In rehabilitation jargon, *professional placement* generally means developing client employment opportunities which require at least a college education. Bauman and Yoder (1962) offer excellent coverage of this area of placement as it pertains to work for the blind. Professional placement is *facilitative* work for the counselor. The counselor can help his client in terms of giving advice and information; however, he must be certain not to take the place of the client in securing actual jobs. The client must be ready to meet with the employer without the counselor in order to discuss his professional qualifications for work. When he has a particular problem, the counselor should be able to assist him with information which could be helpful during the employer interview. For example, he should be coached on how to present himself most favorably. The counselor might help his client develop a resume or portfolio which would outline his training and give examples of any previous work done in the job field in which he wants employment. Other procedures usually followed in placement may or may not be appropriate according to the judgment of the counselor.

A worker in charge of professional placement may want to organize pre-college orientation groups for clients. It will be necessary, also, for the counselor who is dealing with persons in training to inform them about services available while they are in training and away from their home area. If, for instance, clients are attending college, the rehabilitation counselor should help them become acquainted with college counseling center services at the institution they attend (Hardy, 1965).

Effective professional placement requires long-range planning on the part of both counselor and client. Two years before placement (in training cases) is not too early for the client to begin planning with his counselor in order to solve problems related to his securing the type of employment he wants. The counselor will need to prepare by knowing who the prospective employers are and the requirements of the job.

Getting the Client Ready for Employment

Planning for placement does not begin once the client has had vocational training and is ready *skillwise* for employment, but when the counselor first reads the client's rehabilitation referral form. The rehabilitation worker must constantly learn about his client in order to effectively help him secure the type of employment he needs. Jeffrey (1969) has developed a job readiness test which helps in the evaluation of job preparedness of clients. While the total instrument is not applicable to all rehabilitation clients, certain questions are quite helpful with most rehabilitation clients.

Role playing is an excellent method to use in preparing a client for employment interviews. After going through a mock interview which includes a variety of questions, the counselor can give suggestions concerning how the client might improve the impression he makes with the employer. In role playing, it is helpful for the counselor as well as the client to play the role of the employer. Once this is tried, counselors will immediately realize the usefulness of this procedure. The client should realize that getting a job is not an easy task and that he, to the best of his ability, should participate in the job-securing aspects of placement. In some cases, it is an indicator of effective rehabilitation procedures when the client is able to, in fact, *get his own job,* assuming of course that he is ready for employment. The ability with which the client will be able to do this will vary with his motivation and the severity of his social, mental, or physical handicap.

The rehabilitation counselor must stress *training* as a partial answer to many of the problems of the handicapped worker. Overtraining a worker for a job which will affect his personal and family adjustment for many years to come is seldom done. In each case, the counselor must take an individual approach to helping his client. In the case of those who are educationally or socially retarded, various remedial programs may be necessary before actual work training programs can begin. In each case, the counselor must exercise considerable judgment concerning what his client needs in order to be totally ready for employment.

On-the-job training can be a very effective arrangement for

client training. In many of these cases, the state rehabilitation agency will make *tuition* payments to the employer-trainer in order that the rehabilitation counselor may get the employer interested in training a client and evaluating his work. It may be necessary for the counselor to help the employer arrange the appropriate payment schedule for the client since he is not a trained employee and would not receive an amount equal to a regularly salaried employee.

Bridges (1946) offered four major factors which are involved in successful employment of handicapped workers. These remain as highly important considerations for the counselor and are listed below:

1. The worker should have the ability to accomplish the task efficiently, i.e. to be able to meet the physical demands of the job.
2. The worker should not be a hazard to himself.
3. The worker must not jeopardize the safety of others.
4. The job should not aggravate the disability or handicap of the worker.

Common Misconceptions about Vocational Placement

Misconceptions about vocational placement are as follows:

1. Because placement occurs toward the end of the rehabilitation process, the counselor's responsibility to the client diminishes.
2. Placement is an activity which requires no counselor training and is a matter of matching an available client with an available job.
3. Client location of his job (*self-placement*) cannot be effective rehabilitation work.
4. When a client is ready for vocational placement, the information in his case folder is no longer of value to his counselor since the client has been, in a sense, readied for employment.
5. Follow-up after placement always can be handled easily by phone or mail communications with the employer or client.
6. Labor market trends and job information and analysis are

the responsibilities of placement specialists and employment service counselors, not of general rehabilitation
counselors.

7. An employer will notify the counselor and the rehabilitation agency when he is dissatisfied with a client placement.
8. An employer will automatically call upon the rehabilitation agency to furnish him with additional employees
when he needs them.

Rehabilitation counselors should be certain that their clients
understand that it is not necessarily bad to be turned down for
a job. Counselors should understand that experience has shown
that nine or ten employer contacts often must be made before
the counselor makes a placement.

Job Analysis

Every rehabilitation counselor should be thoroughly familiar
with the techniques of job analysis for use in selective placement.
The rehabilitation counselor has to be able to match the prospective worker's social, mental, and physical qualifications with
requirements of the job. Factors such as judgment, initiative,
alertness, and general health and capability must always be taken
into consideration as well as the individual's social and economic
background.

Job analysis should answer certain questions concerning the
job. *What* does the worker do in terms of physical and mental
effort that goes into the work situation? How is the work done?
In other words, does this job involve the use of equipment,
mathematics, or does it require travel. *Why* does the worker
perform the job? This component of the job analysis answers
the question concerning the overall purpose or the sum total of
the task and is the reason for doing the job. The worker also
should understand the relationship of his task to other tasks that
make up the total job.

Generally, the rehabilitation counselor should attempt to
place clients on jobs which they can *handle* and which do not
require modification. In some cases, however, minor modifications can be made with little or no reengineering effort. The
counselor will have to be careful in suggesting reengineering of a

job, since this can be a costly undertaking in many instances. The major objective should be that of helping handicapped workers integrate effectively into the total work force without major modification or change in the work situation.

The following outline can be used in evaluating a job which is to be performed by a handicapped worker:

1. Name used for position surveyed:
    a. D.O.T. title:
    b. Alternate titles:
    c. D.O.T. definitions:
    d. Items worked on in plant surveyed:
2. Usual operator:
    a. Sex:
    b. General characteristics:
3. Physical and psychological demands:
    a. Activities:
    b. Working conditions:
    c. Skill required:
    d. Intelligence:
    e. Temperament:
    f. Other:
4. Description of physical activities:
5. Description of working conditions:
6. Description of hazards:
7. Steps required to accomplish the goal of the work:
    a.
    b.
    c.
    d.
    e.
8. Equipment found in the particular plant surveyed:
    a. Identification:
    b. Set-up and maintenance:
    c. Modification (if required for blind persons):
9. Equipment variations which may be found in other plants:
10. Pre-employment training required:
11. Training procedure:

12. Production:
     a. Full production definition:
     b. Time to reach normal efficency:
13. Interrelation with preceding and succeeding jobs:

Relating Psychological Data to Job Analysis Information in Vocational Placement

As a first step in getting to know clients well, the counselor should make arrangements to secure appropriate psychological information about them. He should either complete job analyses or use available job evaluation data to make decisions about types of information which will be of value to his clients in the job selection and placement procedure. In many instances, however, the counselor fails to synthesize information obtained from two of his most important sources: the psychological evaluation and the job analysis.

The counselor should take five basic steps, as described by Hardy (1969), in developing a successful procedure for interrelating and using important information. He should do the following:

1. Study the needs of the client and the types of satisfaction meaningful to him.
2. Make certain that valid psychological and job analysis data have been gathered.
3. Review the requirements of the job and evaluate the individual traits needed to meet job requirements.
4. Consider the environmental pressures with which the individual must interact.
5. Discuss the job analysis and psychological evaluation with the client so that he will understand what the work will require of him and what it will offer.

Both client and counselor need to have an understanding of job requirements in order to make realistic decisions. One important move should be structuring a set of goals—a guide to help the client avoid useless foundering that gets him nowhere. What satisfaction is he seeking? What is important to him in the long run and what types of work or work settings will provide these satisfactions? These are questions which the counselor must help the client answer.

Maslow (1954) has suggested a hierarchy of the individual needs which the counselor must understand in order to evaluate a client's psychological status—his satisfactions and frustrations. In the usual order of prepotency these needs are for the following:

1. Physiological satisfaction.
2. Safety.
3. Belongingness and love.
4. Importance, respect, self-esteem, independence.
5. Information.
6. Understanding.
7. Beauty.
8. Self-actualization.

In our society, there is no single situation which is potentially more capable of giving satisfaction at all levels of these needs than a person's work, and it is the responsibility of the counselor to help his counselee plan for future happiness through adjustment on the job.

The worker needs to help his client become fully aware of the social pressures of the job, because these are as important to the individual as the actual job pressures. A client's ability to adapt to the social interactions of the work environment will directly affect his job performance.

The counselor always must ask himself what the requirements of the job are. This question can be answered superficially or in considerable detail. A lay job analyst can give superficial requirements, but the responsibility for an in-depth job description belongs to the expert—the counselor who will often have to give direct advice to the client.

Effective placement requires effective planning. Planning cannot be really useful unless appropriate information has been obtained, interrelated, and skillfully utilized so that the client and the counselor have a clear understanding of possible problems and possible solutions.

Follow-up After Placement

A rehabilitation counselor often is tempted to consider his job completed when the client is placed on a job which appears suitable for him; however, the phase of rehabilitation which begins immediately after the person has been placed in employment is one of the most complex. Follow-up involves the counselor's ability to work as a middleman between employer and client in order to help the client solve problems related to his handicap which may arise after being hired. The counselor must be diplomatic and resourceful in maintaining the employer's confidence in his client's ability to do the job. At the same time, he must let the client know that he has full faith in him. The counselor, however, must somehow evaluate how his client is performing on the job and make certain that he is available to help if problems arise which the client cannot solve.

In addition to the worker's service to the client during follow-up, this period can offer real public relations opportunities for the counselor, especially when the employer notes the interest with which the counselor *follows* his client. The frequency of follow-up varies according to the couneslor's judgment of the client's job ability and adjustment.

Agency regulations usually require that a final follow-up be done after thirty days in order to make certain that placement is successful before a *case* can be closed as rehabilitated. Counselors should also consider follow-up periods of sixty to eighty days after placement. Again, this helps reassure the client of the interest of the agency and the counselor in his success and can be of value to the counselor in further developing employment opportunities for handicapped persons.

In follow-up after professional placement, however, the counselor must increase the sixty to ninety day period which is usually adequate in the placement of clients in nonprofessional jobs. A longer period will be necessary and this period will vary with job complications and severity of the client's handicap. Bauman and Yoder (1962) have recommended six months to a year for follow-up in most cases where blind persons have been placed in professional work.

Counselors will probably wish to schedule specific days for

follow-up in the field. Generally, the period of follow-up is a time when the counselor sees the efforts of the entire rehabilitation process coming to fruition. If the job has been well analyzed and the client well evaluated and placed, follow-up will be a pleasurable experience for the counselor.

Summary

The counselor's responsibility in vocational placement must not be underrated. The decisions made at this stage in the rehabilitation process not only affect the client's immediate feelings of satisfaction and achievement but also, of course, his long-term physical and mental health. The counselor has a real responsibility to *ready* the client for employment by giving him the type of information that he needs about the job and about holding employment once it is achieved. Placement should be *client-centered* with strong emphasis given to the client's opinions about work and how it will affect him and his family. Counselors must be ready to answer the questions that employers will ask about hiring handicapped persons and about the rehabilitation program. Vocational placement is high level public relations work.

The counselor must be knowledgeable about job analysis and must interrelate all medical, psychological, and social data with job analysis information in order to be successful in client-centered placement. Once placement has been achieved, the counselor must follow-up the client in order to make certain that he is doing well on the job. The client should have an opportunity to evaluate his job and also the efforts of his counselor in helping him decide on and obtain the job. Effective placement requires effective planning, and counselors must constantly evaluate their knowledge of the world of work and their ability to interrelate information in order to assure real placement success.

REFERENCES

American Mutual Insurance Alliance: *Workers Worth Their Hire*. Chicago,
American Psychiatric Association: *Diagnostic and Statistical Manual of Mental Disorders*. Washington, D.C., American Psychiatric Association, 1965.

Bauman, Mary K., and Yoder, Norman M.: *Adjustment to Blindness—Re-Viewed.* Springfield, Thomas, 1966.

Bauman, M. K., and Yoder, N. M.: *Placing the Blind and Visually Handicapped in Professional Occupations.* Office of Vocational Rehabilitation, Department of Health, Education and Welfare, Washington, D.C., 1962.

Bridges, C. C.: *Job Placement of the Physically Handicapped.* New York, McGraw-Hill, 1946.

Carroll, Thomas J.: *Blindness: What It Is, What It Does, and How to Live With It.* Boston, Little, 1961.

Department of Veterans' Benefits, Veterans' Administration: *They Return to Work.* Washington, D.C., U.S. Government Printing Office, 1963.

English, H. B., and English, A. C.: *A Comprehensive Dictionary of Psychological and Psychoanalytical Terms.* New York, McKay, 1966.

Gustard, J. W.: The definition of counseling. In Berdie, R. F.: *Roles and Relationship in Counseling.* Minneapolis, U. of Minn., 1953.

Hardy, Richard E.: Counseling physically handicapped college students. *New Outlook for Blind,* 59:5:182-183, 1965.

Hardy, Richard E.: Relating psychological data to job analysis information in vocational counseling. *New Outlook for Blind,* 63:7:202-204, 1969.

Hardy, Richard E.: Vocational placement. In Cull, John G. and Hardy, Richard E.: *Vocational Rehabilitation: Profession and Process.* Springfield, Thomas, 1972.

International Society for the Welfare of Cripples: *Selective Placement of the Handicapped.* New York, 1955.

Jeffrey, David L.: Pertinent points on placement. *Clearing House,* Oklahoma State University, November 1969.

Jones, J. W.: Problems in defining and classifying blindness. *New Outlook for Blind,* 56:4:115-121, 1962.

Jordan, John E.: Counseling the blind. *Personnel and Guidance Journal,* 39:3:10-214, 1962.

Lofquist, L. H., and Dawis, R. V.: *Adjustment to Work—A Psychological View of Man's Problems in Work-Oriented Society.* New York, Appleton, July, 1967.

McGowan, J. F., and Porter, T. L.: *An Introduction to the Vocational Rehabilitation Process.* Rehabilitation Services Administration, July, 1967.

McNamee, H. T., and Jeffrey, R. P.: *Service to the Handicapped 1960.* Phoenix, Arizona State Employment Service, 1960.

Maslow, A. H.: A theory of human motivation. *Psychological Review,* 50:370-396, 1954.

Morgan, Clayton A.: Personality of counseling. *Blindness,* AAWB Annual American Association of Workers for the Blind, Inc., Washington, D.C., 1969.

Office of Vocational Rehabilitation. *Training Personnel for the State Vocational Rehabilitation Programs—A Guide for Administrators.* Washington, D.C., U.S. Government Printing Office, 1957.

Sinick, D.: *Placement Training Handbook.* Washington, D.C., Office of Vocational Rehabilitation, 1962.

Stalmaker, W. O.; Wright, K. C., and Johnston, L. T.: *Small Business Enterprises in Vocational Rehabilitation.* U.S. Department of Health, Education and Welfare, Vocational Rehabilitation Administration, Rehabilitation Services Series No. 63-47, 1963.

Thomason, B., and Barrett, A.: *The Placement Process in Vocational Rehabilitation Counseling,* U.S. Department of Health, Education and Welfare, Office of Vocational Rehabilitation, GTP Bull. No. 2, Rehabilitation Services Series No. 545, 1960.

Truax, Charles B., and Cartkuff, Robert R.: *Toward Effective Counseling and Psychotherapy: Training and Practice.* Chicago, Aldine, 1967.

U.S. Employment Service: *Dictionary of Occupational Titles.* Washington, D.C., U.S. Government Printing Office, 1965.

U.S. Employment Service: *Selected Placement for the Handicapped* (Revised ed), Washington, D.C., 1945.

Weiss, D. J.; Dawis, R. V.; Lofquist, L. H., and England, G. W.: *Minnesota Studies in Vocational Rehabilitation.* University of Minnesota, Industrial Relations Center. (Series published since 1954.)

CHAPTER VI

REHABILITATION OF THE MENTALLY ILL

ROBERT A. MACGUFFIE

Medical Model
Appropriate-Inappropriate Behavior Model
Institutionalized *Mentally Ill*
The *Mentally Ill* in the Community
Consultant———→Mediator———→Target

T HE DIFFICULTIES rehabilitation counselors face in the rehabilitation of the *mentally ill* is best illustrated by a political incident in the 1972 election year. The withdrawal of a vice-presidential candidate because of public knowledge that he had experienced psychiatric difficulties exemplifies the suspicion and mistrust the general public has regarding *mental illness*. One newspaper account that I read stated in its headline that the candidate *confessed* to experiencing psychiatric difficulties. The fact that the man had received electroshock therapy as part of the treatment was brought out suggesting not only is the public suspicious of the person experiencing *mental illness* but the treatment methods as well.

Further indication of this attitude has been demonstrated by Tringo (1970) in research with the Attitude Toward Disabled Persons (ATDP) scales. The purpose of his study was to identify an hierarchy of preference toward major disabled groups. The results suggested that the least preferred group was *mental illness*. Thus, rehabilitation counselors find not only must they deal

118

with the person experiencing *mental illness* but with the attitude of the public toward the disability itself. The public asks in a variety of overt and covert ways: "Can the mentally ill be trusted? Are they dangerous? Are they ever *cured*?

Like the criminal offender, the *mentally ill* person finds himself labeled for life experiencing all the aversive reactions such a label brings from society. It will be the intent of this chapter to discuss factors contributing to this perception of *mental illness* as well as suggesting ways rehabilitation counselors can best cope with this and other problems in the rehabilitation of the *mentally ill.*

The major point I am attempting to relate in this chapter is: The first goal of a rehabilitation counselor should be to bring some positiveness in the life of the *mentally ill* person. I am firmly convinced the *mentally ill* tend to be people who feel badly about themselves and have experienced little positive feedback in their lives. Too much of our treatment has been based on aversiveness and negativism and I believe this is one reason why we are not more successful. Aversiveness reinforces the negative self-image that most *mentally ill* people seem to have. Remember the first rule: *Create a Positive Experience.*

Medical Model

I believe that one of the major difficulties in the rehabilitation of the *mentally ill* relates to the fact that they are referred to as *mentally ill.* This labeling is the result of the application of a medical or illness model to a population experiencing environmental problems. From this frame of reference a person experiencing psychiatric difficulties is perceived as ill in much the same manner as if he were to suffer from a virus or a broken leg. The procedure would be to determine the cause of the illness (diagnosis) and *cure* the illness (treatment).

The initial process of diagnosis brings with it certain problems which, in my opinion, make the value of the procedure questionable. In the first place, most diagnoses are much too subjective. The validity of well known instruments (such as the Rorschach) used in diagnosis of *mental illness* have been questioned. The clinician is forced to label a behavior whether he wants to or not and many times the labels are *rubber stamped*. For example, I have seen hospitals in which almost all patients had the label of *paranoid schizophrenic*. At times the diagnosis is merely a reflection of the predilection of the diagnostician and has little to do with the patient's behavior. The point is, that in spite of our efforts to do otherwise, the process remains too subjective to continue using labels that have vast repercussions on the patients who wear them.

A second problem is the diagnosis does not tell the person much about his behavior and, in my opinion, does more to frighten or confuse him than anything else. The term schizophrenia may be a frightening term and, unless one knows what specific behaviors are implied, the term tends to be meaningless. To cite an example I will relate an incident with a patient recently discharged from a mental institution. I was engaged in a conversation with the man in a restaurant. After he learned that I was a psychologist he related he was recently discharged from a state mental institution. I asked him what he had learned about himself during his stay in the hospital. He replied that he knew he was schizophenic and must *pass* a Rorschach to return to his previous employment as an airplane pilot. I asked him what a schizophrenic was and if he he knew anything about himself other than he was schizophrenic. He replied that he did not know what schizophrenia was other than a *disease* and asked me to explain it to him and teach him how to *pass* the Rorschach so he could return to work. The point is that the person learned little about himself as a person except he had been labeled schizophrenic and that his performance on the Rorschach determines if he is *fit* to return to his former employment. This instance certainly did not give the person the feeling he has control over his behavior or the opportunity to learn about himself and his feelings.

Another problem with diagnosis was discussed by Glasser (1965). He suggests that a person will use the label as a *crutch* to explain his behavior and do nothing about changing it. This is apparent to me from consultation duties I am engaged in at a hospital for the *criminally insane*. In that setting the therapists are, in essence, asking people excused of crimes because of *insanity* not to be *insane* anymore so they can face the consequences of their behavior and, in all probability, go to prison. As one can see, this is a very difficult situation, and for some, there may be some benefit to remain *mentally ill.*

I realize in spite of my feeling, diagnostic procedures are going to continue in the field of mental health. However, diagnosis should be established as a tentative hypothesis. If we perceive the diagnosis as a hypothesis subject to change and search for more data about the person's behavior, the procedure may have merit. In any case, we must move away from the finality which tends to accompany diagnostic labels.

How do we know when a *mentally ill* person is *cured?* Is it when the psychotic patient tells the hospital staffing team he no longer hears voices and they recommend discharge? Is it when a person stops denying he engaged in a behavior and says he is sorry? Obviously these are difficult questions to answer and whether or not a person is *cured* is, in my opinion, the wrong question. A better question may be: How does the person behave and how closely does his behavior approximate what is generally referred to as normal behavior in the community? Can the person carry on an intelligent conversation? How well does he relate to others? Can he make his own decisions? How does he feel about himself? These seem to be more appropriate questions.

How does he feel about himself? It is this that interests me the most and is the one question about a person being discharged from a mental hospital I would ask. If the person feels positive about himself, there is a greater probability that his stay in the hospital taught him something constructive. How much has the person learned about himself is a much more productive question to ask than *is he cured?* When we start asking these questions about the *mentally ill* then I believe that we will be moving in a positive direction toward understanding *mental illness* and moving away from some of the traditional flaws of the medical model.

Appropriate-Inappropriate Behavior Model

Rehabilitation counselors should develop some model for perceiving *mental illness.* The model I suggest is one that works for me. This model is primarily based upon my experiences as a counselor with the *mentally ill.*

Generally speaking, people are referred to as *mentally ill* when of people in their environment. The majority of people determine the norms for appropriate or acceptable behavior. What is perceived as appropriate behavior in a mining camp may not be appropriate in a Mennonite community. In addition, there bar. The person who deals with his environment successfully possesses the ability to read *cues,* and acts within reasonable boundaries of acceptable behavior for that setting. However, the person who does not possess this ability experiences a great deal of frustration. People feel he is unable or does not want to conform. If he is perceived as unable to behave appropriately and is not mentally retarded or physically ill then he tends to be referred to as *mentally ill.* The criminal offender would be an example of a person who acts inappropriately because he does not desire to act otherwise.

To further illustrate my point I will cite an example. In each school there are certain norms for classroom behavior. Students are expected to sit and pay attention to the teacher in carrying out tasks for learning. However, if one child hits the teacher, cries when the teacher calls on him or acts in a manner outside the classroom norms the probability is that eventually the child will be referred to as *emotionally disturbed.* The point is that the behavior is situationally defined with certain standards or guidelines as to acceptable behavior.

One might perceive the psychotic person as one whose behavior is inappropriate in most settings and is only appropriate in an institution for the *mentally ill.* On the other hand, the neurotic person may behave erratically and inappropriately at times but generally speaking is able to meet the behavioral norms. It is also possible his inappropriate behavior is not as bizarre or traumatic. Frankly, I do not find the terms to be very useful and do not use them. It is not the label psychotic or neurotic that tells us about a person, but a description of how the person behaves in his environment.

I concede the model has the same problems as the medical model in being subjective. However, the results of the subjectiveness do not appear to be as detrimental to the person. To say a person acts inappropriately most of the time seems more positive than to refer to the person as being psychotic or schizophrenic. All of us can see ourselves as acting inappropriately at times, but few of us would refer to ourselves as *mentally ill*.

The key to this model is to become a keen observer of behavior and, in addition to listening with the third ear to look with the third eye. One must continually ask: "What is appropriate behavior in this situation?" One can develop skills in perceiving any situation involving people. For example, the next time you are at a supermarket, make it a point to observe what people are doing and how they are interacting. Make some attempt to categorize what you feel is generally appropriate behavior in this setting. This gives you cues as to how a *mentally ill* person should act in the same situation and places you in a better position to teach him these skills or to see that someone else does.

If one acts appropriately in most situations he is more likely to receive positive reinforcement from people with whom he is interacting. If he receives positive reinforcement, he should feel better about himself and develop a more positive self-concept. *Mentally ill* people tend to be people who have experienced too little positive reinforcement in their lives. Through the teaching of more appropriate behavior we should increase the probability of a *mentally ill* person being treated in a positive manner and enable him to learn how to adapt favorably to his environment.

I have suggested a frame of reference from which rehabilitation counselors may consider mental illness and will proceed to discuss strategy in the rehabilitation process. For convenience, and because I believe they involve different elements, I separated the *mentally ill* into those who are institutionalized and those who are living in the community.

Institutionalized Mentally Ill

This group includes people referred to as *patients* who reside full time in some institution for the *mentally ill*. The focal point of their existence is the institution where they reside, although they may have visitation privileges and passes.

Generally speaking, most rehabilitation counselors working with this population are either employed directly by the institution or are a member of a service team assigned to the institution by the state rehabilitation agency. Regardless of the arrangement, the initial concern of the counselor should be: *What is my role and function? How do I add another dimension to the services being provided these people?*

The institutionally employed rehabilitation counselor may experience less ambiguity in his initial role since the institution should have a fairly clear idea of their expectations. On the other hand, the state agency counselor may find more ambiguity initially since he is employed by an *outside* agency. Obviously, there are advantages and disadvantages to either arrangement. However, it is the intent here to focus on the commonalities applicable to both settings.

Typically, the counselor will find whatever he does must be as a member of a team since most institutions utilize the team concept. The counselor finds himself surrounded by psychiatrists, ward physicians, psychologists, psychiatric social workers, nurses, attendants, and other personnel engaged in providing service to this population. Each has his function clearly defined and the rehabilitation counselor must ask, *How do I complement the team?*

This is not an easy assignment as it has been my experience that people employed in institutions tend to be very protective of their roles. The rehabilitation counselor will encounter what I refer to as *turfism*. Turfism is the concept that each professional has his role, his place and his area within the setting. The rehabilitation counselor will be well aware when he *steps on someone else's turf* or is infringing upon some duties or skills that others feel are exclusively theirs. Turfism breeds battles such as who conducts psychotherapy with patients, or who on the team makes decisions regarding treatment. Turfism is reinforced throughout most institutions and involves such issues as who has the closest parking spot to the building. Turfism, in my opinions, is what is wrong with many institutions because it does not encourage the cohesiveness needed to provide the patient with the best team effort. For example, if the attendant (who is usually *low* man in the hierarchy) has the best relationship with the patient, why shouldn't he engage in what we refer to as psychotherapy or counseling? If turfism prevails he will be *out of his area*, since psychotherapy is the job of the psychologist or social worker.

Thus, the counselor must first demonstrate what dimension he is adding to the team. He must communicate he is not there to *take* but is there to complement. Initially he will probably justify his role as a vocational rehabilitation counselor. Most of the team members will accept the fact he is the *man* with the knowledge about jobs and training and will utilize his expertise in this area in team staffings. However, the vocational rehabilitation counselor image may be a limited role and the more important role might be that of a *facilitator of the rehabilitation process* through offering patients the opportunity to return to the community regardless of a vocational objective. It is the philosophy of rehabilitation, to help a person rise to the fullest level of functioning in his environment. This is the important concept the counselor must convey.

Generally speaking, mental institutions have not been rehabilitative in nature but have been merely custodial. If they were rehabilitative in nature then presumably they would not need the services of a rehabilitation counselor since competent psychotherapists should be capable of developing worthwhile rehabilitation plans with patients. However, problems most institutions face such as conservatism, rigidity, crowded facilities lack of money and staff make successful rehabilitation in these settings difficult. Thus, the rehabilitation counselor should assure himself that his services are needed and that he must add a dimension to the setting by *bridging the gap* between the community and the institution and contribute to a philosophy of rehabilitation rather than one of custody.

Another issue involved in the rehabilitation process of this population concerns the point at which the rehabilitation counselor should become involved. Should he become involved with the patient when the patient is admitted or when the patient shows indications of being able to return to the community and might be in need of training or job assistance? I believe that the rehabilitation counselor should be involved in every case as early in the process as possible. If he is to be a facilitator of rehabilitation he should begin immediately. There are too many people living on *back wards* of mental institutions because they become lost in the *shuffle*. To combat factors of institutionalization the rehabilitation process should begin immediately. Therefore, it is necessary for the counselor to be involved in at least planning for the patient's return to the community.

Once the counselor has helped initiate the rehabilitation process, he must concern himself with developing job training and employment opportunities for the patient. This presents some problems with this population since the nature of psychiatric difficulties may not permit the patient to crystallize his vocational preference. Initially, the counselor would probably utilize the institution as a training resource. There should be many opportunities for patients to engage in work-related activities on the grounds. This should give the counselor the opportunity to gather data concerning the work habits of the patient as well as his interpersonal behavior in a work setting. It provides the opportunity to utilize the institution as a learning of appropriate skills useful in the employment market.

Initially, the counselor should engage in a detailed analysis of each job training possibility the institution provides. This will provide useful data and each setting can be rated as to degree of job skill and other variables. The counselor will then be able to develop a *job training hierarchy*. The initial training situation should be one where chances of the patient experiencing failure are also nonexistent. This is extremely important as the initial training experience, like the initial interview in counseling, is one in which the foundation for positive attitudes and relationships are established. If this initial experience is successful the patient should be able to progress through the hierarchy of more complex training to ultimate employment in the community. The counselor must permit the patient to progress through this hierarchy at his own pace spending as long in each setting as is necessary to learn the essential job skills and attitudes.

In addition to the actual training in work skills in different settings like the kitchen or the laundry, the patient must grasp the more important social skills. It will be his ability to respond appropriately to the environment that will keep him in the community and on a job. Thus, the counselor must continually assess the growth of the patients in this area and be aware that these skills are necessary in addition to specific vocational skills.

The rehabilitation counselor must become aware of the phenomenon of *institutionalization*. Institutionalization suggests the patient does not want to leave the institution. This may be difficult for counselors to understand since most feel being a patient in a mental institution is aversive. However, the patient may not feel this way. The patient is fed, cared for and in most situations makes few decisions. He is told when to eat, to a person who feel the world *outside* is a cruel and frustrating place. The institution becomes a *refuge from reality* and the patient may not want to leave although he may verbalize otherwise. Most patients I have talked with say they want to leave the institution as soon as possible. However, by observing their behavior it is possible to find just the opposite. The patient may be *too content* and foil rehabilitation plans while providing *lip service*. The counselor must become adept in observing the patient's behavior, considering what the patient does as well as what he says, to determine whether or not the patient is institutionalized. The counselor must try to perceive the institution through the eyes of the patient. If the patient appears to be institutionalized, the counselor will have to use his creativity to help the person develop the initiative to try again in a world he finds aversive. If this initative is lacking, the patient may possess all the employment potential in the world and still remain institutionalized.

The Mentally Ill in the Community

A rehabilitation counselor working with the *mentally ill* person who is residing in the community has certain advantages not present in the institutional setting. In the first place, he is working with people residing physically in the *real* world as opposed to an isolated environment. Thus, he has at his disposal all of the resources he would have for any disabled client. Also, if we can make the assumption that it requires more skills to reside in the *real world* than it does in a mental institution, it seems reasonable to expect that the *mentally ill* person living in the community has more potential than the institutionalized client.

A workable model for rehabilitation counselors with this population is the triadic model suggested by Tharp and Wetzel (1969). Basically the model is: a consultant (rehabilitation counselor) working through a mediator (rehabilitation aid, community worker, friend, relative, etc.) to help a target (client).

$$\text{Consultant} \longrightarrow \text{Mediator} \longrightarrow \text{Target}$$

The sole criterion for the function of the consultant is the possession of knowledge. A trained rehabilitation counselor at the master's level or a bachelor's level with several years experience should be able to meet this criterion.

The role of the mediator requires the person have direct contact with the target. He receives instruction from the consultant as how to help the target. Tharp and Wetzel (1969) suggests there are five, ten, or a hundred potential mediators in the social network of any target. The consultant must be skillful enough to identify these people and organize them as resources for the target.

The target is anyone with a problem. Thus, the eligibility process of the agencies would identify the target under this model.

The major advantage of this model appears to be it permits the rehabilitation counselor, through his function as a consultant the opportunity to provide services to many people. The traditional dyadic model limits the number of clients a counselor can serve and raises questions whether or not it is the most productive model of treatment.

The triadic model offers a great deal of flexibility in the roles provided. For example, in an alcoholic population, a criminal population or a minority population, a paraprofessional could serve as a consultant advising the rehabilitation counselor who could be utilized as the mediator. This flexibility provides the opportunity to place the person with the knowledge in the best position to influence the services being provided to clients.

The rehabilitation counselor utilizing this model must know a great deal about the client and his problem. He must become knowledgeable about the community where the client resides to identify the mediators. This model demands that counselors become involved in the community and not spend their time in their offices away from the world of the client. Through this community involvement the counselor should be in a better position to influence community attitudes toward the *mentally ill* and counteract some of the myths that have been with us over the years.

Finally, what can be more reinforcing than helping someone? This model provides the opportunity for a friend to help a friend, a mother to help her child, a businessman to help a derelict. This involvement of non-professionals should be a positive factor in improving the attitudes toward *mental illness* and remove some of the stigmas.

In addition, we will stop wasting a great deal of talent that could be utilized effectively in the helping profession. In the past we have insisted that one must be a psychiatrist, psychologist, social worker or counselor to help someone. This model should enable the rehabilitation counselor to utilize this resource of talent to help provide more and better services to clients.

Considerations for Rehabilitation Counselors

In this chapter I have attempted to relate my feelings about the rehabilitation counselor's role with the *mentally ill*. My bias should be fairly obvious in that I prefer an environmental approach emphasizing teaching the *mentally ill* person better ways to adapt to his environment. In conclusion, the following considerations are concerns I would have if I were working as a rehabilitation counselor with this group of people.

1. Rehabilitation counselors working with the *mentally ill* must become excellent observers of behavior. They should not assume that clients have skills without checking them out. For example, if the counselor feels that the patient should be able to utilize the public transportation system on his own initiative then he should ask the person to demonstrate it.

2. Because of the emphasis of the team concept in work with the *mentally ill*, it should be beneficial for the rehabilitation counselor to have some training in group interaction. This should increase the probability of his becoming successful as a team member.

3. Rehabilitation counselors should develop a *job training hierarchy*. Although this was included primarily for counselors working with the institutionalized population it should be considered a concept for counselors working in the community as well.

4. Because of the problems of *labeling* people, rehabilitation counselors should refrain from doing this. Counselors should be aware that inadvertantly the label may become the disability.

5. Rehabilitation counselors should be aware of some of the flaws of the *medical or illness* model of treatment and consider other models such as the *triadic* approach.

6. Rehabilitation counselors must be involved in bringing about environmental changes leading to more positive attitudes and treatment of the *mentally ill*. Effective use of community resources will be an important tool in this behalf.

7. Last and most important, rehabilitation counselors must commit themselves to create positive experiences for people who have been denied such experiences. Through such experiences the *mentally ill* may be able to learn better ways of coping with the world in which they live.

REFERENCES

Glasser, W.: *Reality Therapy*. New York, Harper & Row, 1965.

Tharp, R. G., and Wetzel, R. J.: *Behavior Modification in the Natural Environment*. New York, Academic Press, 1969.

Tringo, J. L.: The hierarchy of preference toward disability groups, *The Journal of Special Education, 4* (No. 3):295-306, 1970.

CHAPTER VII

THE SPINAL CORD INJURED PATIENT

SENA SWORD AND M. M. ROBERTS

The Spinal Cord
Damage to the Spinal Cord
Medical Treatment of the Cord Injured Patient
Physical and Occupational Therapy
Emotional Adjustment
Emotional Problems
Vocational Rehabilitation

T HE REHABILITATION OF the victim of spinal cord damage is one of the most challenging tasks undertaken by the rehabilitation team. This disability, in particular, requires the highest quality of services from all those professionals who are involved in the rehabilitation process. Physicians, surgeons, nurses, physical therapists, occupational therapists, psychotherapists, social workers and vocational rehabilitation personnel—all of these persons have a vital role in assisting the paralyzed client if he or she is to return to some approximation of a normal life, to home and family, to community, and to gainful employment where this is possible and appropriate.

For many years the most visible efforts to assist cord injured people in the United States have been undertaken on behalf of war veterans. The organizations and agencies which have been responsible for this fine work have accumulated much knowledge and experience and have contributed significantly to the development of effective medical, surgical, nursing and after-care techniques used in the treatment of this disability. They have also advanced new procedures for, and approaches to, assisting patients in developing self-care and self-help skills so that they can learn to function in and out of their homes, and be employed in a vocation or profession.

More recently, interest in the severely disabled has grown considerably, and new programs for civilian victims of cord injury have been initiated in various types of medical and rehabilitation facilities all over the country.

In 1972 the 92nd Congress, in its second session, passed HR 8395, a bill providing for many types of rehabilitation programs and services. Under Title II, Special Federal Responsibilities, Section 207 reads as follows:

(a) For the purpose of establishing and operating National Centers for Spinal Cord Injuries, there is authorized to be appropriated $15,000,000 for the fiscal year ending June 30, 1973; $25,000,000 for the fiscal year ending June 30, 1974; and $30,000,000 for the fiscal year ending June 30, 1975. Funds appropriated under this section shall remain available until expended.

(b)

in order—

(1) to help form national networks of centers with special competencies in providing complete vocational and comprehensive rehabilitation services and acute medical care to individuals with spinal cord injuries;

(2) to assist meeting the cost of such services to such individuals;

(3) to encourage and assist the study and development of methods for the provision of such services and;

(4) to develop new methods of achieving cooperation with and among community and other public and non-profit organizations concerned with the problems of spinal cord injury; The Secretary, subject to the provisions of section 212, is authorized to enter into an agreement with any public or non-profit agency or organization to pay all or part of the costs of the

establishment and operation, including construction and equipment, of centers to carry out the purposes of this subsection, which centers shall be known as National Centers for Spinal Cord Injuries."

Unfortunately, HR. 8395, The Rehabilitation Act of 1972, did not win administration approval. However, its basic provisions will almost certainly be introduced in new bills to be considered by the Congress when it convenes again in 1973. At any rate there seems to be growing awareness of the special needs of quadraplegic and paraplegic Americans from every part of the population.

The Spinal Cord

The spinal cord is a large bundle of nerve cells and fibers which helps connect the brain with all parts of the body. Nerve messages from the brain keep many different types of bodily processes functioning properly and make movement of the body possible. Messages from all parts of the body to the brain provide sensation and keep the brain informed of the body's position, contacts with outside objects, exposure to heat and cold, etc.

The cord runs the length of the trunk from the base of the skull to the lower back. It lies inside the boney vertebral column which supports the trunk and provides protection for the soft nerve tissue of the cord. From between each vertebra there emerges four nerves, two of which carry impulses from the brain (motor), and two of which carry messages to the brain (sensory). These root nerves connect the nerve fibers of the cord with the peripheral nerve fibers, thereby providing for movement and sensation in all body parts.

The vertebral column is composed of thirty-three bones. Counting downward from the base of the skull the first seven vetrebrae are called cervical vertebrae. These are the bones of the neck. Below the cervical vertebrae are twelve additional vertebrae known as the thoracic vertebrae. These are the bones of the upper back. Below the thoracic vertebrae are the five vertebrae of the lower back. These are called the lumbar vertebrae. Below the lumbar vertebrae are the bones of the sacrum and coccyx (tailbone). Between the vertebrae are the softer discs of cartilage which give flexibility to the spine and permit a wide range of movement in the torso.

Damage to the Spinal Cord

The spinal cord can be damaged in many ways. Various diseases such as tumors of the cord, infections, genetic disorders like spinal bifida, and other neurological conditions may injure cord tissue and produce marked interference in function. Likewise all types of traumatic injuries which partially or totally sever the cord will cause grave difficulties and result in loss of sensation and paralysis. The parts of the body affected and the extent of the loss of function will depend on the level of the injury to the cord and how severe the damage is.

When a foreign object such as a bullet penetrates the spine the cord is often severed. In other types of accidents however, the cord is frequently damaged without being completely cut. An injury to the cord in the neck area will affect both upper and lower extremities, and the victim will suffer loss of feeling and movement in the body parts below the injury. An injury to the cord in the thoracic area (upper back) generally leaves the victim with some feeling and movement in the upper torso and arms. These conditions are both referred to as quadraplegia. Injury to the cord in the lower back produces loss of feeling and paralysis in the lower extremities only, a condition known as paraplegia.

Injuries to the vertebrae (backbones), do not necessarily injure the cord inside. It is quite possible to have a *broken neck* or a *broken back* with no loss of sensation or movement in body parts. Frequently loss of sensation and paralysis are temporary, caused by pressure on the cord by a foreign object, by dislocated and damaged vertebrae, or by bleeding and swelling in the area of the injury. Surgical intervention to relieve such pressure and the effects of natural healing over a period of time may restore feeling and movement to body parts which were without sensation or movement. Whatever restoration of function is possible generally occurs within a few months. After longer periods of time have elapsed the damage should probably be considered permanent. Scientists and medical researchers continue to seek new procedures to promote healing in damaged cord tissue.

The most common cause of cord injury in the United States is automobile accidents. Next are accidents of other types. Falls and athletic injuries, especially among divers, skiers, and motorcycle enthusiasts, take their toll. Unfortunately a very large percentage of the victims of cord damage are young and active people with their whole lives before them. Most researchers report a preponderance of male victims, generally around 75 percent—80 percent of the total. World War II, the Korean War and now the war in Vietnam have resulted in thousands of cord injuries to young American military personnel. The ever increasing numbers of paraplegic and quadraplegic individuals is apparently a significant factor in the growth of national associations and organizations for the spinal cord damaged in addition to powerful lobbies which bring pressure to bear on political leaders to recognize the problems and make provision for the services needed by this large group of handicapped citizens.

Medical Treatment of the Cord Injured Patient

Appropriate medical and surgical treatment of the victim of spinal cord damage is best administered in a medical facility which has equipment and personnel specifically designated for this purpose. The care needed for this kind of injury requires highly specialized training and experience on the part of the staff and the very best of modern medical implements and devices designed to avoid further injury to the patient and to facilitate his or her recovery.

The physicians and medical personnel responsible for the cord injured patient must conduct comprehensive examinations and decide what treatment is appropriate. In many cases traction is applied to the spine; in some cases surgical intervention is indicated. In all cases the patient must be immobilized for a period of time, and during this immobilization, expert nursing care is required. If the individual has lost control of the bladder and the bowel, then the functions of these organs must be performed mechanically by the nursing staff. If the patient has lost sensation and movement in body parts he will not be aware of pressure on these parts. Pressure sores may develop on the weight bearing protuberances of those parts, and these ulcers can become severe enough very rapidly to be a threat to the recovery and even to the life of the individual. Medical experts in the field recommend that the spine injured patient be strapped firmly to a frame which can be turned at least once every two hours. The most modern medical facilities which have special areas for the spine injured are now equipped with electrically operated, bed-like support frames to which the patient can be firmly attached in an immobile position. The frames can be moved from the horizontal position to the vertical and vice versa with the touch of a lever, and greatly facilitate the proper care of the patient.

The nursing staff must also be meticulous in the care of the patient's skin. If it is not kept clean and dry at all times sores may develop because of skin irritation, and these can be as dangerous and difficult a problem as the pressure sores.

Several other medical problems which the spine injured individual encounters during the initial phases of medical care include pain of various sorts, autonomic disturbances, respiration difficulties, an abnormal blood picture, and infections of the urinary and digestive systems.

The amount of pain suffered by victims of spinal damage varies considerably. A large percentage, eighty-five to ninety-five percent, report significant discomfort. However, only a small number, less than ten percent, have pain intense enough to hamper rehabilitation. In these cases surgical treatment may become necessary to relieve the root causes of the pain. Most of the discomfort can be tolerated by the patient. Eventually, as recovery takes place and he becomes active again he can learn to live with it.

Autonomic disturbances occur most frequently when the injury to the spine is in the upper back or neck. The patient may suffer a rapid rise in blood pressure, perspiration, chills, and occasionally a severe headache. The mechanism which triggers these disturbances may be associated with a bladder spasm, skin sores, or other conditions related to the cord injury. Medication and sometimes surgery are used to control this problem.

Respiratory difficulties are most often found in patients with cervical lesions of the spine. The intercostal muscles (muscles of the rib cage), are paralyzed and the diaphram must carry the whole load. If digestive or urinary problems develop the abdomen may become distended and inhibit the proper movement of the diaphram. The proper use of urinary catheters (drainage tubes), and enemas will relieve the congestion in the abdomenal cavity and restore proper function to the diaphram.

Abnormalities of blood content are treated by careful control of substances ingested by the patient, and in some cases by the administration of whole blood by transfusion.

The possibility of urinary and digestive infections will remain with the quadraplegic and paraplegic patient for the rest of his life. When normal controls of the bladder and bowel have been lost the elimination functions must be performed in some other way. A catheter may be inserted to resolve the urinary problems. The bowel may be emptied by means of enemas and manual manipulation through the anal opening. Eventually, with special training, many patients develop some bladder control and can discard the catheter or other type of drainage device. They can also learn to take over the control of elimination of feces, by learning dietary control procedures, and by developing the manual evacuation skills themselves. Patients who are not able to acquire these self-care skills will always need the assistance of a trained individual if they are to maintain their health. When the patient returns to his home this individual may have to be a member of the family. If so, this person needs instruction while the patient is still in the hospital or medical facility. The necessity of using mechanical devices as well as manual techniques for emptying the bladder and bowel greatly increases the chance of infection in the tissues and organs affected. Great care must be taken to insure antiseptic conditions at all times. Infections which do develop must be treated immediately with antibiotics and other appropriate medical procedures.

Finally, the medical treatment of the cord damaged individual must include the stabilization of the vertebral column and the control of severe muscle spasms, especially of the flexor type.

If these measures are not accomplished the patient will not be able to get out of bed, learn to function in a wheelchair, or learn to walk with the help of braces and crutches.

The stabilization of the backbone may occur without elaborate medical procedures, but frequently it requires additional surgery and the design of supports and braces to fit the individual needs of each person. It is important that whatever activities the patient undertakes, he will be able to move without undue pain or discomfort, and he will not cause further damage to his health and physical condition.

Severe muscle spasm can so distort the patient's posture and body position that further rehabilitation measures become almost impossible. Most spine damaged individuals experience some muscle spasms but can learn to function in spite of them. Extreme ones, however, which hamper movement and activity, will probably have to be treated surgically if the rehabilitation process is to continue.

Physical and Occupational Therapy

Once the medical care of the victim of spinal cord damage has been completed, the next step in the rehabilitation process is the initiation of physical and occupational therapy. These therapeutic procedures provide the means to increased strength, endurance, and mobility. They are vital to the health and fitness of the patient, and skilled therapists can teach the individual many self-care and self-help skills which will contribute greatly to his rehabilitation. Under their supervision the patient can exercise to develop unusual power in whatever muscles of the upper torso which are still functional. He can learn to move himself around in bed and assume responsibiilty for much of the routine care of his own body. With the assistance of his physician and therapists he can select a wheelchair which is just right for his disability and life situation. He can learn to get in and out of it efficiently or provide the maximum possible assistance to an individual who is attempting to move him. He can learn to operate his wheelchair inside his home and out.

With the help of members of the patient's family, the therapists can devise ways of modifying the home situation-bedroom, bathroom and kitchen, so that the utmost in self reliance for the paraplegic or quadraplegic individual is possible. The patient can learn to use the scores of *gadgets* which have been designed to help paralyzed individuals accomplish certain specific tasks which must be performed in their daily routine or as part of some educational, occupational or recreational activity in which they wish to participate.

The paraplegic patient can even become ambulatory. With the help of long leg braces with locked knees, and with crutches, he can master the *paraplegic walk.* (This type of locomotion is executed with a swinging forward movement of both legs while the weight is supported on the crutches. The patient then pulls his torso over his feet which support his weight until he can lean forward and place his crutches ahead for the next *step.*)

There is some difference of opinion among doctors, therapists and even patients themselves as to the practicality of ambulation as the primary method of movement for the paralyzed individual. It is a valuable form of exercise as it promotes circulation and the retention of calcium in the bones. It is, however, tiring and time-consuming. Many experts in the field believe that the paraplegic's real base of operation should be the wheelchair and that most of his time and energy should be spent in learning new skills, training or retraining for a vocation, or actually working in a job or profession. It should be noted, nevertheless, that many patients report a real psychological *lift* when they are able to *get on their feet* again when they can get around in something approximating the way they used to move, and when they can *look others in the eye* instead of *always being looked down on.* (These paralyzed individual's use of language here is interesting. It seems to have both literal and figurative meanings.)

Last, but certainly not least, the paraplegic patient can learn to drive an automobile which has been fitted with special hand controls. In this society, the automobile is both a symbol of independence and a necessary fact of life for most citizens. Many paralyzed patients indicate that after they found they could get in and out of their cars alone or with some assistance and could drive safely, they finally begin to experience a return of self confidence and optimism about the future.

All of the skills which cord damaged individuals develop with the assistance of physical and occupational therapists contribute directly to the speed and effectiveness with which they begin to rebuild their lives. It is fortunate that these services are becoming available to the majority of paraplegic and quaddraplegic patients. However, individuals who for one reason or another do not have access to this type of assistance need to be aware of the possibilities. Sometimes it is necessary for the rehabilitation counselor or one or the other social service staff who work with paralyzed clients to *open these doors*. Often a program somewhere can be found which will accept the client even belatedly and give him the help he needs. If not, the client and his family can at least be provided with some of the many excellent materials which have been developed specifically for the victims of spinal cord damage and their families, to assist them in their readjustments. All social service personnel who work with the clients that are paralyzed should have an extensive library of these materials, not only for their own information, but in order to have them on hand for clients who need them. Materials published by the following organizations may be especially helpful:

> American Rehabilitation Foundation
> 1800 Chicago Avenue
> Minneapolis, Minnesoa 54404
> Institute for the Crippled and Disabled
> 340 E. 24th Street
> New York, New York 10010
> National Society for Crippled Children and Adults
> 2023 W. Ogden Avenue
> Chicago, Illinois 60612
> The Institute of Rehabilitation Medicine
> New York University Medical Center
> 400 E. 34th Street
> New York, New York 10016
> Paralyzed Veterans of America
> 3636 Sixteenth Street
> Washington, D.C.
> National Paraplegia Foundation
> 333 N. Michigan Avenue
> Chicago, Illinois 60601

Emotional Readjustment

While the medical and related problems of paralyzed patients are formidable, the emotional adjustments which they and their families must make are often more difficult. Like most individuals who suffer a severe disability, the victims of cord injury tend to go through several stages of emotional reactions.

The initial stage is generally one of shock and confusion. The individual seems stunned, unable to comprehend what has happened to him or her. This phase may last only a few hours or a few days after the accident or injury.

The second stage is usually more protracted. It is often a highly emotional phase as the victim becomes aware of the extent and significance of his or her loss. This is a period of great anguish and often great anger. Some rehabilitation professionals call this the *Why me, God?* period. During this stage of recovery the treatment personnel and the victim's family will need a great deal of patience and compassion. The victim may lash out at anyone and everyone and be totally unaccepting of efforts to be of assistance. The manner and attitude of those around the patient will assume great importance to him. Paraplegics and quadraplegics who have survived this period describe some rather interesting reactions which they had to certain types of individuals with whom they had contacts in this phase of recovery.

One common complaint centers around the *bright, brisk, cheerful staff member* who seems to feel that the victim's situation is *really not so bad,* and *everything's going to be fine if he will just cooperate with the staff and not waste time feeling sorry for himself.* It is interesting that various patients have reported having similar fantasies regarding this type of individual. Their fantasies go something like this: The staff person finishes work and goes along home in his brisk, bright, cheerful manner. But on the way home he has an accident similar to the victim's, and the next morning the staff member ends up in a nearby bed— paralyzed like the patients. The patients then report what enormous delight they took in saying, "Well, Doctor! Not so brisk, bright and cheerful this morning are you?" (Or words to that effect.)

On the other hand, severely disabled patients often report

irritation and anger at expressions of sympathy, especially from family members. These seem to injure their pride and cause them greater distress. Few people enjoy being objects of pity. So it is difficult to know exactly what type of manner will be the most supportive and helpful to the individual who is struggling to adjust to the tragedy of paralysis. Each person is different, of course, and will react differently to being handicapped. Both treatment staff and family members need to respond in sensitive and perceptive ways during these trying times.

After the stormy second period many victims of cord injury suffer a period of extreme depression. During this stage of emotional readjustment the individual seems to lose interest in everything. He or she accepts the situation, but feels that life is really over and there is little possibility that he can have a happy or satisfying future. Occasionally, a paralyzed patient will attempt suicide during this period. If either the second or third stage is extended, the patient may need the aid of a psychotherapist. This highly trained professional can work directly with the patient but can also give treatment staff and family members suggestions regarding the best way to relate to the patient during the adjustment period.

Social workers and social services personnel can assist the patient and his family by providing information concerning sources of financial assistance, usually a factor of much concern to the paralyzed individual, and assist them with various other adjustment problems they will have in their community.

One of the most important contributions to the emotional adjustment of the cord injured patient can be made by the rehabilitation counselor. For it is the professional, more than any other, who offers the paralyzed client real hope that he or she can learn new ways to function so that return to a previous vocation may become possible; or that he or she can benefit from additional education or training and learn a new vocation or enter a new profession. The idea that one can contribute to one's family, help support them, and become productive again seems to reduce anxiety and depression and generate enthusiasm for life once again. When this happens, the individual is ready to enter the final period of emotional adjustment. This is the phase of recovery during which the victim of cord damage resolves to build a new life in spite of his handicap. He becomes more objective and philosophical about his situation. He begins to plan and work to overcome problems. There are almost certainly difficult times ahead, and the individual will suffer failures and frustrations, but once he achieves this final stage of adjustment the chances are that the worst is over.

Emotional Problems

Emotional disturbance is a common occurrence in our society today. It is not surprising, therefore, that a number of cord damaged patients have emotional problems which existed before their illness or accident. In many of these cases the patient who already had difficulties in relating to people, working successfully or functioning as a member of a family finds that his problems are compounded by his handicapped condition. His already poor self-image may deteriorate further. His inadequate relationships with family and friends may grow more strained. Since most paraplegics and quadraplegics lose the ability to function very well sexually their relationships with their spouses usually have to be re-examined. Most patients are reluctant to speak openly of this problem, but it is a concern of the first magnitude, especially to the young and vigorous male who is so often the victim of spinal cord injury. In a society which places great emphasis on sexual expression as a reflection of *manhood* or *womanhood* it is not surprising that so many paralyzed patients feel that they are no longer *whole*. The rehabilitation counselor and the social services personnel who work with cord injured clients need to be aware of these problems, and be prepared to obtain additional guidance and family counseling services for their clients if the need arises.

Vocational Rehabilitation

Statistics indicate that a large percentage of spinal cord injured people never become employed. Of course, work opportunities for the quadraplegic individuals who have little or no use of arms and hands are extremely limited. They need a great

deal of assistance, and unless they are intelligent and well
educated people, or have an unusual talent or skill, vocational
rehabilitation may be a difficult process. For paraplegics, too,
return to previous employment may be unrealistic and many
other types of work are now impossible.

Although it is fortunate that there are many sources of funds
available to the severely disabled, the amount of financial aid
which they receive, often labeled compensation for *total disability* not only influences their views of themselves but decreases
their motivation to become employed. In many cases these funds
are terminated when they begin to work, and the whole venture
constitutes a risk which they are reluctant to take.

The paralyzed individuals who are most often successful in
going to work, are generally young, well educated, and highly
motivated. The aging, the educationally disadvantaged, and
those with additional physical or mental handicaps encounter
many problems. Nevertheless, no matter what the situation may
be, a minimal level or rehabilitation is nearly always possible.
That is, the client may be assisted in the achievement of the
maximum amount of independence and self reliance he can
attain so that other members of his family can be free to seek
employment if they need to, or wish to do so. Arrangements can
be made with the telephone company to install equipment which
is especially suited to the paralyzed client's needs. A checking
system for routine hourly calls, or a *drop by* system involving
members of the family or friends can be developed to assure the
client's safety and welfare while he or she is alone.

The female victim of cord damage who has been an enthusi-
astic homemaker will usually find that many of the tasks which
she used to perform for her family are still possible with a few
modifications of the physical structure of her house, and the
addition of a few *gadgets* to help her reach hard-to-get-to places
and things. If she can become adept in handling her wheelchair
(motor driven chairs are recommended for those who have little
arm strength or control) or if she can learn the *paraplegic walk,*
she can soon learn new ways to manage her household. She will
need her family's help in many instances, but proper organization
of time and tasks can be the key to a smoothly functioning home.

The rehabilitation counselor may wish to suggest that the client talk with another paralyzed homemaker who has had more experience and has become skillful in adjusting her daily routine to her handicap.

Many cord injured clients can become self-employed or work part-time in their own homes. This type of arrangement permits them to set their own hours, structure the situation to fit their individual needs, and at the same time gain some economic and personal independence. Some quadraplegics who have been fitted with special hand braces and supports, or with *mechanical hands,* have learned to use electric typewriters and calculators. With these skills a number of jobs can be done from a wheelchair or even from a bed. Vocational activities which have been performed by severely paralyzed individuals include commercial writing, accounting, bookkeeping and tax computation, tutoring of students in academic subjects, surveying and sales promotion by telephone, and many others.

The rehabilitation counselor who works with paraplegic and quadraplegic clients must acquire some expertise in vocational evaluation. He or she must know how to obtain a comprehensive assessment of each client's current abilities and potential, and must also be able to secure very precise analyses of the work requirements of a variety of vocations and professions. If the counselor is working in a comprehensive rehabilitation facility much of the information needed concerning each client can be provided by those professional staff members who specialize in psychometry and work evaluation. Also available in most of these centers are simulated, practice situations and workshops where the handicapped individual can test his capacities and abilities and can obtain additional experience and training to enhance his employment potential. In this type of setting the counselor has only to work closely with the other rehabilitation professionals and his client in planning for the future and in locating an appropriate job placement when the client is ready to leave the facility.

However, if a client has not had the advantages of a comprehensive rehabilitation program it may be necessary for the counselor to participate more directly in the vocational evaluation process or to make arrangements with a sheltered workshop or similar program to secure the information which is needed to make valid decisions concerning the client's employment prognosis.

Many paraplegics and a few quadraplegics will be able to return to their former vocation or profession. This is generally a most satisfactory arrangement, if the client was doing well in the work and enjoyed it. The total situation must be analyzed carefully, however, to ascertain whether the modifications necessary for the client to return to his job and to work effectively can be arranged. It must also be determined if all employers and co-workers are willing and able to accept the new situation and assist the client in his work adjustment. In most cases it is the rehabilitation counselor who will be called upon to explain how these things can be accomplished and convince all those involved that it will be worth the effort. This aspect of the counselor's work is most important, and must be done carefully and with complete honesty. He will do the client no favor by placing him in a job which he cannot manage adequately, or where other individuals involved will not accept him.

In cases where the client was self-employed prior to paralysis many difficulties are eliminated. The individual can gradually resume those activities which are possible and at a pace which is comfortable. Clients in professions such as law, medicine, the creative arts, business administration and others may find they need to reduce their work load initially, and some will have to specialize in one particular phase of their profession, but on the whole, their prospects are bright so long as they retain their health and strength.

The paralyzed client who cannot return to any aspect of the former vocation or profession presents a challenge to the rehabilitation counselor. Together, counselor and client must explore new and different possibilities. A type of work which is similar in many ways to the previous job may appeal to the client. However, other factors must be taken into consideration, including the current job market. If additional education or training are involved the client must consider the length of time involved and the status of his or her family. These decisions are all of the utmost importance and should be made with great care. Too often both counselor and client are anxious to proceed quickly and they neglect to take into account some factor which later will present many problems. This can mean significant waste of time, effort and money, and it is frustrating and discouraging to the paralyzed individual.

Whatever vocation or profession the cord injured client attempts, whether part-time or full-time, in the home or in some other place of employment, he or she will almost certainly require the assistance, support and encouragement of the rehabilitation counselor for an extended period of time. There is really no way that either can anticipate all the difficulties—physical, emotional, social or vocational—that may be encountered in the actual work situation. But the professional knowledge and skills of the counselor together with a moderate amount of courage and patience on the part of the client can generally resolve most problems. This is being proven all over the country as paralyzed individuals are becoming productive people.

REFERENCES

1. Felton, J. S.; Perkins, D. C., and Lewin, B. A.: *A Survey of Medicine and Medical Practice for the Rehabilitation Counselor.* Washington, D.C., Vocational Rehabilitation Administration, U.S. Department of Health, Education and Welfare, 1966.
2. Freeman, L. W.: Treatment of acute spinal cord injury. *G.P.*, V (No. 5), May, 1952.
3. French, J. J., and Porter, R. W.: *Basic Research in Paraplegia.* Springfield, Charles C Thomas, 1962.
4. Frost, A.: *Handbook for Paraplegics and Quadraplegic.* National Paraplegia Foundation. Chicago, Wallace Press, 1964.
5. Howorth, M. B.; Petrie, J. G., and Bennett, George: *Injuries of the Spine.* Baltimore, The Williams and Wilkins Co., 1964.
6. Jousse, A. T.: The management of paraplegia. *Manitoba Medical Review*, 43 (No. 7):383-391, August-September, 1963.
7. Lofquist, L. H., and Dawis, R. V.: *Adjustment to Work—A Psychological View of Man's Problems in a Work-Oriented Society.* New York, Appleton-Century-Crofts, 1969.
8. Reynolds, F. C. (Chairman, Committee on Publications): *American Academy of Orthopaedic Surgeons Symposium on the Spine* (A Monograph). St. Louis, C. V. Mosby Co., 1969.

9. Rosenburg, Charlot: *Assistive Devices for the Handicapped.* Rehabilitation Publication No. 705. Minneapolis, American Rehabilitation Foundation, 1968.

10. Vocational Rehabilitation Administration: *Guidelines for Organization and Operation of Vocational Evaluation Units: A Training Guide,* Rehabilitation Service Series No. 67-50. Washington, D.C., U.S. Department of Health, Education and Welfare, 1966.

CHAPTER VIII

THE DEAF

RICHARD K. JOHNSON

The Deaf Population
Their Education
Deaf People and the Community
The National Organization

DURING THE PAST decade an increasing awareness of the plight of minority groups seeking equal status in American society has become evident. Deaf people, especially the adult deaf, are such a minority who have only recently begun to emerge from relative obscurity. Historically, deaf people have tended to seek out each other, forming in the process many sub-cultural deaf communities within the larger society (Furfey and Harte, 1964). As a positive force toward self-deterministic goals, these groups of deaf people throughout the nation have exerted only limited, sporadic influence. One reason for the lengthy obscurity of deaf people stems from a lack of effective representation by the various organizations of the deaf, at the local, state, and national levels (Friedman, 1961; and Garretson, 1961). Other weaknesses have been insufficient aggressive leadership at all levels, particularly at the local level, a lack of adequate interaction with non-deaf organizations and the impetus necessary to generate more involvement by deaf people in identifying their own rehabilitation needs (O'Brien, 1961; and Pettingill, 1964). Williams (1961), speaking for the (then) United States Office of Vocational

Rehabilitation, noted that this latter type involvement is critically needed:

> In its work for the deaf, however, the rehabilitation service has faced a frustrating, persistent problem that other public agencies may also experience when trying to discharge their responsibilities for a similar minority group. Deaf people have been quite passive. They and their associates have not manifested the vigorous responsiveness, the hard driving realism through which needs are first identified and then fulfilled. The net has been a considerable sociological vacuum resulting in unawareness of and inattention to the special needs of deaf people within the rapidly growing service institutions for society at large (p. 5).

Specifically, the goals of rehabilitation include the need to expand systems of assistance available to deaf people in order to provide them with equal opportunities to compete in society.

Although there have been fragmented efforts to upgrade services to the deaf, these have met with only limited success. One reason for the marginal acceptance has been the lack of involvement of deaf people themselves in planning and initiating these programs (Mayes, 1970).

Sussman (1965) suggested that those in authority were more frequently preoccupied with the intent to do things *for* the deaf rather than determining what deaf people really wanted. He also suggested that time and energy were being wasted on maintaining several competing systems whereas efforts should be channeled into greater understanding of what the adult deaf person wants and how he plans to approach the rehabilitation which he thinks desirable.

The Deaf Population

In the United States, there are an estimated 15,000,000 adults and 3,000,000 children who have sustained some degree of hearing loss. According to the preliminary findings of the National Census of the Deaf, approximately 450,000 to 550,000 are classified as deaf or deafened. About 20 percent to 35 percent of these people may be multiple handicapped, that is, having one or more disabilities in addition to their deafness (Adler, 1968; and Williams, 1967).

The term *deaf* refers specifically to those whose hearing loss prevents auditory reception and the acquisition of normal speech. Such persons are distinguished from the hard of hearing, who have some functional reception of auditory communication (Furth, 1966; and Myklebust, 1960). Deafness may be further defined as an invisible physical disability which presupposes an audiological loss of some seventy decibels in the speech range (Garretson, 1972). However, in selecting a single factor as being descriptive of deaf people in general, the most widely accepted would be their dependence on their visual perception as a primary means of receptive communication (Babbidge, 1965).

Deafness has always been a social stigma. Deaf people have often been portrayed in the classics of literature and drama as fools, wretches, demons and sub-humans (Kohl, 1966). This traditional image has evidently been carried over into our present day society. Klinghammer (1964) conducted an experiment to determine the extent to which a deaf person's voice and speech play in the development of the *deaf stereotype* (which he describes as one who is considered by his hearing peers to be overly suspicious, irritable and stupid). In his experiment Klinghammer tested the perception of hearing individuals towards the deaf and the blind by pre-recording the voices of both deaf people and blind people, and then playing these tapes back to hearing subjects under controlled conditions. The overall result indicated that the blind were viewed in a very positive light, while the deaf were considered in a very negative manner.

Deaf persons have, historically, been considered legally and humanly incompetent, based on the assumption that speech is the distinguishing mark of the rational as compared to the irrational animal (Hodgson, 1954; and Kohl, 1966). Although this theory has been conclusively refuted, Furth (1966) noted that the myths remain prominent in today's society, and that speech or language is still the passport required to admit the deaf into the society of fully developed human beings.

There is ample evidence that deaf people are not, in terms of intelligence, dumb (MacKane, 1933; Ross, 1966; and Vernon and Makowsky, 1969). Nor, as commonly believed, are they dumb, in the sense that they cannot speak. Frequently, however, as Sanderson (1969) notes, they choose to remain mute in the face of repeated failure to be accepted, as deaf people with speech limitations, by their hearing peers in the community. Another problem is that many in the hearing community, as a result of misinformation, believe that any person, regardless of hearing loss, can be taught to speak and lipread *normally* if he has normal intelligence. Such thinking has deprived deaf people of a positive self-image and caused the general public to expect performance in the area of communication which is, frequently, both unattainable and unrealistic for the average deaf person.

Deaf people range widely in general classifications of personality and achievement variables. Among them are found extroverts and introverts; college graduates and illiterates; rich and poor; the good and the bad (Burns, 1958; and Johnson, 1969).

The great majority of deaf people are products of state residential school programs, and most who go on to higher education do so by attending Gallaudet College or the National Technical Institute for the Deaf. Their medium of communication tends to be the American manual language of signs (Switzer and Williams, 1967).

There is a tendency for deaf people to mingle socially with other deaf persons with whom they can communicate freely by manual means. Also, as in other sub-cultural groups, deaf people frequently prefer deaf marriage partners. Most of them are well adjusted average citizens, regularly, although under-employed, own their own homes and drive their own automobiles (Burke, 1961; Furfey and Harte, 1964; and Kohl, 1966). The deaf maintain their own social clubs, sports groups, churches and state and national organizations. Those who are comfortably situated do not need special assistance from rehabilitation or welfare programs. However, there are many deaf who do need such support services, just as there are those in the hearing population who need assistance of one type or another (Johnson, 1969). Finally, there are people who become deaf in later life, but, due to strong, established ties outside of the *deaf community*, are seldom seen as a part of the existing deaf social structure (Burns, 1958; and Levine, 1960).

Their Education

Most of the adult deaf in America are the products of one of four methods of educating the deaf used in this country. The first, known as the *pure oral method,* was developed during the latter part of the nineteenth century. This method broke down the language of normal children to certain developmental stages and attempted to teach deaf children, at much later ages, to work through these developmental stages. All sign language was forbidden in favor of the *talk, talk, talk* approach (Scouten, 1964). The second was the *oral method.* While basically similar to the *pure oral method,* it added and emphasized the reading and writing of orthographic forms of the English language (Greenaway, 1964).

A further modification of the oral approach, known as the *natural method,* was developed in the early part of the twentieth century. This method was built on the theory that deaf children could be taught to speak through a permissive program of broad ranging activities. In this method, also, sign language was prohibited, and only speech and lip reading were allowed. The fourth method, the *Rochester Method,* differed markedly from the others in that the use of manual finger spelling was permitted (Hester, 1964).

The fact that sign language is almost universally preferred by the deaf themselves has been consistently ignored by those in charge of preparing the young deaf individual for later adulthood (Rainer, Altschuler, Kallman, and Deming, 1963).

Kohl (1966) conducted a study of the education of deaf children for the Center for Urban Education. This study included residential and day school programs for the deaf. Kohl could find no evidence that manual communication was being taught in the classroom, although there was an evident emphasis on the teaching of speech and lip reading skills. However, he noted that the majority of the children used some form of manual communication outside of the classroom, rather than the oral skills which were being taught. Kohl concluded that educators were amiss in neglecting the perfection of manual communication as a teaching tool for work with deaf children. Although research has shown that manual communication is quite conducive both to the educational achievement and psychological adjustment of the deaf child, the trend continues against using it in the classroom (Meadows, 1967; Montgomery, 1968; Stuckless and Birch, 1966; and Vernon and Makowsky, 1969). In recent years there has been introduced in education circles a fifth method, known as *total communication*. In this approach manual as well as oral-aural methods are used during preschool years and by parents in the home. Although this recent trend has not been in wide-spread use long enough to measure its overall impact on deaf students, from preschool through secondary and post-secondary levels, the results obtained thus far indicate that Total Communication may well provide the breakthrough long sought in educating deaf youth (Newman, 1972).

Babbidge (1965), reporting on education of the deaf in America, stated, "The American people have no reason to be satisfied with their limited success in educating deaf children and preparing them for full participation in our society (p. xv)." This report noted that less than half of the deaf children in need of specialized education are receiving it.

Another indicator of the failure of the educational approach used with the deaf is identified in a study of the occupational status of young deaf adults. Boatner, Stuckless and Moore (1964) surveyed a sample of deaf youth from the New England area and concluded they were employed considerably below their basic aptitude levels. Comparing GATB scores, Boatner, *et al.*, further concluded that, although the young adult deaf in the study group appeared to be significantly superior to the general population in areas of form perception and manual dexterity, they were significantly inferior in verbal areas.

The unemployment rate for young deaf adults in the New England survey was approximately four times that of the general population in the area. The occupational status of the young deaf adults in New England, not only in unemployment rate but in wages and employment levels, was found to be lower than that of the hearing. Similar studies on the occupational status of deaf people in other regions of the country have supported these findings (Kronenberg and Blake, 1966; and Lunde and Bigman, 1959).

The Babbidge Report (1965) noted that more than 80 percent of the deaf adults work in manual jobs as contrasted to 50 percent of the hearing population. It recommended that special effort be made to provide deaf people with access to a full range of post-secondary occupational and adult education programs with appropriate support services at the community level to bring about a greater parity.

The major conclusion to be drawn from an investigation of the literature on education of the deaf is that the schools do not appear to be fulfilling their responsibilities of providing adequate education to deaf youth.

As a result of past efforts of those responsible for education of deaf people there is now an adult deaf population in which a disproportionate number are educationally deprived and lacking in general knowledge. In addition to having created an educational gap, Vernon (1969) believes the failure of past methods seriously undermined the efforts of rehabilitation and contributed to a denial, on the part of deaf people, of their individual handicaps.

Deaf People and the Community

According to Sanger (1956), the best evidence of social maturity in any community is the capacity and ability of various agencies and organizations to cooperate, day after day.

Cooperation among organizations with similar interests had its beginnings in this country in the latter part of the 1800's. However, such cooperation did not flourish until the 1940's when the social needs generated by World War II resulted in a merging of efforts (Ullman, 1958).

In the case of organizations of deaf people and organizations of persons interested in the problems of deafness, interest in cooperation is a relatively recent development of the past decade. Moreover, such efforts are all too few and have not always met with complete acceptance by the parties involved.

After studying the interaction of deaf and hearing people

in Frederick County, Maryland, Furfey and Harte (1964) concluded that if the hearing community is to participate effectively in planning for the welfare of deaf people, it must develop social contacts with the deaf community and must have a practical knowledge of deafness and the problems of deaf people. In addition, hearing people need to realize that the hearing loss is not always the only factor affecting cases involving deaf individuals.

In working with deaf people, as with other physically disabled people, the scope of treatment must be broad enough to include not only the deaf person but also the significant others whose attitudes may contribute to successful adjustment. In order to better understand the naivete frequently manifested by deaf individuals it is necessary to understand the relationship which frequently exists between the deaf individual, his home and family. It is not an exaggeration, in many cases, to say that the deaf child grows up in a household where he is a stranger. In the case of the child who has been a student in a residential school for the deaf, one might assume that this could be attributed to a physical absence from the home. However, when one views the deaf child who is a pupil in a day porgram and who, like his hearing peer, commutes daily from his home to his school, it will be frequently noted that this situation of strangeness to the family household continues to be present. The reason for this, as Grinker (1969), points out, is that communication between the family, the child and frequently his siblings, is carried on at an extremely superficial level, which makes a continuous and meaningful exchange of ideas, feelings and emotions quite difficult if not impossible.

This breakdown of communication within the family unit, accompanied by the frequently inadequate and frustrating educational methods commonly in use in most of our school programs for deaf youngsters, frequently leaves the rehabilitation counselor with a client who is ill-prepared socially, emotionally, educationally and vocationally for entry into today's competitive world of work.

Immediate family members, friends, co-workers as well as many other persons in a deaf man's life are of major importance in understanding how he reacts to his disability. This disability is, or should be a, family, community and societal responsibility, insofar as each is, or should be, involved in a disabled person's framework of therapeutic adjustment (Levine, 1960; and Wright, 1960).

Best (1943) felt that society as a whole knows very little about deaf people. Since they do not form a large part of the population many people seldom, if ever, come into contact with them. He noted that their affliction tends to remove them from the usual community avenues and makes them, more or less, a class apart from the general community.

The problem then is in getting people involved. Rainer and Altschuler (1966), in reviewing a special mental health program for deaf people in New York, noted that the most frequent causes for referral were family problems, social conflicts, poor work adjustment as well as acute psychiatric illness. One of the major implications drawn from this study has been the need for better education of both the hearing and deaf communities toward greater understanding of the problems of deaf people, and proper referral to appropriate facilities.

In the last decade, there has come into being throughout the nation, a network of skilled interpreters for the deaf. These people are members of the Registry of Interpreters for the Deaf, a national organization with headquarters in Washington, D.C. While use of interpreters should in no way be considered a substitute for a counselor's skill in manual communication, the use of such people should not be overlooked when the time comes to place the deaf client in training situations, or when mobilizing community action groups. In the community, the classroom and on-the-job interpreters have been found invaluable for providing the deaf client with meaningful input from whatever learning situation in which he may be involved. For the counselor this means using interpreters as a catalyst within the community, developing situations where people get together and mobilize greater participation by deaf and hearing people in local activities.

Recently there has been an increasing awareness that, for the deaf person, there are many needs still to be met. Stewart (1969)

believed that efforts to prepare deaf people for earning a livelihood, and to be as much like hearing people as possible, have
overlooked the deaf person's more important psychological needs.
Lauritsen (1969) also took this view and suggested that deaf
people, as individuals, must first be understood and accepted as
unique human beings by their hearing peers:

> Integration of the isolated deaf person into the deaf community,
> of the large masses of deaf people into hearing society, is based on
> understanding through communication. If we can achieve under-
> standing, we can achieve communication. Improved communication
> will permit the deaf man to integrate more fully into the world
> (Lauritsen, 1969, p. 52).

Furth (1966) pointed out, however, that today, despite all
the progress that has been made, deaf people remain relatively
unknown to *outsiders*. Largely excluded from the larger community by their communication handicap, they naturally tend to
group together and form their own *community* within the wider
society.

Vernon and Makowsky (1969) used knowledge available
about the relationship of minority groups to the majority society
to analyze the position of deaf people in America. They concluded that deaf people share many of the problems that face
other minority groups in this country. They cited, for example,
the paternalism which denies deaf persons important roles in
education, habilitation and rehabilitation programs which are
ostensibly designed to help them. Vernon and Makowsky noted
similar parallels in roles delegated to minorities such as the
Blacks, Indians and Mexican-Americans. The attempts to de-
prive the deaf of manual communication, and to make them
ashamed of using such medium in public have analogs in hair
straightening, skin bleaching and other examples of minority
attempts to deny their identities and become something they are
not. These authors further concluded that those in positions of
authority in the field of deafness have preferred to ignore
individual problems rather than come to grips with them.

> Authoritarian personalities tend to divide the world into the
> strong and the weak. They associate minority groups with the latter,
> which for them is minimally respected. In some cases, minorities

are depersonalized as implied in the concept of *the deaf* which suggests a lumping together of all deaf persons. This results in an effort to treat unequal people equally, usually by taking the lowest common denominator as a frame of reference (Vernon and Makowsky, 1969, p. 6).

Wright (1960), in discussing the psychological implications of disabilities, pointed out that, although a person with a disability shares problems common to those of other minority groups, there are differences. The greatest is that the disabled person seldom has the sanction of parents, teachers or friends who endorse the behavior stemming from the disability. Instead, the typical advice offered is to appear as much like non-disabled people as possible.

A limited view of the potential of the deaf individual is prevalent in the history of education of the deaf. Rather than accepting his disability and teaching him to live with it, educators of the deaf have been stressing *hearing* attributes, with the end result that the deaf person develops devaluative feelings about himself and his handicap (Rainer and Altschuler, 1966).

In a study of the interaction between deaf and hearing people Furfey and Harte (1964) found that deafness interfered with family life and this was likely to be more severe when some members of the deaf person's family were hearing persons. They also found that the variety of jobs available to the deaf were limited. In addition, deaf people met with difficulties in pursuing their educational goals and in matters related to daily living. Many of these problems were directly related to their hearing handicap. Furfey and Harte concluded that successful adjustment of a deaf person demanded planning, and this planning must involve the entire community as well as the deaf individual himself.

According to Sanderson (1967) the majority of deaf leaders in the organized deaf community are inexpert and unsophisticated. He believed they knew little or nothing about the power structure of the hearing community and, therefore, had failed in dealing with hearing leaders. He felt that these failures had conditioned deaf leaders to believe that the hearing community did not care about the deaf community, and thus isolation was reinforced. As a result, he thought, the leadership of the deaf community has developed a set of attitudes which work against successful integration.

Sanderson also felt that the attitude of deaf leaders toward problems of securing satisfactory vocational training and jobs were strongly colored by the success or failure of their own efforts in the community. He thought they may view rehabilitation as ineffective because they lacked understanding of the complex problems faced by the counselors; they may view the efforts of educators as equally ineffective, because they sense that their own inadequacies as leaders are in a large measure, due to deficiencies in their own education.

Every few years the question arises in the field as to whether the rehabilitation counselor should be a generalist or a specialist. Without becoming embroiled in the overall controversy, there is little doubt that in the area of deafness the specialist has a very definite role in the rehabilitation process of deaf clients. Not only must such an individual be a specialist in the general area of rehabilitation and deafness, but he must also be a jack-of-all-trades in terms of playing a vital role in several areas which, with the non-deaf client, are normally handled by a variety of counselor associates. For example, in the evaluation process the counselor who is working with deaf clients will frequently find that he cannot merely refer such an individual over to one of his co-workers or to the cooperating agency. In many cases such a counselor will find that he must accompany the deaf individual for his medical examination, interpreting as may be needed, to insure that an adequate medical is obtained and then follow through on psychological and vocational evaluations to be sure that the results of such evaluations are indeed valid for his deaf client. Furthermore, since the whole process of counseling is based on communication between the counselor and his client, the counselor who possesses a high degree of skill in manual communication is not merely desirable, but absolutely necessary if we are to avoid turning the whole counseling process into a farce.

Speaking from his personal experience in working with adult deaf people, Pettingill (1967) noted that their problems of finding and holding jobs were due more to their insecurity and inability to adjust rather than to their lack of comprehensive training. He also felt that deaf people in general have a poor public image. Pettingill believed the greatest need was for a strong program to teach deaf people how to *grow up*, and shake off the attitude of dependency which they seem to develop in schools for the deaf. Such a program, he thought, could include orientation for hearing people to inform them of the abilities of deaf people.

In summarizing remarks made at a national workshop, Thomure (1967) noted the inter-related problems faced by deaf people, as delineated by the speakers, encompassed the following: lack of sufficient general educational achievement; lack of sufficient maturity to attain good personal and social adjustment; lack of motivational forces to help in shaping life goals; lower status employment which keeps the deaf primarily in blue-collar positions; public attitudes which stereotype deaf individuals into lesser employable positions; lack of success in the hearing community; and a lack of enough interpreter services. Concern was also expresed regarding the gap between what the schools are doing, especially in the prevocational areas, and the requirements of the world of work.

These observations were supported by the Hicks (1967) report on the occupational levels of 269 young deaf adults surveyed in the southwestern part of the United States.

According to this data almost 70 percent of these young deaf

TABLE I

OCCUPATIONAL LEVELS OF 269 YOUNG DEAF ADULTS SURVEYED
IN THE SOUTHWESTERN UNITED STATES

Occupational Level	*N*
Professional and management	3
Semi-professional	1
Clerical and sales	34
Service	35
Agriculture, fishery, forestry	9
Skilled	72
Semi-skilled	75
Unskilled	40
Total	269

adults were employed in skilled, semi-skilled or unskilled jobs. Very few were in professional and managerial occupations. They made their living with their hands, in occupations hardest hit by automation.

Hicks also noted that more than half of the young people involved in the study were working in areas other than in which they received their secondary school vocational training. The reasons given for this condition, in order of greatest frequency, were: inadequacy of training; inability to find a job in the training area; acceptance of a job requiring no previous training; and acceptance of post-secondary or on-the-job training.

Stahler (1967) believed deaf youth should be taught how to go after better jobs, especially in view of the stiff competition they have been and will be facing with other youths. Specifically, he thought they should be taught how to look for jobs, fill out applications, groom themselves properly, present their qualifications effectively during interviews and how to take tests. He believed that knowing these things often made the difference between getting and not getting the job.

In order to accomplish the job of preparing deaf people for greater employment opportunities, Congressman Hugh L. Carey (1967) suggested an increase in the need for more adult education programs for these people.

Although adult education has come into sharper focus in the past few years, this emphasis has rarely included any provision for the adult deaf. The fact that most adult deaf people communicate principally by the language of signs has discouraged significant steps in this direction. However, this does not lessen the need for providing whatever special assistance may be necessary to make more such opportunities available to the deaf. The deaf need access to more courses offering such basics as facts about jobs, insurance, social security, taxes, local government, legal matters and the raising of children (Babbidge, 1965).

Karnes (1967) also thought local adult education programs should be established, or expanded, both as classes for the deaf alone and as integrated classes with hearing individuals. However, he felt that additional research is necessary to determine the optimum use of adult education techniques for the deaf.

Such areas as motivational and attitude changes, the use of new methods and programs for the multiple handicapped should be studied.

Post-secondary opportunities for deaf individuals also continue to be severely limited. Although Gallaudet College and the National Technical Institute for the Deaf, both subsidized in part by direct Federal appropriations, continue to offer the best liberal arts and technical vocational programs available to deaf citizens in the United States, there have come into being during the past two years a number of new post-secondary programs. These programs are predominantly of a junior college or vocational school nature. At the present time very little direct evaluation is available on most of these newly founded programs. Although some of them may offer adequate services, the counselor should make every effort to evaluate such programs in view of the particular needs of his specific client. Too frequently, counselors are inclined to pick the program which is closest to the client's home and therefore the cheapest in terms of case money expenditure. However, if such a program does not offer a strong support service the student may not be able to make satisfactory progress. In such cases what may, at first seem to be the most economical approach to training may indeed turn out to be the most expensive in terms of long-range benefits.

The National Organization

Although there are several groups working with the deaf in this country The National Association of the Deaf (NAD) has the longest history and continues to be the foremost example of its type of organization in existence anywhere in the world today.

According to their by-laws, NAD and its affiliates comprise a national non-profit organization composed primarily of deaf adults who have banded together in an effort to improve, develop and extend schools for the deaf; to provide information; to prevent discrimination against the deaf in employment, legislation and other areas; to promote economical, intellectual, professional and social betterment of the deaf; and to improve standards for teachers of the deaf. The organization's present structure has grown from a small group founded in 1880 to its present operation.

Membership is open to any deaf citizen of the United States, in addition, special categories of membership are also available to non-deaf individuals and people from other countries.

NAD also conducts various surveys in areas pertinent to the welfare of deaf people and, in cooperation with the United States Bureau of Census, a national census of the deaf. It has affiliated with state organizations which generally served two purposes; one of bringing deaf people together for mutual progress; the other that of providing opportunity to meet at regular intervals and renew old friendships.

REFERENCES

Adler, E. P.: The severely disadvantaged deaf. In G. T. Lloyd (Ed.), *International Reseach Seminar on the Vocational Rehabilitation of Deaf Persons.* Washington, D.C., Social and Rehabilitation Services, U.S. Department of Health, Education, and Welfare, 1968, pp. 224-226.

Babbidge, H. D. (Ed.): *Education of the Deaf, a Report to the Secretary of Health, Education, and Welfare by His Advisory Committee on the Education of the Deaf.* Washington, D.C., U.S. Department of Health, Education, and Welfare, 1965.

Best, H.: *Deafness and the Deaf in the United States.* New York, Macmillan, 1943.

Boatner, E. B.; Stuckless, E. R., and Moore, D. F.: *Occupational Status of the Young Deaf Adult of New England and Demand for a Regional Technical-Vocational Training Center.* West Hartford, Conn., American School for the Deaf, 1964.

Burke, D. J.: The District of Columbia plan for the coordination of local organizations of the deaf. In A. B. Crammatte (Ed.), *Proceedings of the Workshop on Communication Development Through Organizations of and for the Deaf.* Washington, D.C., Office of Vocational Rehabilitation, Government Printing Office, 1961, pp. 57-61.

Burns, B. B.: Who are the deaf? *American Annals of the Deaf, 103:*224-228, 1958.

Carey, H. L.: Legislation and education of the deaf. In F. E. Thomure (Ed.), *New Trends in Vocational and Technical Training for Deaf Youth.* Chicago, DePaul University, 1967, pp. 49-63.

Friedman, M.: Existing organizations of deaf persons and their potential functions. In A. B. Crammatte (Ed.), *Proceedings of the Workshop on Communication Development Through Organizations of and for the*

Deaf. Washington, D.C., Office of Vocational Rehabilitation, Government Printing Office, 1961, pp. 35-40.

Furfey, P. H., and Harte, T. J.: *Interaction of Deaf and Hearing in Fredrick County, Maryland.* Washington, D.C., Catholic University Press, 1964.

Furth, H. G.: *Thinking Without Language: Psychological Implications of Deafness.* New York, The Free Press, 1966.

Garretson, M. D.: Coordination and teamwork among national state and local organizations of and for the deaf. In A. B. Crammatte (Ed.), *Proceedings of the Workshp on Communication Development Through Organizations of and for the Deaf.* Washington, D.C., Office of Vocational Rehabilitation, Government Printing Office, 1961, pp. 66-70.

Garretson, M. D.: The handicap of deafness, *The Deaf American, 24*:15-16, 1972.

Greenaway, E. S.: The communication needs of the deaf child. In P. V. Doctor (Ed.), *Proceedings of the International Congress on Education of the Deaf.* Washington, D.C., Gallaudet College, 1964, pp. 433-439.

Grinker, R. R.: *Psychiatric Diagnosis, Therapy and Research on the Psychotic Deaf.* Washington, D.C., Social and Rehabilitation Service, U.S. Department of Health, Education, and Welfare, 1969, Research Grant Number, RD-2407-5.

Hester, M. S.: Manual Communication. In P. V. Doctor (Ed.), *Proceedings of the International Congress on Education of the Deaf.* Washington, D.C., Gallaudet College, 1964, pp. 211-221.

Hicks, D.: Vocational education and occupational status. In F. E. Thomure (Ed.), *New Trends in Vocational and Technical Training for Deaf Youth.* Chicago, Ill., DePaul University, 1967, pp. 37-44.

Hodgson, K. W.: *The Deaf and Their Problems.* New York, Philosophical Library, 1954.

Johnson, R. K.: Personal counseling. In R. L. Jones (Ed.), *Proceedings of the Council of Organizations Serving the Deaf Forum.* New Orleans, La., 1969, pp. 49-55.

Karnes, R.: Problems of the 22 and over age group. In F. E. Thomure (Ed.), *New Trends in Vocational and Technical Training for Deaf Youth.* Chicago, DePaul University, 1967, pp. 122-136.

Klinghammer, H. D.: Social perception of the deaf and of the blind by their voices and their speech. In P. V. Doctor (Ed.), *Proceedings of the International Congress on Educatin of the Deaf.* Washington, D.C., Gallaudet College, 1964, pp. 615-618.

Kohl, H. R.: Language and education of the deaf. *Center for Urban Education,* 1966, No. 1.

Kronenberg, H. H., and Blake, G. D.: *Youth Deaf Adults; An Occupational Survey.* Washington, D.C., Vocational Rehabilitation Administration, U.S. Department of Health, Education and Welfare, 1966.

Lauritsen, R. R.: Community integration of deaf people. In R. L. Jones (Ed.), *The Deaf Man and the World*. Washington, D.C., Council of Organizations Serving the Deaf, 1969, pp. 62-66.

Levine, E. S.: *The Psychology of Deafness*. New York, Columbia University Press, 1960.

Lunde, A. S., and Bigman, S. K.: *Occupational Conditions Among the Deaf*. Washington, D.C., Gallaudet College, 1959.

MacKane, K.: *A Comparison of the Intelligence of Deaf and Hearing Children*. New York, Columbia University, 1933.

Mayes, T. A.: Education and rehabilitation of the deaf, A candid view. *The Deaf American, 22*:9-11, 1970.

Meadows, K.: The effects of early manual communication and family climate. Unpublished doctoral dissertation, University of California, 1967.

Montgomery, G.: Proper case services depend upon proper diagnosis and evaluation. In G. T. Lloyd (Ed.), *International Research Seminar on the Vocational Rehabilitation of Deaf Persons*. Washington, D.C., Social and Rehabilitation Service, U.S. Department of Health, Education, and Welfare, 1968, pp. 183-186.

Myklebust, H. R.: *The Psychology of Deafness*. New York, Grune and Stratton, 1960.

Newman, L.: The handicap of deafness. *The Deaf American, 24*:18, 1972.

O'Brien, J. G.: Cooperation with community organizations. In A. B. Crammatte (Ed.), *Proceedings of the Workshop on Communication Development Through Organizations of and for the Deaf*. Washington, D.C., Office of Vocational Rehabilitation, Government Printing Office, 1961, pp. 41-44.

Peterson, E. W. (Ed.): *Deaf Leadership Training for Community Interaction*. Washington, D.C., Rehabilitation Services Administration, U.S. Department of Health, Education, and Welfare, 1969.

Pettingill, D. G.: Adjustment of the deaf. In S. R. Silverman (Ed.), *A Report on the Summer Workshop for Vocational Rehabilitation Counselors—Understanding the Deaf Client*. Boulder, University of Colorado, 1964, pp. 1-11.

Ranier, J. D., and Altschuler, K. Z.: *Comprehensive Mental Health Services for the Deaf*. New York, Department of Medical Genetics, New York Psychiatric Institute, 1966.

Ranier, J. D.; Altschuler, K. Z.; Kallman, F. J., and Deming, W. E.: *Family and Mental Health Problems in a Deaf Population*. New York, Columbia University, 1963.

Ross, D. R.: Test Performance of Deaf Adults Under Two Modes of Test Administration. Unpublished doctoral dissertation, University of Arizona, 1966.

Sanderson, R. G.: Implications of deafness in the world of work. In F. E.

Thomure (Ed.), *New Trends in Vocational and Technical Training for Deaf Youth.* Chicago, DePaul University, 1967, pp. 18-30.

Sanderson, R. G.: The deaf man and the world. In R. L. Jones (Ed.), *Proceedings of the Council of Organizations Serving the Deaf Forum.* New Orleans, 1969, pp. 9-17.

Sanger, W. T.: Factors inherent in mobilization to serve the handicapped. Conference and workshop on the handicapped. Washington, D.C., U.S. Department of Health, Education, and Welfare, 1956, pp. 42-46.

Scouten, E. L.: The place of the Rochester method in American education of the deaf. In P. V. Doctor (Ed.), *Proceedings of the International Congress on Education of the Deaf.* Washington, D.C., Gallaudet College, 1964, pp. 429-433.

Stahler, A.: Manpower. In F. E. Thomure (Ed.), *New Trends in Vocational and Technical Training for Deaf Youth.* Chicago, DePaul University, 1967, pp. 10-17.

Stewart, L. G.: Fostering independence in deaf people. In R. L. Jones (Ed.), *The Deaf Man and the World.* Washington, D.C., Council of Organizations Serving the Deaf, 1969, pp. 56-61.

Stuckless, E. R., and Birch, J. M.: The influence of early manual communication on the linguistic development of deaf children. *American Annals of the Deaf, 111*:452-462, 1966.

Sussman, M. B.: Sociological theory and deafness: Problems and prospects. In E. R. Stuckless (Ed.), *Research and Behavioral Aspects of Deafness.* Washington, D.C., Vocational Rehabilitation Administration, U.S. Department of Health, Education, and Welfare, 1965, pp. 38-53.

Switzer, M. E., and Williams, B. R.: Life problems of deaf people. *Archives of Environment Health, 15*:249-256, 1967.

Thomure, F. E. (Ed.): *New Trends in Vocational and Technical Training for Deaf Youth.* Chicago, DePaul University, 1967.

Ullman, D. C. (Ed.): *Respective Roles and Responsibilities of Private and Public Agencies in Advancing Community Relations Objectives.* New York, National Community Relations Advisory Council, 1958.

Vernon, M.: Mental health, deafness and communication. In D. M. Denton (Ed.), *Proceedings of the Teachers Institute.* Fredrick, Maryland School for the Deaf, 1969, pp. 16-18.

Vernon, M., and Makowsky, B.: Deafness and minority group dynamics. *The Deaf American, 21*:3-6, 1969.

Williams, B. R.: Foreword. In A. B. Crammatte (Ed.), *Proceedings of the Workshop on Community Development Through Organizations of and for the Deaf.* Washington, D.C., Office of Vocational Rehabilitation, U.S. Department of Health, Education, and Welfare, 1961, p. 5.

Williams, B. R.: Challenge and opportunity. *Journal of Rehabilitation of the Deaf, 1*:3-9, 1967.

Wright, B. A.: *Physical Disability—A Psychological Approach.* New York, Harper & Row, 1960.

TABLE II*
SERVICES PROVIDED FOR THE DEAF

Title and Address	Director	Full-Time Deaf Students	Interpreting	Notetaking	Tutoring	Career Counseling	Personal Counseling	Placement
CALIFORNIA								
Hacienda LaPuente Valley Vocational School 15359 E. Proctor City of Industry 91744	Jean Smith (213) 968-4638	77	X	X	X	X	X	X
Golden West College 15744 Golden West Street Huntington Beach 92647	Paul Culton (714) 847-4489	70	X	X	X	X	X	
Pasadena City College 1570 E. Colorado Blvd. Pasadena 91106	I. G. Lewis (213) 795-6961	20	X	X	X	X	X	
Riverside City College 4800 Magnolia Avenue Riverside 92506	Wm. May (714) 684-3240	27	X	X	X	X	X	
San Diego Community Colleges 835 Twelfth Avenue San Diego 92101	Beverly McGee (714) 232-7497		X	X	X	X	X	X
San Fernando Valley State College Northridge 91324	Ray L. Jones	52	X	X	X	X	X	X
American River College 4700 College Oak Drive Sacramento 95841	R. E. Allerton (916) 484-8261							
Santa Ana College 17th and Bristol Santa Ana 92706	L. J. Cloria (714) 547-9561	8				X	X	X
COLORADO								
Community College of Denver 1001 East 62nd Avenue Denver 80216	S. T. Guttadore (303) 287-3311	86	X	X	X	X	X	X
DISTRICT OF COLUMBIA								
Gallaudet College Florida Avenue at 7th St., N.E. Washington, D.C. 20002	B. Greenberg (202) 447-0841	1009	X		X	X	X	X
FLORIDA								
St. Petersburg Junior College 2465 Drew Street Clearwater 33515	T. M. Howze (813) 544-2551	20	X	X	X	X	X	X

* Delgado, G., and Stuckless, R.: An Information Publication of Post-Secondary Programs for the Deaf. From a manuscript to be published early in 1973.

TABLE II
SERVICES PROVIDED FOR THE DEAF

Speech and Hearing	Academic Advisement	Manual Communication Tr.	Supervised Housing	Tuition	Fees	Room	Board (State Resident)	Tuition	Fees	Room	Board (Out-of-State Resident)	Certificate	Diploma	Associate Degree	Bachelor Degree	Masters Degree	Technical-Vocational	Liberal Arts	Religion
X	X	X	X									X	X				X		
X	X	X		X			$ 80.	X	X		$ 110.	X	X	X			X		
	X			X	X		$ 130.	X	X		$ 130.	X	X	X			X		
	X	X		X			$ 100.					X	X	X			X	X	
X	X	X										X	X	X			X	X	
X	X	X		X	X	X	$1383.	X	X	X	$2493.				X	X		X	
												X	X	X			X	X	
	X											X	X	X			X	X	
	X	X		X	X		$ 112.	X	X		$ 382.	X	X	X			X		
X	X	X	X	X	X	X	$1917.	X	X	X	$1917.				X	X		X	
	X	X		X			$ 125.	X			$ 325.				X			X	X

TABLE II (Continued)
SERVICES PROVIDED FOR THE DEAF

Title and Address	Director	Full-Time Deaf Students	Interpreting	Notetaking	Tutoring	Career Counseling	Personal Counseling	Placement
IDAHO								
College of Southern Idaho 1300 Kemberly Road Twin Falls	Neil Cross (208) 733-9554	5	X		X	X		
ILLINOIS								
Northern Illinois University Speech and Hearing Clinic DeKalb 60115	K. Bosch (815) 753-1481	40	X	X	X	X	X	X
INDIANA								
Hyles-Anderson College Box 1007 Hammond 46325	R. J. Billings (219) 836-3350							
IOWA								
Iowa Western Community College 2700 College Road Council Bluffs 51501	B. N. Hicks (712) 328-3831	12	X	X	X	X	X	X
KANSAS								
Johnson County Community College 57 and Merriam Drive Shawnee Mission 66202	D. E. Matthews	14	X	X	X	X	X	X
KENTUCKY								
Jefferson County Area Vocational School 3101 Bluebird Lane Jeffersontown 40299	J. L. Wright (502) 267-7431	18	X		X	X	X	X
LOUISIANA								
Delgado Vocational Technical Junior College 615 City Park Avenue New Orleans 70119	D. O. Wells (504) 486-5403	75	X	X	X	X	X	
MICHIGAN								
Genesee Community College 1401 East Court Street Flint 48503	B. E. Poss (313) 238-1631		X	X	X			X
State Technical Institute and Rehabilitation Center Alber Drive Plainwell 49080	Fred Daniels (616) 664-4461	18	X	X	X	X	X	X
MINNESOTA								
St. Paul Technical Vocational Institute 235 Marshall Avenue St. Paul 55102	Roger Reddan (612) 227-9121	90	X	X	X	X	X	X

TABLE II (CONTINUED)
SERVICES PROVIDED FOR THE DEAF

Speech and Hearing	Academic Advisement	Manual Communication Tr.	Supervised Housing	Tuition (State)	Fees (State)	Room (State)	Board (State)	Annual Cost (State Resident)	Tuition (Out)	Fees (Out)	Room (Out)	Board (Out)	Annual Cost (Out-of-State Resident)	Certificate	Diploma	Associate Degree	Bachelor Degree	Masters Degree	Technical-Vocational	Liberal Arts	Religion
				X		X	X	$1090.	X		X	X	$1090.	X	X				X		
X	X	X	X	X		X	X	$2774.						X	X	X	X	X			
				X	X	X	X	$1780.	X	X	X	X	$1780.				X	X			X
	X	X		X	X	X	X	$1005.	X	X	X	X	$1145.	X	X	X			X		
X	X	X	X	X	X			$ 345.	X	X			$ 795.	X	X	X			X		
X	X	X		X	X			$ 200.	X	X			$ 200.	X	X				X		
		X	X	X	X	X	X	$1770.	X	X	X	X	$1875.	X	X	X			X		
X	X	X		X	X			$ 700.	X	X			$1000.	X	X	X			X		
X	X	X	X	X	X	X	X	$ 649.	X	X	X	X	$1300.	X	X				X		
X	X	X	X	X	X	X	X	$2060.	X		X	X	$2060.	X	X				X		

TABLE II (CONTINUED)
SERVICES PROVIDED FOR THE DEAF

Title and Address	Director	Full-Time Deaf Students	Interpreting	Notetaking	Tutoring	Career Counseling	Personal Counseling	Placement
NEW YORK								
National Technical Institute for the Deaf One Lomb Memorial Drive Rochester 14623	J. Dengler (716) 464-2197	338	X	X	X	X		X
OHIO								
Columbus Technical Institute 550 East Spring Street Columbus 43215	D. Slasor (614) 221-6743		X	X		X	X	X
PENNSYLVANIA								
Community College of Philadelphia 34 South 11th Street Philadelphia 19107	Aram Terzian (215) 569-3680							
TENNESSEE								
Tennessee Temple Schools Chattanooga 37404	L. D. Lockery (615) 698-1535	7	X			X		
TEXAS								
Eastfield College 3737 Motley Drive Mesquite 75149	W. Dennis (214) 746-3100	7	X	X	X	X	X	X
Lee College Box 818 Baytown 77520	T. S. McGee (713) 427-6531	50	X	X	X	X	X	X
Tarrant County Junior College Northeast Campus 828 Harwood Road Hurst 76053	Jim Reed (817) 336-7851		X	X	X	X		X
UTAH								
Utah State University Department of Communicative Disorders Mechanical Arts Building Logan 84321	J. R. Jensen (801) 752-4100	25		X	X	X	X	X
WASHINGTON								
Seattle Community College 1625 Broadway Seattle 98122	S. R. Traxler (206) 587-4183	92	X	X	X	X	X	

TABLE II (Continued)
SERVICES PROVIDED FOR THE DEAF

Column groups: columns 5–9 = Annual Cost, State Resident (Tuition, Fees, Room, Board, total); columns 10–14 = Annual Cost, Out-of-State Resident (Tuition, Fees, Room, Board, total); columns 15–22 = Leads to Emphasis.

Speech and Hearing	Academic Advisement	Manual Communication Tr.	Supervised Housing	Tuition (St)	Fees (St)	Room (St)	Board (St)	State Cost	Tuition (OS)	Fees (OS)	Room (OS)	Board (OS)	Out-of-State Cost	Certificate	Diploma	Associate Degree	Bachelor Degree	Masters Degree	Technical-Vocational	Liberal Arts	Religion
X	X	X	X	X	X	X	X	$1448.	X	X	X	X	$1448.	X	X		X	X	X	X	
	X	X		X	X			$ 630.	X	X			$1110.	X	X	X			X		
																			X		
	X		X	X	X	X	X	$1765.	X	X	X	X	$1765.	X	X						X
X	X	X		X				$ 212.	X				$ 504.	X	X	X				X	X
X	X	X		X	X			$ 242.						X	X	X			X		
	X					X	X	$ 250.			X	X	$ 840.	X	X	X			X		
X	X	X		X	X	X	X	$1354.	X	X	X	X	$1354.				X	X	X	X	X
X	X	X	X	X	X	X	X	$1375.	X	X	X	X	$1707.	X	X	X			X		

CHAPTER IX

THE DIABETIC

AMOS SALES

Diabetes Defined
Orientation for Rehabilitation Counseling
Special Considerations
Summary
References

DIABETES IS A serious and widespread health problem. It is a chronic disease that is found all over the world and affects males and females of all ages. In the United States diabetes is ten times more prevalent after age 45, with the chance of it occurring among children under age 15 being minimal. Although a cure is not yet known, the introduction of insulin therapy during the 1920's and the increased awareness of the importance of diet have greatly improved the prognosis for diabetes. However, even with advances in treatment procedures, the life expectancy of a diabetic is still only two-thirds that of the general population.

A family history of diabetes and obesity are factors that are generally associated with diabetes. With these family characteristics, the over forty, obese individual would be a likely candidate for this disease. Estimates have indicated that approximately 4.4 million persons in the United States have diabetes. About 1.6 million of these do not know that they have the disease and probably have not yet developed symptoms. Some may have developed symptoms but may not be sufficiently aware of the implications or seriousness of the symptoms to seek medical care. Approximately 325,000 persons each year learn for the first time that they have the disease (U.S. Department of Health, Education and Welfare, 1968).

Indications of the wide prevalence of other chronic complications associated with diabetes have been provided by a national health survey. In this study, four out of five diabetic respondents reported one or more conditions in addition to diabetes. Approximately two of every five indicated having either heart disease or high blood pressure in conjunction with the diabetes. Other reported conditions with a comparatively high prevalence among diabetics were genito-urinary conditions and visual impairment. Comparisons of groups of diabetics with non-diabetics have revealed that eye lesions are far more frequent among the diabetics. This seems to be true for all age groups. Cataracts, for instance, are found in approximately 27 percent of the diabetics and only 9 percent of the non-diabetics. About 7 percent of the diabetics reported they were totally blind but not necessarily as a result of their diabetes. The National Society for the Prevention of Blindness has indicated that diabetes is presently the third leading cause of blindness in this country (U.S. Department of Health, Education and Welfare, 1968).

It would appear that approximately 562,000 diabetics are limited in their ability to work, keep house, or engage in scholastic activity. Approximately 168,000 of these are entirely unable to perform their major activity, with 6 percent of all diabetics confined to their homes and unable to move about without difficulty. Such limitations from a humanitarian point of view would provide adequate indication of the need for provision of rehabilitation services to diabetics. A closer look at the annual cost of diabetes to United States' economy clearly indicates the simple economic need for the rehabilitation of diabetics. Potential earnings losses have been estimated to be approximately $442,000,000 annually, with sickness absenteeism among persons who are currently working estimated at $74,000,000 per year. The total annual cost to the United States economy is estimated to be at least $2,000,000,000 for such areas as earnings losses, homemaker services losses and medical services costs. The cost data developed for many of these items are admittedly rough estimates, but they do provide some indication of the problem (U.S. Department of Health, Education and Welfare, 1968).

In determining an appropriate rehabilitation approach with diabetics, any practitioner will readily agree that the ability to understand and interpret information about health and disease is essential. A basic understanding of body functioning and of body dysfunction allows the rehabilitation counselor to better understand the client and his situation. This understanding also enables him to be more effective in his professional contacts with other professionals, with potential employers, or with the client's family.

Diabetes Defined

The following description of diabetes is an attempt to sufficiently describe the dysfunction to allow the rehabilitation counselor to work effectively with his client, whether the setting is a hospital, private or state facility, or general DVR agency. The purpose here is not to provide a full medical analysis of the total disease entity of diabetes but to provide a minimal amount of medical information necessary for the rehabilitation counselor to serve as an effective client advocate with diabetics. The rehabilitation counselor who is interested in a similar exposition on diabetes mellitus, should check Felton, Perkins and Lewin's (1966) work. A more detailed exposition of diabetes is to be found in Best and Taylor's (1950) reference book.

One of the major endocrine glands is the pancreas, which produces the hormone, insulin. Insulin is normally passed directly into the blood stream. There it acts as a chemical messenger to function according to bodily demands to hasten or slow down various processes. When the pancreas produces an inadequate supply of insulin or, in some cases, completely fails to produce it as a result of possible destruction of portions of the cells of the pancreas, the body dysfunction is termed diabetes.

Diabetes is a term used principally with reference to the disease, diabetes mellitus. Diabetes means *to-go-through,* and mellitus means *sweetened with honey;* together they refer to the disease popularly known as sugar diabetes.

Insulin, produced by the pancreas, should regulate the use)f sugar by the body and its storage in the liver. When the pancreas does not secrete enough insulin there is an excessive amount of sugar in the blood (hyperglycemia) and sugar in the urine (glycosuria). The amount of urine also is greatly increased (polyuria) because of the effort of the kidneys to remove the extra sugar from the blood. In diabetes, the blood sugar may be as high as 5 or 6 percent, whereas in normal blood the sugar content is from .09 to 0.15 percent. Increase in thirst is caused by the excessive urination. There may also be hunger, emaciation, weakness, and an accumulation of acids in the blood, causing acidosis, which in turn, may cause death.

The function of insulin is to promote the storage of glycogin, an animal starch in the liver, muscles, and skin, to facilitate the combustion of glucose, which is the chief source of energy for the tissue cells, and to support the utilization of protein and fat. Without adequate insulin, sugar is not utilized and is present or collects in increased amounts in the blood. When this condition comes about, the excessive sugar spills over into the urine. Since the body fails to derive energy from its normal source of supply, it draws upon its stored fats. By-products of this fat metabolism, acetone and ketone bodies, characteristically appear in the urine of the diabetic whose disease is not under control. The radical dislocation of the acid base equilibrium cannot be tolerated by the body for a sustained period of time. Accordingly, severe diabetes, undiagnosed and untreated, can result in death. Early detection and painstaking control are mandatory in maintaining the health and employability of the diabetic.

The major symptoms of diabetes are increased amounts of urine (polyurine), thirst (polydypsia), and hunger (polyphagia). These symptoms appear classically in severe diabetes in young persons. Other symptoms are loss of weight, loss of strength, and itching. At times the patient may be totally asymptomatic, with the only indication of diabetes being through a urinalysis or blood sugar test. Prolonged presence in the blood of waste products of fat metabolism, a condition called acidosis or ketosis, will at times result in the diabetic coma. Associated with the coma are dehydration, circulatory collapse, kidney failure, and, at times, the coma may be fatal.

When not under medical care and not practicing good personal care, the diabetic has lower resistance than the normal individual and is more susceptible to pulmonary tuberculosis, pneumonia, skin diseases, pimples, boils and eye diseases such as cataracts, inflammation or hemorrhage of the retina, and occasionally total loss of vision. There is also danger of slow or defective healing of wounds, cuts, and breaks in the skin and non-union of bone fractures. Gangrene is a prominent hazard in injuries to the legs and feet, especially with older diabetics, where there is a tendency toward arteriosclerosis which causes poor circulation in the legs, feet and toes.

A major treatment for diabetes is the control of hyperglycemia, which is accomplished by limiting the intake of carbohydrates and by stimulating the glucose utilization through chemotherapy. The plan of treatment is unique and individualized for each patient to meet his specific needs. The amount of insulin administered, the amount and types of food permitted, and the amount of exercise included in the patient's normal life pattern must be maintained and balanced.

Early diagnosis and treatment are considered essential for a positive prognosis. Treatment early after onset of the disorder with good control of the condition helps not only to prolong life but helps prevent or delay the development of complications. Treatment has included some oral medications; however, recent findings regarding effectiveness of various oral medications have raised some doubts regarding the efficacy of their past use. The most effective treatment appears to be control of diet and of insulin. Enlisting cooperation from the diabetic in the controlling of both diet and insulin is most important, and enlisting the diabetic's cooperation would appear to be most easily attained through a positive educational approach to the disability. Ample literature is available through sources such as the State Departments of Public Health to make the diabetic an *expert* in terms of awareness and control of his diabetes. Armed with such awareness, the diabetic will be better able to cooperate in the successful treatment of the disorder.

If the individual knows he is diabetic and has been properly instructed, diabetic coma is no longer the serious hazard to life that it formerly was. Insulin shock, a complication of treatment, is characterized by rapid onset of tremor, excessive perspiration, headache, pronounced weakness, anxiety, and finally loss of consciousness. Prompt administration of glucose will correct hyperinsulinism and diabetics are often cautioned to carry with them a cube of sugar, a candy bar, or a small box of raisins which can be consumed at the first symptom of insulin shock. Coma (stupor or unconsciousness) can also result from giving up or taking too much insulin. The onset of coma is slow, preceded by a feeling of sickness and nausea, but its course is fast, death or recovery taking place usually within twenty-four to thirty-six hours. Treatment must be immediate and active and includes calling the personal doctor and going to bed at once. Treatment given during the first few hours is exceedingly important. The essential factor is that, when being sent to other than their own personal physician, diabetics should be identified as such to preclude the possibility of erroneous diagnosis, which can happen easily, and incorrect treatment, which may be fatal (Felton *et al.*, 1966).

The above medical overview is, of course, quite brief. Further study of the disorder will be helpful for any rehabilitation counselor working with diabetics. As one gains further knowledge of the disorder, however, he should continually keep in mind that any attempt at definition of diabetes usually deals exclusively with the nature of the physical impairment and not with the physically impaired person. The logic of disease classification is not at all the logic of person classification. Too often the medical practice of classification, with the potential for stereotyping, invades counselor practice. Generalizations regarding disability serve a good purpose in acquainting the counselor with the disease entity and factors associated with it. Ultimately, however, these generalizations may often inhibit as much as they aid the process of rehabilitation counseling.

Orientation for Rehabilitation Counseling

Counseling, as well as rehabilitation counseling, has been defined in a great variety of ways by a great number of experts. To provide a list of such definitions probably would take more pages than are in this book. Although the variety of definitions and orientations is great, certain commonalities in practice have been identified and bear consideration here.

Research indicates that, regardless of the counselor's espoused school or theory of counseling, certain measurable personality in-counseling characteristics of the counselor appear to be correlated with outcome criteria. The counselor's expression of these is correlated with substantial changes in his client. When high levels of these conditions are evident, client change is for the better. However, counseling relationships characterized by low levels of these counselor conditions result in a worsening of the client's situation.

The first of these conditions is empathic understanding. This is not the diagnostic, information-gathering type of understanding which is common in our society. Empathic understanding is, instead, characterized by the ability to understand a person from his own frame of reference and to communicate this understanding to the client. Counseling experts' emphasis on the ability to listen and be in tune with a client reflects their awareness of this singularly important counselor quality.

The second necessary condition of any helping relationship is acceptance of or respect for the client as a capable and responsible person. The counselor non-possessively cares for and shows concern for his client as a human being without prejudging him as a person or imposing conditions upon his behavior.

The third prerequisite is that the counselor must be genuine. The counselor must consistently be himself and not play out a role, a technique, or a facade as a counselor. He must be a real person if he is to be a therapeutic person. Genuineness, warmth, and empathic understanding when offered at high levels by counselors result in clients feeling, possibly for the first time, understood, accepted, and valued as a human being. Within a safe, non-evaluative relationship, this feeling of acceptance allows the client to verbally express and clarify for himself the full range of emotion he feels relative to his present situation. This is the necessary first step to establishing an effective counseling relationship which, depending on counselor competence and client need, may later follow a variety of techniques to reach their specified goal.

Rehabilitation counseling requires the counselor conditions discussed above. Although much of the rehabilitation counselor's work consists of providing advice and information and coordinating various needed services, the basic ability to establish an effective relationship characterized by the above qualities is considered to be a pre-requisite to professional functioning in the field. The majority of clients seeking the services of the rehabilitation counselor do not require that the client and counselor enter into continuing *in-depth* counseling sessions. However, to meet the needs of the percentage that do require this continuing counseling contact and to be truly able to understand the client well enough to provide the type of help needed for the client to solve his own problems, the rehabilitation counselor must be able to establish a therapeutic counseling relationship.

The rehabilitation counselor's *raison d'etre* is to assist the client to reach his optimal vocational adjustment. He works in this capacity while being fully aware that one cannot isolate vocational adjustment from personal/social adjustment. Rehabilitation counselors realize they must be able to relate to the total person in order to help him move toward successful personal and vocational adjustment. Client need will determine to a great extent the type of counselor-client interaction. No unique counseling technique or theory has to be developed for the rehabilitation counselor to provide services to individuals with diabetes. There are special areas of knowledge which the rehabilition counselor must have in order to be truly effective in his full range of contacts with his client who has diabetes. A basic awareness of the medical dysfunction helps the rehabilitation counselor to not only more easily understand the diabetic client from his frame of reference but also more readily anticipate the full range of vocational implications of the disorder. The following are some special considerations to keep in mind when counseling with individuals with diabetes.

Special Considerations

Keeping in mind that it is very difficult to apply a general set of rules to all patients falling in this disease category, it is felt that the typical client with diabetes presents fewer initial counseling problems because he generally comes to the counselor well aware of the established diagnosis of diabetes. Indications are (Kessler, 1953) that half of all diabetics require no insulin and no special need to establish any special restrictions to their work activity. Many experts feel that diabetics who follow their insulin and diet schedule faithfully do not require specialized aid in securing a job unless their condition warrants change from heavier to lighter work. The typical diabetic seeking services through rehabilitation agencies is one who has developed secondary problems because of complications of the disease. Complications would include impairment of visual acuity, impairment of vascular circulatory system, which often results in amputation of an extremity, and impairment of the neurological system. The counselor's major client contact will be with individuals suffering from complications of the disease.

In working with diabetics, the rehabilitation counselor would probably have concerns or questions to be resolved with the physician. Several of the following considerations are paraphrased from Lofquist's (1957) excellent presentation regarding vocational counseling with the diabetic. From the medical case file and other available information, the rehabilitation counselor would be concerned with identifying the type of dietary program or schedule which the client must follow in order to maintain control of his condition. He would also be most interested in who has explained the importance of diet and the dietary regulations to the client and to his family. Vocational implications of answers to dietary questions are, of course, of primary concern to the rehabilitation counselor and the client in clarifying future vocational direction.

The rehabilitation counselor would also be most interested in attempting to determine whether or not the client would be particularly vulnerable to ill effects from injuries or infections. A minor industrial accident might possibly be a major problem for a diabetic if his disorder is complicated by serious peripheral vascular difficulties. The rehabilitation counselor must creatively review the diabetic's medical situation to identify potential occupational hazards whenever considering vocational possibilities with him.

Other rehabilitation considerations would include an identification of possible physical defects and their influence on training or ability to work. Also, circulatory problems necessitate increased concern over personal hygiene. Therefore, personal care and the quality of it have vocational implications. Certain kinds of employment might interfere with or preclude good personal care. These should possibly be avoided since increased susceptibility to infections, a result of poor circulation within diabetes, are often prevalent with poor personal care.

A major consideration will be the client's emotional reaction to knowledge of his condition and the regimen he must follow to keep the conditions under control. The degree of acceptance of the disability and the extent to which the client is coping with the effects of it are most significant indicators of future rehabilitation success. Readers interested in further discussion of the emotional reaction to disability are referred to Wright's (1960) text.

The general thought that individuals with disabilities are more emotionally disturbed than are individuals without disabilities lacks support in research fact. The more adequate the controls, the more often no differences between comparison groups exist. Research attempts to discover personality differences unique to a disability such as diabetes carry with them the hazard of misinterpretation. Overgeneralization of the findings tends to ascribe group trends to individual cases. The rehabilitation counselor must keep in mind that each client is a unique person. He must be able to avoid preconceived expectations regarding his client. Disability labels do not reveal a client's unique problems, only the client can provide such information (Wright, 1971). However, diabetes is one of many disorders in which fluctuations of one's emotional state greatly influence the stability of the disorder. Anxiety often influences the ability to control the disorder and the rehabilitation counselor must be prepared to serve in a supportive role in these cases.

Diabetic clients are often limited in terms of the amount of energy they can expend on the job. Often, a work setting wherein the scheduled daily energy output is comparable to a restricted energy intake must be found. Other work considerations should include the question of whether or not different work hours, such as late shifts or rotating shifts, will influence the medical problem.

Another consideration for the rehabilitation counselor is that of control of the disorder. Is the condition *brittle* and almost unmanageable or is the diabetes controlled well enough that possible dizziness, faintness, or loss of consciousness will not be present? If the above symptoms are present, any decisions regarding future vocational choice must insure that the person not be placed around dangerous equipment where he might be a hazard to himself or others if these conditions arose. Other types of physical involvement or complications may be present which would impose other types of limitations. For instance, degrees of proneness to infection might present a particular hazard to one individual with diabetes but be only a minor concern to another individual. The range of complications and personal limitations is great among diabetics and no set rules can be established regarding what situations should be avoided. The above are but a few of the general kinds of questions the counselor will want to consider in his consultations with medical specialists and in his interaction with his client.

If complications related to diabetes force an individual to change his job or to seek more regular work hours, the counselor must assist the client plan more realistically within, of course, the labor market framework of the community to which he plans to return. Too often vocational rehabilitation plans are developed, training programs set up, and eventually diabetics trained for occupations in which employment possibilities are limited or non-existent.

In developing a rehabilitation plan, sources of information in addition to that gathered during the actual counseling contacts may be of help with the diabetic client. Helpful information might be obtained from observing dates of treatment to gain some awareness of the progress of treatment of conditions such as insulin shock. This information can be utilized as an indicator of the duration and control of the diabetic condition as well as the cooperation and adjustment to the treatment process by the particular client. The number of and the nature of job changes may also indicate difficulty of control or failure to even observe measures prescribed to maintain control. The creative counselor will make use of all information available to assist him in identifying potential problems which his client may have to confront. Utilization of such information need not interfere with the experiential interaction within counseling contacts.

It would seem that the diabetic who suffers no complications and whose illness is under control is readily employable if certain restrictions are observed. Work, of course, should be relatively free of stress since emotional stress tends to exacerbate the severity of the disease. Rotating shifts may have to be avoided since the program of insulin and food intake should not be disrupted in some cases. In some instances, the diabetic should avoid certain jobs in which injury hazards would cause a high risk of infection.

Industry has not experienced a major absentee problem with diabetics. However, there is some reluctance to employ a diabetic without reassuring information concerning control of the disease and its prognosis. Many employers are quite concerned about insulin shock problems, and some general employer education would be helpful when it comes to job placement of a diabetic. Even though experience has shown that some employers are hesitant to hire a known diabetic, it is still advised that the employer probably should be aware of medical conditions when he hires the diabetic. This would seem to be necessary so that key people in the plant could be alerted to possible coma or insulin reactions. The developing trend is toward a more liberal attitude in the hiring and employing of diabetics.

The above specific considerations in the rehabilitation counseling of the diabetic should not be presumed to be the major factors to be considered in effective rehabilitation counseling of diabetics. These are specific considerations common to many individuals with diabetes which may be helpful to the counselor in identifying some problem areas or points of consideration in working with them. The rehabilitation counselor's major concern with diabetics, as with other clients, is with developing an effective counseling relationship with his client which is characterized by understanding the full ramifications of the medical problem and the resulting personal-vocational problems that the client presents. Understanding and sensitivity to client needs are prerequisites to the rehabilitation counselor's being able to assist the client to clarify for himself his own situation, his own potentials, and his own direction in the future.

Summary

Individuals with diabetes present a wide variety of individual differences. They vary greatly in the nature and severity of their disorder as well as in the number and severity of accompanying complications resulting from it. Their scholastic aptitude and intellectual ability may range from excellent to poor. Because of their heterogeneity, no universal personal characteristics of diabetics as a group provide a guide to understanding an individual with diabetes. Any attempt to identify unique characteristics of individuals with diabetes carries with it the hazard of rehabilitation counselors' relying on stereotyped notions as a guide to reacting to and working with individuals with diabetes.

Assisting the client with diabetes toward ever-increasing independence and a clarification and determination of a new vocational future is the major problem faced by the rehabilitation counselor. An awareness of medical information and considerations relative to the body dysfunction, diabetes, will help the rehabilitation counselor better understand the diabetic client and his particular vocational needs. A realization and appreciation of each individual's uniqueness and his unique reaction to disability are necessary in assisting the client with diabetes to reach a realistic vocational objective. Armed with a familiarity with the disorder, the following suggestions should assist in the rehabilitation counselor's effectiveness:

> Determine your course of action on the basis of behavioral and functional evidence of abilities and disabilities as opposed to stereotyped thinking about categories of physical impairment.

View the disability in its perspective as not the individual's most significant characteristic but only one of many important attributes. Value knowing the client as well as knowing about him.

REFERENCES

Best, C. H., and Taylor, N. B.: *Physiological Basis of Medical Practice,* 5th ed., Baltimore, Williams and Wilkins Co., 1950.

Felton, J. S.; Perkins, D. C., and Lewin, M.: *A Survey of Medicine and Medical Practice for the Rehabilitation Counselor,* Washington, D.C., V.R.A. Department of Health, Education and Welfare, 1966.

Kessler, H. H.: *Rehabilitation of the Physically Handicapped.* New York, McGraw-Hill, 1946.

Lofquist, L. H.: *Vocational Counseling With the Physically Handicapped.* New York, Appleton-Century-Crofts, 1957.

U.S. Department of Health, Education and Welfare, Public Health Service, *Diabetes Source Book,* Publication No. 1168, Washington, U.S. Government Printing Office, 1968.

Wright, B. A.: *Physical Disability—A Psychological Approach.* New York, Harper & Row, 1960.

Wright, B. A.: Some Problems, Some Concepts, and Some Solutions, in A. Sales (ed.), *Supervision of Rehabilitation Counseling Contacts, Selected Psychological Considerations,* Emporia, Kansas, Kansas State Teachers College Press, 1971.

CHAPTER X

REHABILITATION AND CANCER

KENT M. SAMUELSON AND CECIL O. SAMUELSON

Introduction

CANCER IS PROBABLY as old as life itself. Signs of it have been found in the bones of animals that lived anciently. It is found today in every kind of living thing—plants, animals, and humans. The Egyptians knew it and treated it with ointments, prayers, and spells and, no doubt, other peoples in other places at other times had their peculiar remedies, none of which were particularly helpful. Since so little was known about cancer and so little could be done about it and because it so often affected the most intimate parts of the body, it came to be regarded with particular dread as an unmentionable or disgraceful condition (*Youth Looks at Cancer*, American Cancer Society). But what actually is cancer?

Definition

Cancer may be defined in various ways depending upon who is giving the definition. In a medical sense, cancer is a disease that is characterized by abnormal growth and spread of cells. Cancer typically begins as a *localized* disease. At the start, just one of the tiny cells of the body—or perhaps a few cells—undergoes an unfortunate change; it becomes a malignant cell, cancer. The cancer cell reproduces itself by dividing into two cells which in turn divide, etc. All of the cells that started from the original cancer cell or cells are themselves cancer cells. Thus, the cancer grows (American Cancer Society, 1970).

The person afflicted with cancer, or those involved, may not think of this relatively simple-sounding biological process. The person so afflicted may define it as a death sentence preceded by untold agony.

Philosophy

Over the years cancer has been regarded generally as a horrible, incurable disease. Those who became so afflicted were unfortunate and there was not much hope for them. Once the diagnosis was made, it became basically a waiting game—waiting for death which was assumed to be inevitable. Perhaps worst of all was the emptiness of this waiting period which contained little thought for the possibilities of constructive activity on the part of the person caught by this dreadful disease. The posture on the part of all concerned typically was one of hopelessness.

This negative attitude might be expected on the part of the subject and those close to him. What else was there to think in the absence of encouragement from any source? Pondering such an ailment in the atmosphere of its distressing symptoms could bring despair to even the stoutest soul. Healy (1968) says it is easy to understand the lay person's defeatest attitude toward the disease. He learns little about cancer except for the publicity given the fatal cases, reports on the increase in incidence of lung cancer, or the fear tactics used by various cancer societies and insurance agencies. Rarely does he learn of the successes of cancer therapy. But, perhaps the greatest negative influence has come from the attitudes of the individuals in the professional groups to which persons with cancer are exposed. The applicant with cancer who found his way to the vocational rehabilitation office was scarcely reassured by his need to meet the criterion of employability after the rehabilitation service had been rendered. The fears of such an applicant may be further kindled by the need to wait a year or two after the final treatment to make certain that he had been *cured*. While from an agency point of view this procedure may appear to reflect sound policy and good judgment on the part of the counselor, it could be devastating to the subject. His morale might waste away at the time when he needed the greatest support, and, from a realistic standpoint, the loss of time waiting for the *cure* to be verified could not be recovered.

Even some physicians may harbor attitudes out of keeping with the facts about cancer. Healey (1968) reflects this possibility concerning physicians in these words:

> Unfortunately, however, the practicing physician also maintains a negative attitude toward cancer and the rehabilitation potential of patients afflicted with this disease. This attitude generates from certain deficits in his medical education. The average physician, during his medical training, has very limited exposure to cancer patients, and therefore, is poorly informed about the facts of cancer. His training in rehabilitation procedures is even more limited (p. 23).

The substance of this is to stress the need for improving the attitudes and changing the philosophy of all those concerned in the treatment and care of cancer patients. This is more than a platitudinous call for improvement. There is a substantial basis for a more constructive philosophy toward cancer. While there does not seem to be a *cure* for cancer at the present time, the outlook is far from discouraging. Again Healey (1968) points out that in the 1920's cancer was considered to be an incurable disease. Today, according to the statistics of the American Cancer Society, one of every three patients obtains a *clinical cure*. Holleb (1970) writing about the cancer cures we have now believes that if every cancer were detected and treated in the early stage the cure rate would be increased to one of every two patients despite the fact that we do not know the cause of cancer. This great achievement is possible with the therapeutic methods which are available today. Improved medical and surgical procedures and especially early diagnosis have served to increase the numbers who have survived a five year period. Time has brought improvement in the outlook for cancer patients.

From a vocational rehabilitation point of view cancer has always presented practical problems. Since the state rehabilitation agency was charged with the ultimate employment of the persons it served, the dull future of the cancer patient did not make him a bright prospect for rehabilitation services. Furthermore, a distinction had to be made between physical restoration services which were primarily for purposes of medical care and those that were for purposes of vocational rehabilitation. The long standing concern of the Federal Vocational Rehabilitation Administration for the cancer patient and the need to make the above mentioned distinction in selecting applicants for rehabilitation services was set forth in the guidelines embraced in the ADMINISTRATIVE SERVICE SERIES NUMBER 64-6 of August 8, 1963. In the COMMISSIONER'S LETTER NUMBER 68-5, dated August 29, 1967, further instructions were issued concerning eligibility of cancer patients. Among other helpful directions this letter states that, "Accordingly we believe that cancer at all stages may be considered a disability which constitutes a substantial handicap to employment." The effect of this statement is to emphasize that cancer is a qualifying disability for rehabilitation purposes and to encourage the state agencies to look with greater receptiveness at applicants so afflicted. Five years ago the Vocational Rehabilitation Administration and the American Cancer Society as indicated in the COMMISSIONER'S LETTER NUMBER 68-11, November 9, 1967, entered into a cooperative agreement embracing joint efforts that included liaison between the organizations, patient referral, professional education, research and demonstration, public education, and consulting services. These developments indicate substantial movement in the rehabilitation of the cancer-afflicted person. Other agencies, organizations, and concerned individuals are moving toward a more realistic and at the same time constructive attitude toward cancer and the person it attacks. The future merits our calm and confident reassurance.

Medical Information

In discussing cancer there are a number of terms that are used by physicians which warrant a general definition that might be helpful to the counselor. The following list is intended to include only some of the more general terms that might be encountered. For definitions of those terms not listed it is suggested that the reader refer to books such as Dorland's *Illustrated Medical Dictionary*, 24th Edition, S. B. Saunders Company, Philadelphia, 1965, or Taber's *Cyclopedic Medical Dictionary*, 9th Edition Illustrated, F. A. Davis Company, Philadelphia, 1962.

Cancer—An uncontrolled growth of abnormal cells that have a tendency to invade tissues locally and also spread to distant sites. If untreated, the cancer will usually cause death.

Tumor—An abnormal swelling or enlargement made up of a mass of cells which grow as an independent cluster and serve no useful purpose.

Neoplasm—A tumor.

Malignancy—Cancer.

Benign—Non-malignant.

Carcinoma—A cancer originating in epithelial (covering) tissue.

Sarcoma—A cancer originating in connective tissues, such as muscle, bone, and cartilage.

Leukemia—Cancer of the blood-forming organs (bone marrow, lymph nodes, spleen) characterized by excessive formation of white blood cells.

Lymphoma—Malignant growths of lymph nodes.

Metastasis—The spread of disease from one part of the body to another by direct extension or through the lymph or blood vessels, carrying the characteristic cells from the first lesion to a new location in the body. It is applied to secondary tumors arising at a distance from the primary growth.

Biopsy—The removal of a small part of a living tissue for microscopic examination to determine whether cancer cells are present.

(Adapted from *Teaching About Cancer,* a publication of the American Cancer Society.)

Cancer is usually thought of as a process which starts in one location of the body and then spreads to other sites. The major symptoms experienced by the patient may be due to either the primary or metastatic proliferation, or to the systemic effects caused by the abnormal metabolism of cancerous cells. Often cancer is first discovered when the patient has symptoms from a secondary growth and it is sometimes the metastatic lesion that is life threatening and produces the major problems. Some patients will present only some of the systemic complaints that are usually seen with cancer—weight loss, weakness, anemia, easy fatigability.

Depending upon its type and location the cancer will usually cause various nutritional deficiencies to occur in the rest of the body which account for the systemic effects. This may be due to loss of nutrients appropriated by the growing tumor or those lost to malabsorption with tumors involving the digestive system. Special dietary and nutritional care may offset this problem temporarily, but long-term nutritional therapy cannot adequately supply the nutrients lost to the tumor (Mayer, Part 1, 1971).

Nutritional and systemic problems can further be compounded by the various forms of treating the malignancy. Surgery, radiation, and anti-cancer drugs can and frequently do cause problems, such as, nausea, vomiting, diarrhea, fluid loss, malabsorption, and hemorrhage, to name a few. Nutritional deficiencies secondary to cancer therapy often respond fairly well to dietary management as opposed to those secondary to the disease itself. In such cases, dietary monitoring and management become an important part of the therapy (Mayer, Part 2, 1971).

In planning an appropriate rehabilitation program for a patient, the question of prognosis becomes an important consideration. There are many factors which influence a prognosis, such as, type and location of the malignancy, the stage or degree of advancement when diagnosed, the availability of appropriate therapy, and the response of the body and tumor to the therapy. The evaluation of the many variables involved in each particular patient is the province of the physician, and the counselor must depend upon him for adequate information on this subject.

Prognosis is often given on the basis of five year survival

rates. This simply represents the number of patients in a given series who have had a specific tumor and treatment and who are alive after five years. The period of five years does not carry special significance regarding the cure of cancer as some believe; figures could just as well be given as four or six year survival rates. There are many investigators who use other methods of reporting survival rates and this information is just as valuable. Of course, the longer the follow-up, the more valuable the study becomes in accurately estimating survival.

Shimkin (1951) reported on a review of the literature on the natural history of untreated cancer and gives survival rates in the form of a coordinate graph with survivals extending up to seven years. A method of computing survival rates for patients with chronic diseases has been published by Axtell (1963). This is another approach which may be used in dealing with cancer statistics and may be more meaningful than five year survival rates. The details of these procedures are presented in these references.

Cutler and Heise (1971) published twenty year survival rates for cancer of the uterus, ovary, colon, rectum, and bladder. Cancer of these organs accounted for 56 percent of all cancers in females and 19 percent of all cancers in males that were reported for their study. The data show an upward trend in survival rates, which although confirming the dreaded nature of cancer, offer an encouraging prospect.

The computation of survival rates constitutes important information about cancer, but such data apply to groups and should not be used as a basis for a decision as to whether a particular person is suited for rehabilitative efforts. The following research summary reflects a constructive way of considering the rehabilitation of the cancer patient.

> No accurate judgment of life expectancy or time for useful activity can be estimated for the cancer patient, in spite of the general tables available. Therefore, it is unrealistic and contrary to the concept of total care to defer rehabilitation attention for a waiting period in order to determine the status of the disease or possibility of its spread. Disability from cancer or its treatment can be considered by the same criteria as are used for non-cancer related disability. The need for supportive care for the patient with ad-

vanced cancer should be stressed (*Research Brief of Significant Findings—Rehabilitation of Cancer Patients,* Memorial Hospital for Cancer and Allied Diseases, New York, New York).

As with any disease, the cancer patient's family, friends, and contacts are often concerned about the possibility of their contracting the disease. The big questions are: "Is it hereditary?" and "Is it contagious?" Knowing the answers to these questions would certainly influence the way friends and relatives react to and interact with the patient and his disease. It has generally been taught to the public that "There is no scientific proof that cancer in humans is contagious or inherited" (*Teaching About Cancer*). While this statement is true as far as actual proof is concerned, there are some interesting and provocative reports in the literature which suggest that in the future we may not be able to be quite so dogmatic.

The medical literature contains numerous reports of certain types of cancer occurring in various families much more frequently than would be expected statistically (Li, 1970). While such reports certainly do not prove an hereditary basis for cancer, the incidence of such cases is, indeed suggestive. Knudson (1970) in writing on *Genetics and Cancer* states that, "For most cancers it may be said that heredity plays a role, but clarification of this role is not possible at present."

There has also been considerable interest in the relationship between viruses and cancer. Viruses are minute infectious agents that are generally composed of either DNA or RNA and covered by a protein coat. Viruses have been known for a number of years to cause cancer in animals and viral particles have been shown to be present in some malignancies in man (Henke, 1968). The demonstration of a cause-effect relationship between viruses and some cancers in animals, obviously, does not mean that the same is true for man, but the possibility is worthy of consideration. Considerable investigation is being carried out on this subject and Milt (1969) has written a good review of the problem of viruses and cancer.

Incidence

It appears that cancer is assuming an increasingly important role as a cause of death and disability among people for whom such statistics are kept. Cancer is found among all peoples who have been studied, although some forms of cancer appear to be more common among the more affluent societies than among primitive peoples (Mozden, 1965). In the United States cancer is the second leading cause of death, exceeded only by cardiovascular diseases. Regarding the incidence of cancer, this statement from the American Cancer Society (1970) is sobering in the magnitude it suggests:

> More than fifty-two million Americans now living will eventually have cancer; one in four persons according to the present rates. Cancer will strike over the years in approximately two of three families. In the 70's there will be an estimated 3.5 million cancer deaths, 6.5 million new cancer cases, and 10.0 million under medical care for cancer (p. 3).

As the life span increases the problem of cancer increases. The development of the means to prolong life coupled with the current trends to restrict births will tend to increase the proportion of the population most susceptible to the ravages of cancer.

Treatment Success

The picture of cancer is a grim one indeed. Each year thousands die or become disabled as a result of its ravages. However, the perspective of *cure* rates over time presents a more encouraging situation.

> In the early 1900's few cancer patients had any hope of cure. In the late 1930's fewer than one in five was being saved—that is, alive five years after first being treated. Ten years later one in four was being saved. Since 1956 the ratio has been one in three. The gain from one to four to one to three currently amounts to some 54,000 lives each year. Of every six persons who get cancer today, two will be saved and four will die. Numbers one and two will be saved. Number three will die but might have been saved had proper treatment been received in time. Numbers four, five, and six will die of cancers which cannot yet be controlled; only the results of research can save these patients. This means that about half of those who get cancer could and should be saved—by early diagnosis and prompt treatment. Thus, the immediate goal of cancer control in the country is the annual saving of 325,000 lives, or half of those who develop cancer each year (*Cancer Facts and Figures*, 1970, p. 4).

However, it should be noted that this same publication points out that there are 1,500,000 Americans, alive today, who have been cured of cancer. An additional 700,000 cancer patients diagnosed and treated within the past five years will live to be counted as cured. This means that there are more than 2,000,000 Americans cured of cancer.

While many people will survive their attack of cancer, the treatment may have caused a loss of limb or radical alteration of some body function that requires major rehabilitation adjustment. Rehabilitation must develop and refine such techniques, skills, and facilities as will keep pace with the needs of this problem.

Indications for Rehabilitation Involvement

The problems presented by cancer are no doubt manifold and to an extent overlapping. The presenting physiologic symptoms, of course, command the initial attention of the patient and those involved in his treatment. Usually these physiologic abnormalities were the impetus in causing the patient to seek medical advice and in such cases usually the fear of cancer is a very strong component. As the disease progresses the physical problems become more apparent and are more debilitating, painful and worrisome. Regardless of his knowledge or sophistication, the person experiencing the physiological effects of cancer knows he has something seriously wrong with him. He may know, suspect, or even deny that he has cancer but the deep concern is always present. There are those in whom cancer has been diagnosed by various means who, at the time, have minimal or no symptoms. Upon learning of their diagnosis they, in a sense, join those in whom the ravages of the disease are more apparent in that they must come to grips with their new situation.

How the patient responds to this situation is, indeed, critical. No doubt, a basic question concerns the extent to which the subject is aware of his condition. Does he know he has cancer and does he know the extent of his involvement with it? What is his attitude toward cancer? If it is one of fear he may hesitate to seek aid until the chance of optimum care is past. Or, even after seeking aid his fears may dominate his thoughts and behavior to the point of rendering him ineffectual.

If his attitude toward cancer is one of revulsion, he may devalue himself and withdraw from all possible social interaction. The attitude of self pity is likewise present. Why did this happen to me is a common question reflecting this point of view. In addition to these fears and attitudes the cancer patient is often confronted with the loss of a body part, change in function and appearance, and marked limitation of previously enjoyable and satisfying activities. Such a person has indeed suffered a loss and his reaction to this loss is a definite factor in his overall adjustment.

The person who suffers a loss of a body part, loss of or impairment of function, or disfigurement not only suffers the inconvenience of not being able to do what he could do formerly, but he suffers a psychological loss as well. As others without these limitations may look upon the injured with pity and accordingly devalue them, so the person so afflicted may come to pity and devalue himself. If he feels that he is repulsive to others he will likely become repulsive to himself, and this may interfere with what would be normal social relations (Demke, 1952).

It is possible that people who have sustained such a loss never get to the point where they can fully accept it. It does seem important to recognize that such a person may equate his personal loss with his personal worth. It is imperative that these two be kept separate so that even in the face of substantial loss the individual can still regard himself as a valuable member of society.

The main problem appears to be that the non-injured is considered to be the norm or model toward which all should orient themselves. Modern day advertising stresses the perfection, beauty, and strength of the young and whole with the implication that we should all be like that. Most of us are not. Nonetheless, there is a tendency to view these near perfect states as the ideal toward which we should all strive. The feelings one has about himself are crucial and, consequently, the concern of physician and counselor alike.

The above comments tend to reflect the negative aspects of subject attitude. There is also the positive side in which the individual knows his condition, is accepting whatever treatment is appropriate, and is trying to get on with his life in the best way he can. The point is, the attitude of the subject is an important fact to be considered in both treatment and rehabilitation.

Another problem area presented by cancer concerns the counselor himself. What is the extent of his familiarity with cancer, the extent of his information, and the nature and magnitude of the problems it represents to the particular subject. What are the counselor's attitudes toward cancer. Since he is typically not a medical person, his attitudes—fears, biases, values, etc.—may roughly parallel those of the client. If the counselor sees the problem as offering little or no hope for a lifetime that would merit substantial rehabilitation effort, there may be a disinclination on the part of the counselor to become really involved in the rehabilitation process. The counselor is prone to think in terms of longevity and function in relation to employment and his attitudes determine how he interprets this in regard to particular subjects.

From a rehabilitation point of view, the differences in cancer subjects is profound. There is no doubt small commonality among them and consequently there is likely no special counseling technique that will serve them all. The differences in the disease itself as it affects the individual coupled with the idosyncratic reaction to it combine to make the rehabilitation problems very unique indeed. For subjects for whom a cure cannot be achieved, the pertinent medical and counseling questions would relate to what can be done to allay symptoms, prolong life and well being, and permit significant rehabilitation in terms of economic and family needs.

Should the Patient Be Told

In working with cancer patients the question usually arises, "Should the patient be told that he has cancer?" There is no single right answer to this question, but there are a number of considerations that should be kept in mind when confronted with this problem. Cancer is a disease that is often thought by the public to be incurable and associated with untold agony, suffering, and death. Further, that a knowledge of the diagnosis would only cause undue worry, depression, fear, and anxiety, and that by withholding this information the patient is spared considerable mental anguish and trauma.

Those actively working with cancer patients are well aware that this is not usually the case. There are many who have been cured of cancer and countless others with this disease who have had their lives significantly prolonged and have been able to function in an essentially normal manner. There is also the question of whether withholding the diagnosis actually does prevent or decrease the mental strain associated with the disease and whether there are other significant factors entering into the decision to follow this practice. Wangensteen (1950) has suggested that the family plays a big role in this decision in that in addition to protecting the patient they are actually protecting themselves from needless uneasiness. It is quite unlikely that withholding the diagnosis actually does cause the patient to be less concerned. The present day patient is typically reasonably sophisticated in his knowledge of certain aspects of medicine. Most people know the warning signs of cancer and when they have an illness which doesn't remit and have to undergo radical treatment they usually are very suspicious that they have cancer even though they might have been told otherwise.

Consideration must also be given to whether patients want to know and whether it is harmful for them not to know. An interesting survey of this question was carried out by Kelly and Friesen (1950). They surveyed two groups of patients; one group with known cancer and another group in whom there was no evidence of cancer. Of these subjects who did not have cancer, 82 percent said they would want to be told if it were to be diagnosed in them, and 14 percent said they would not want to be told. In the group with cancer, 89 percent said they would prefer to know about having cancer themselves. In regard to telling others with cancer, 73 percent of the cancer patients stated that they thought such people should be told; 4 percent said that people shouldn't be told; and 20 percent thought that it could be individualized for each patient. These authors further state that

Many of the patients remarked that they would be more willing and careful to follow directions in regard to necessary follow-up examinations if they knew they had cancer. Moreover, many of them stated that they worried more about the unknown and felt they preferred to know they had cancer, even if it was bad news, because it removed the indefiniteness of the situation (pp. 822-826).

Wright (1960) made an extensive study of the literature relating to this problem. After considering the available data she offers these conclusions:

1. In by far the majority of cases it is wiser to inform the patient of his condition than to conceal it.

2. Certainly where the patient is mature as a person, this course carries little risk.

3. Where the patient appears markedly immature and dependent, one may act more cautiously; but even in this case, if it is incumbent that the patient act realistically, sharing the state of affairs with him under the sustaining power of hope may be more efficacious.

4. Facing the situation realistically need not deny hope, for the two are psychologically not incompatible. Moreover, hope for a *possible* favorable turn of events may even sustain one's resources in acting realistically in terms of the *probable* turn of events.

5. Further research is needed to enable the practitioner more reliably to select those cases where concealment is desirable. We ought not rest content with speculation, for this is an area amenable to investigation. Concealing difficult facts from children, for example, may or may not have the consequences we assume. (Our prejudice, probably shared by most people, is that children should be shielded, but let us remember that this is a prejudice until put to more objective test.)

6. As in all matters of counselor-client relationships, the effects of different rules of behavior or procedure depend on the attributes of the counselor as well as of the client. If the counselor has an abhorrence of cancer, multiple sclerosis, or death, forces in him will resist mention of these facts. Or if the counselor devaluates the person who is ill or who has a disability, he will tend to overestimate the vulnerability of the patient to distressing information (pp. 360-361).

Family Aspects of Cancer

The cancer patient who lives in a family is surrounded—literally immersed—in a complex of attitudes related to cancer. It cannot be assumed that the family knows and understands and appreciates the fears of the cancer subject even though they are all living together in the same house. Further, it cannot be assumed that the family members will minimize their own anxieties over the fact that one of their members is so afflicted.

Indeed, the family members themselves may be very upset about the situation. They may have some fears about the possibility of becoming infected themselves since they are exposed in various ways to the disease. There may be a reluctance to touch the subject, his personal belongings, or even the dishes, towels, and other things he may use. There are also fears they may have about the hereditary aspects of the disease. If a family member has it, what are the prospects of other family members getting it, and what about the possibility of its being transmitted to any offspring. In addition, if the cancer problem has been in process any substantial amount of time there may be mounting medical bills that sorely drain the family resources. These factors may produce fears, apprehension, and resentments on the part of the family toward the afflicted member. The subject is bound to sense these negative feelings on the part of the family members and this may be detrimental to his morale and response to the treatment process. This may produce a guarded relationship among them rather than the supportive, loving relationship needed. Also, the client senses these family feelings and concerns and in his preoccupation with his own symptoms, particularly if the prognosis is guarded, may feel that the family knows something he does not. This conclusion on his part may convince him that his condition is more serious than he thought.

So important is the family that if the client is not making the expected progress, the family situation may merit study. The generalization would be that all professional people concerned with a particular case must do all they can to help the family to accept the subject and to be prepared for his continued care.

Social and Community Aspects of Cancer

The cancer subject frequently demeans himself in various ways. He may be embarrassed by the nature of his affliction and because of his own negative attitudes toward cancer assumes that everyone else feels the same way about it. This general feeling may cause him to avoid contacts with other people, particularly in such public gatherings as dances, games, meetings, theatre, etc. This may be especially true in instances where the individual has had a colostomy, wears an artificial bladder or other device, and fears an accident or worries about an odor that he may not be able to detect.

It seems that the basic problem relates to how the subject himself feels about cancer. The person who feels himself to be unworthy, distasteful to others, etc., will tend to project these attitudes upon others and will behave accordingly. It is of crucial importance in his social adjustment to help the subject learn that many people so afflicted lead normal lives socially. Also, he can be taught the requisites of self care that will minimize the possibility of having embarrassing situations develop.

Cancer is no longer considered to be solely a problem for the individual and his family. It is also a concern of society in general. It is important for the subject, his family, and all others involved in his care to be aware of the various resources in the community that may be of great practical value to him. The American Cancer Society and the various community health agencies are key sources of information about facilities and groups that might be of help in particular instances.

By the very nature of the disease, follow-up over a long period of time is of the utmost importance. This involves not only the motivation on the part of the subject to participate in the follow-up but also community facilities that would encourage this and in many instances make it possible.

Relationship Between Counselor and Physician

The counselor and the physician are inevitably tied closely together in working with the cancer patient. Each has a part to contribute and the other must not stand in the way.

The disease process itself involves medical questions that are basically within the province of the physician and should be left to him. Questions the physician should be permitted to respond to are these:

1. What is the nature of the disease itself? Explanations to the uninformed subject must, of course, be related to the depth and breadth of understanding of which the subject

is capable at the moment.

2. What is the stage of the disease? Where is the disease so far as the particular patient is concerned.
3. What is the general outlook or prognosis? While the physician knows the general course to be expected, this has to be interpreted in terms of the particular patient.
4. Will treatment contemplated for the present or future require hospitalization or proximity to a treatment center?
5. How does the patient feel about his condition? Is he accepting it? Denying it? Resenting it? The question is whether the patient attitude is conducive to the acceptance of treatment procedures.

Considerations more within the province of the counselor that would be useful in helping a particular client would include such information as the following:

1. Aptitudes and interests of the subject.
2. Training facilities.
3. Employment opportunities.
4. Employment requirements.
5. Community agencies available to help the client.
6. Organizations oriented toward particular handicaps.
7. The rehabilitation potential of a particular client.

Relationship Between Counselor and Client

What the counselor does is more likely to convey his feelings about the patient than anything he might say. It isn't likely that the counselor could for very long deceive a client about how he sees the situation. The following considerations adapted from Lofquist (1957) may be of help to the counselor as he tries to work with the cancer client.

Does the counselor believe that his efforts will lead to the rehabilitation of the client? The counselor's actions will likely speak louder than his words. If the counselor is to appear to be sincere to the client, counseling must be complete and he must be consistent in his relationship with the client. If the counselor does not believe in the client's prospects, the client will likely know it.

If the counseling goal is a vocational one, the placement

goals should be achievable as soon as practicable. Training programs should be arranged with this in mind. For practical reasons this will usually be compatible with the client's wishes because lack of money and the uncertainty of the amount of lifetime available.

It is important that the plans for training and placement take into consideration any existing physical limitations that the disease has imposed as well as any additional limitations that might be expected to develop.

It would seem to be important for the counselor to know how completely the family has been informed of the client's status since in counseling it is sometimes desirable to see the spouse and other family members.

The counselor should try to become as involved in the counseling process with the cancer client as he is with other clients. He must try to avoid letting his own fears about cancer become confused with those of the client.

At times such a client may become quite aggressive. While such behavior may be quite disconcerting to the counselor, it must be considered that this behavior may be the client's way of expressing his fears. The counselor may take this as a signal that the personal feelings of the client need more or different attention. The counselor should not abandon the client in this moment of great need.

The counselor, of course, should be informed of the medical and surgical consequences of colostomy, facial disfigurement, plastic surgery, etc., and be prepared to help the client deal with the outcomes as he responds to them personally.

Many clients read extensively concerning their disability and may try to push the counselor into giving further information about the disease. It is not the place of the counselor to tell the client about the client's disease condition.

It scarcely needs to be said that the counselor should keep close liaison with the physician.

Conclusion

Since the report of the President's Commission on Heart Disease, Cancer and Stroke and the subsequent passage and enactment of the Heart Diesase, Cancer and Stroke Amendment of 1965 significant emphasis has been given to the rehabilitation of cancer patients by the federal rehabilitative office. Miss Mary E. Switzer, then United States Commissioner of Vocational Rehabilitation, stated "The rehabilitation of cancer patients has priority over almost anything else we are trying to do." She then pledged the resources of URA to a redoubled effort to help victims of cancer back to productive and satisfying lives (*Rehabilitation Record*, 1966).

This reflects the general spirit and efforts of those concerned with cancer. Much has been done and much progress has been made but the problem has by no means been solved. Medical research is promising and we may be on the brink of discoveries that will provide medical solutions to the problem of cancer. In the meantime, we must work with what we know—early diagnosis and prompt treatment medically and an optimistic and constructive attitude psychologically and socially that will help the individual make the most of his life. Rehabilitation is a most significant vehicle in accomplishing this.

REFERENCES

Administrative Service Series 64-6, August 8, 1963.

Axtell, Lillian M.: Computing Survival Rates for Chronic Disease Patients. *The Journal of the American Medical Association, 186* (No. 13):1126, 1963.

Cancer Facts and Figures, American Cancer Society, 1970.

Commissioner's Letter 68-5, August 29, 1967.

Commissioner's Letter 68-11, November 9, 1967.

Cutler, Sidney J., and Heise, Herman W.: Long-term end results of treatment of cancer. *The Journal of the American Medical Association, 216* (No. 2):293, 1971.

Demke, *et al.*: Acceptance of loss—amputations. In James F. Garrett (Ed.): *Psychological Aspects of Physical Disability.* Rehabilitation Service Series Number 210, Federal Security Agency, Office of Vocational Rehabilitation, U.S. Government Printing Office, Washington, D.C., pp. 80-86.

Gay, Richard L.: The relationship between psychopathology and cancer. *Dissertation Abstracts International, 21* (8-B):4992, 1971.

Healey, J. E., Jr.: Changing philosophy toward rehabilitation. *Cancer Bulletin, 20:*2-3, January-February, 1968.

Henke, Walter: Evidence for viruses in acute leukemia and Burkitt's tumor. *Cancer, 21* (No. 4), April, 1968.

Holleb, A. I.: Using the cancer cures we have now. *Today's Health,* April, 1970.

Kelly, William D., and Friesen, Staley R.: Do cancer patients want to be told? *Surgery, 27* (No. 6):822-826, 1950.

Knudson, Alfred G., Jr.: Genetics and cancer. *Postgraduate Medicine, 48* (No. 5), 1970.

Li, Frederick, P., *et al.*: Familial ovarian carcinoma. *Journal of the American Medical Association, 214* (No. 8), 1970.

Lofquist, Lloyd H.: *Vocational Counseling with the Physically Handicapped.* Appleton-Century-Crofts, Inc., New York, 1957.

Mayer, Jean: Nutrition and cancer, Part 1. *Postgraduate Medicine, 50* (No. 4), 1971.

Mayer, Jean: Nutrition and cancer, Part 2. *Postgraduate Medicine, 50* (No. 5), 1971.

Milt, Harry: Viruses and cancer. *Ca—A Cancer Journal for Clinicians, 19* (No. 4), 1969.

Mozden, Peter J.: Neoplasms, in Julian S. Myers (Ed.), *An Orientation to Chronic Disease and Disability.* The MacMillan Company, New York, 1965, p. 323.

Rehabilitation Record, 7 (No. 1), 1966.

Research Brief of Significant Findings—Rehabilitation of Cancer Patients, Memorial Hospital for Cancer and Allied Diseases, New York.

Rusk, H. A.: Preventive medicine, curative medicine—the rehabilitation. *New Physician, 13:*165-167, 1964.

Shimkin, Michael B.: Duration of life on untreated cancer. *Cancer, 4:*1, 1951.

Teaching About Cancer. Publication of the American Cancer Society.

Wangensteen, Owen H.: Should patients be told they have cancer (Ed.). *Surgery, 27* (No. 6):944-947, 1950.

Wright, Beatrice A.: *Physical Disability—A Psychological Approach.* Harper and Brothers Publishers, New York, 1960.

Youth Looks at Cancer, American Cancer Society.

CHAPTER XI

REHABILITATION OF PERSONS WITH RHEUMATOID ARTHRITIS

WILLIAM H. GRAVES AND JAMES T. BOWMAN

~~~~~~

~~~~~~

"Here, Charlie, wear this copper bracelet. I swear it will help your arthritis. It's the only thing that's worked for me. None of the doctors have done me any good."

CHARLIE AND HIS friends are among the multitudes of humans who have suffered from rheumatoid arthritis since man stepped up and called himself man and maybe even before then. Archaeologists have discovered that chronic arthritis of the spine was present in the ape man of 2,000,000 years ago and in the Java and Lansing men of 500,000 years ago (Hollander, 1966). Of the diseases known to the ancient civilizations, few continue to plague mankind as persistently as rheumatoid arthritis. The Romans built elaborate baths to treat this disease. Few diseases continue to frustrate the physician and patient with its progressive nature, slow response to treatment, sudden remissions and exacerbation, and word of magical cure as does rheumatoid arthritis.

The term arthritis is so misunderstood, misused, and confused that individuals claiming to have rheumatoid arthritis may have any one of several separate and entirely different diseases. The diseases often mistaken by the layman for rheumatoid arthritis, such as osteoarthritis, are similar to this disease because they are all characterized by the involvement of joints (Felton, Perkins & Lewin, 1966). Beyond this resemblance rheumatoid arthritis is very different from, for example, gout or osteoarthritis, two of the more common rheumatic diseases. Gout and osteoarthritis primarily damage joints. Rheumatoid arthritis is, however, a *chronic, systemic disease with major clinical manifestations in the musculoskeletal system and characteristic nonspecific histopathologic findings in the synovial membrane, cartilage and skeletal muscle* (Ivght, Keefer, Lukens, Richards, Sebrell, & Trapnell, 1966). Of the rheumatic disease patients, persons with rheumatoid arthritis are most likely to require the services of the vocational rehabilitation counselor because rheumatoid arthritis characteristically attacks the individual during his prime working years. The characteristic deformities caused by rheumatoid arthritis require the individual to need comprehensive rehabilitation services ranging from training in activities of daily living to vocational training and selective placement.

Arthritis and rheumatic diseases are second only to cardiac disease in causes of chronic limitations of major activities. Approximately thirteen million men and women over the age of fifteen in the United States suffer from arthritis and other rheumatic diseases. Almost nine million of these are twenty-five to sixty-five years old. Forty-two percent are not under medical care and nineteen percent have never received medical care. Twenty-six percent are definitely limited in their activities and ten percent are grossly disabled. There are, therefore, 2.5 million persons between the ages of twenty-five and sixty-five who have significant activity limitations and approximately one million persons who are unemployed because of rheumatoid arthritis.

In 1967-1969, 10,946 persons with rheumatoid arthritis were rehabilitated in the United States by the federal-state programs of vocational rehabilitation (Lesowitz, n.d.). The gap between persons needing comprehensive vocational rehabilitation services for rheumatoid arthritis and those relatively few receiving these services is great. The gap could be due to a number of factors including: (1) lack of referrals from physicians and rehabilitation centers to federal-state programs of vocational rehabilitation, (2) inadequate financial and rehabilitation resources to serve the rheumatoid arthritic client, (3) rehabilitation counselor reluctance to accept the rheumatoid arthritic client for services because of the nature of the disease, and (4) the rheumatoid arthritic client's reluctance to return to the work environment.

The cost of medical and rehabilitation services needed by the rheumatoid arthritic is great, but the effects of rheumatoid arthritis on the social and economic health of this country and its citizens more than justifies each dollar spent. For example, it is estimated that 27 million work days are lost annually in the United States to rheumatic diseases (Hollander, 1966). Chalmer (1972) estimates that 37.6 million work days were lost to rheumatic diseases in Great Britian in one year, more than eight times the number of work days lost to industrial strikes. Brown and Lingg (1961) studied employees of Consolidated Edison Company in New York City for one year. It was found that 15,040 work days were lost to rheumatic diseases at a cost to Consolidated Edison of $300,000. Rheumatoid arthritis with its effects on the functional and work capacity of the individual can then be seen to have a marked influence on the social and financial health of the individual and our society—and is likely to have even more significant effects as death from other diseases continue to be reduced.

Rheumatoid Arthritis

Rheumatoid arthritis is a chronic, progressive, systemic disease marked by inflammation of the joints and tissue surrounding the joints. It usually results in deformity, atrophy, and abnormally immobile and constricted joints. Women are more frequently affected than men. Reports (Ivght *et al.*, 1966) of sex ratio range from 2:1 to 9:1. The disease process is marked by exacerbations and partial remissions. Its onset is usually insidious and frequently associated with physical or emotional stress. The etiology of rheumatoid arthritis is unknown. Diverse theories such as infection, hypersensitivity, metabolic or nutritional defects, endocrine disorders, genetic factors, and psychogenic origins have been offered as causative factors (Hollander, 1966). Clark (1965) suggests that research in the area of autoimmunity, which consists of studying the derangement of the body's own immune mechanisms, holds the most promise for discovering the cause of rheumatoid arthritis.

Pathology

The joints most frequently affected are the proximal joints of the fingers and the joints of the hands, toes, and wrists. More than one joint is usually involved and the involvement is almost always symmetrical. No joint in the body is immune to rheumatoid arthritis, but joint involvement usually proceeds in this order: fingers and toes, wrists, feet and ankles, elbows and knees (Hollander, 1966). The synovial membrane, tissue lining the joint, is usually insulted by the disease first. It then attacks the cartilage or the gliding surface of the joint. The bone itself then undergoes change, and eventually the joint fuses and immobility results. During these changes, there is significant pain and the muscles surrounding the joint go into splitting spasms. Because flexor muscles are stronger than extensors, the joints become stiffened in a flexed position (Felton *et al.,* 1966).

Symptoms and Signs

Because rheumatoid arthritis is a chonic, systemic, progressive disease, it is useful to review its symptomology in terms of early, later, advanced stages, and systemic symptoms.

Early Stages

The rheumatoid arthritic individual reports *morning stiffness;* aching pain in and around joints; slight swelling of small joints which are occasionally warm, but rarely red; and pain on movement of the joint.

Later Stages

As the disease process advances, there is definite swelling of the joints. In muscles surrounding these joints, there is spasm, weakness, and atrophy. The joints typically involved are: the middle joints of the fingers, the wrists, elbows, ankles, middle joints of the toes and the knees.

Advanced Stages

In advanced stages of the disease, skin surrounding the diseased joint shrinks, is glossy, and is usually cold. There are varying degrees of deformity, contractures and joint fusion. The hips and knees may have developed flexion deformities. The shoulders may have become adducted and rotate internally. The jaw may show varying degrees of fusion which can limit the opening and closing of the mouth.

Systemic Symptoms

The onset of rheumatoid arthritis may begin with high fever and multiple joint involvement. Usually, the systemic symptoms consist of low grade fever, weakness, tiredness, poor appetite, weight loss, anemia, and early fatigability. The individual may report nervousness, depression, or anxiety (Felton *et al.*, 1966; Hollander, 1965; Hylbert, 1965; Ivght *et al.*, 1966; McElven, 1966).

Psychological Characteristics

Felton (1966) described a personality type of rheumatoid arthritis patients: "Perfectionist, unable to express rage, extremely sensitive to criticism, incapable of enduring the loss of a close personal relationship, and dependent" [p. 51]. The literature supports this description.

King (1955) describes the personality trait type of the rheumatoid arthritic as an individual who is introverted with feelings of inadequacy and inferiority, is self-sacrificing and over conscientious with a need to serve others, and has a tendency toward depression. King further describes these individuals with rheumatoid arthritis as covertly aggressive and hostile. These individuals also are described as fearful of overt expression of these feelings. Consequently, there may be marked emotional restrictions in their personality makeup, especially the inability to express anger openly. Furthermore, individuals with rheumatoid arthritis seem to have a fear of separation, difficulty in establishing relationships with other people and in making friends. At the same time, they will allow other persons to impose on them rather than risk offense and loss of regard. Scoth and Geiger (1962) reviewed social factors related to rheumatoid arthritis using the case study method. Their findings corroborated much of what King (1955) had reported. As a group, the rheumatoid arthritic individuals demonstrated marked impairment of ego functioning manifested by extreme dependence, insecurity, feelings of inadequacy, difficulty in coping with the environment and with other people, and severe blocking of overt expression of emotions by internalizing feelings. Moos (1969) reviewed factors associated with rheumatoid arthritis using personality data on 5,000 rheumatoid arthritic patients. Commonalities were found among rheumatoid arthritics as compared with control groups on the following factors: the rheumatoid arthritic tends to be self-sacrificing, masochistic, conforming, self-conscious, shy, inhibited, perfectionistic, and interested in sports and games. No commonalities were reported for the following factors: the extent of the expression of anger, the importance of the separation trauma, and the amount of impulsivity and defiance shown.

The reader may conclude since the research generally supports a rheumatoid arthritic personality type that this personality configuration may be related to the etiology of rheumatoid arthritis. The literature does not support this conclusion. For example, the 16 PF was used to examine personality characteristics of persons having rheumatoid arthritis for three years or more (ORA), persons having rheumatoid arthritis six months or less (NRA), and nondisabled diseased controls (Robinson, Kirk, & Frye, 1971). The investigators found that rheumatoid arthritic patients scored higher on indices of anxiety and depression than did nondisabled diseased controls. However, 16 PF profiles of rheumatoid arthritic patients and hypertension and diabetes patients correlated significantly. Also ORA's and NRA's showed similar profiles indicating overall personality similarity.

Two explanations were offered. The first is the personality type predates the disease and plays a part in its development and its progression. The second possible explanation is that the pain and crippling associated with rheumatoid arthritis forces patients to a common personality type regardless of previous personality make up. In order to isolate one of these explanations, a further study of patients with rheumatoid arthritis and other painful diseases was conducted by Robinson, Kirk, Frye, and Robertson (1972). The hypothesis investigated was that any person who suffers from a chronically painful and disabling disease is likely to demonstrate the rheumatoid arthritic personality. Some support for the hypothesis was found. As predicted, pain subjects show greater introversion than normals. The researchers' explanation for this finding was that a painful disease leads to introverted behavior by virtue of greater self-concern and withdrawal from social contact. Although this explanation may involve circular reasoning and the researchers admit that their results were not conclusive, they concluded that the personality traits of the rheumatoid arthritics are disease functional and not predisposing to the development of the disease. The researchers concluded that the personality characteristics of the rheumatoid arthritic represent attempts to cope and adjust to the stresses encountered in the environment as a result of the symptoms of the disease.

A further study (Polley, Swenson, & Steinhelber, 1970) adds some support to Robinson, Kirk, Frye, and Robertson's conclusion. Using the MMPI, the personality characteristics of rheumatoid arthritics, general medical patients, and a healthy group were studied. The findings were that rheumatoid arthritics had higher scores on the hypochondriases, depression, and anxiety scales (the neurotic triad) and lower hypomania scores (measuring physical activity) than the other two groups. The researchers concluded that significant differences of responses to the MMPI by rheumatoid arthritic patients could be explained on the basis of the symptoms and the effects of a disease which is chronic, painful, and potentially disabling. Elevated scores on the neurotic triad have also been noted for patients with other alleged psychosomatic diseases and for patients with only psychoneurotic disorders (Polley *et al.*, 1970). The reactive depression, a common secondary feature of patients with rheumatoid arthritis and patients with other diseases, and the abnormal scores on the MMPI have been considered a reflection of the depressing influence of the disease entity.

Seidenfeld (1962) addresses the question of the relationship between personality factors in the rheumatoid arthritic and etiology:

> The answer to the question of which comes first, the psychic *chicken* or the somatic *egg* must await considerably more research. In the meantime there is little room for doubt that both systems are involved in such diseases as rheumatoid arthritis. This would account for the failing of physical or symptomological treatment in the absence of psychic support (p. 69).

Treatment

There is no known cure for rheumatoid arthritis. No remedy has emerged to deal with rheumatoid arthritis as chemotherapy has dealt with tuberculosis. Chalmer (1972) states there are four goals in the treatment of rheumatoid arthritis:

1. Relief of symptoms and control of the disease activity.
2. Improved general health.
3. Prevention and correction of deformities.
4. Restoration and maintenance of functioning and independence.

Engleman (1966) writes, "Choice of treatment for rheumatoid arthritis is a particular challenge to the physician. . . . The primary objectives (of treatment) are to reduce inflammation and pain, preserve function, and prevent deformity" [p. 295]. Lowman (1959) states that before a realistic treatment program and goal can be established the total patient must be evaluated. He outlines this evaluation in the following manner:

Medically:
    Medical and rheumatological history
    Physical examination
    Specialist consultations
    Laboratory examinations
Functionally:
    Muscle tests
    Joint range of motion
    Activities of daily living

Psychosocially:
  Psychological testing
  Social survey
  Vocational testing
      (p. 540)

A treatment program for the rheumatoid arthritic patient requires a comprehensive team approach with representatives from diverse service areas as internal medicine, orthropedic surgery, physical medicine, psychology, social work, nursing, occupational and physical therapy, and rehabilitation counseling. Because of the integrated efforts of these service areas, persons with rheumatoid arthritis are being successfully managed. Some are experiencing pain relief, deformity prevention and correction, and the maintenance of muscle and joint integrity (Felton *et al.*, 1966). General treatment programs for rheumatoid arthritis include joint rest, systemic, and emotional rest, proper nutrition, physical therapy; and salicylates (Engleman, 1966).

Physical therapy exercises are prescribed to preserve joint motion and muscular strength and endurance (Bowie, 1966). Although no drug has yet been developed to cure arthritis, indomethacin is a valuable *anti-rheumatic agent* (Lockie & Norcross, 1966). The salicylates, such as aspirin, suppress pain (Felton *et al.*, 1966). Gold crystal injections (Freyberg, 1966), corticosteroid injections (Black, 1966), and intrasynoival corticosteroid injection (Hollander, 1966) are helpful to some patients, but must be carefully administered because of possible adverse side effects. Lanyi (1968) and Potter and Kuhns (1966) discuss the positive benefits of advances made in surgery on the arthritic joint (arthroplasty) as well as in the development of artificial joints.

Despite these medically related advances made in the treatment of the arthritic patient, progress can be reversed by emotional stress. As Rusk (1971) has stated, "More than any other factor, the psychologic economy of the arthritic patient is a major force in determining success or failure in attainment of rehabilitation goals" [p. 369]. If this is the case, then the rehabilitation counselor must begin at the time of his initial interview with the arthritic referral to establish a basis for the counseling relationship which will last for the duration of the client's involvement with vocational rehabilitation. The counseling relationship needs to be one that will provide the client with a threat-free, accepting atmosphere which will allow the expression of bottled up feelings and permit the exploration of feelings of inadequacy and inferiority. In short, the relationship that develops must foster an understanding by the client of all the feelings and emotions that have led to the labeling of the *arthritic personality.*

The Rehabilitation Process

That the rehabilitation of the person with rheumatoid arthritis is a difficult process is substantiated by the relatively few persons (approximately 11,000 of 3,000,000 needing rehabilitation services) vocationally rehabilitated from 1965 to 1969 by the federal-state programs of vocational rehabilitation (Lesowitz, n.d.). The complex interrelated problems for the patient and rehabilitation staff created by the chronic, progressive nature of the disease require comprehensive, well planned rehabilitation programs. The goal of a comprehensive rehabilitation program for the rheumatoid arthritic client is to assist him in developing maximum independence—functional, social, personal, and vocational. Some writers, for example, Chalmers (1972) and Felton, Perkins, and Lewin (1966), advocate the initiation of the rehabilitation program of the rheumatoid arthritic in the latter phases of the medical treatment program; others, for example, Lanyi (1968), suggest that the rehabilitation goal must be present at all stages of treatment—even during the acute phases. If the goals of the treatment program are to relieve symptoms and control the disease activity, to improve the general health of the rheumatoid arthritic, to prevent and correct deformities, and to restore and maintain joint functioning and patient independence, it is clear that the rehabilitation program for the rheumatoid arthritic must begin when he first reports symptoms of the disease.

Seven factors have been discussed by Lowman (1959) and Rusk (1971) as critical in the rehabilitation process of the person with rheumatoid arthritis. The factors are as follows: (1)

medical control of the disease process, (2) the extent of the joint damage, (3) the psychological integrity of the client, (4) the functional training the client has received, (5) the success of corrective orthopedic surgery, (6) the client's ability to use self-help devices, and (7) other socioeconomic and vocational factors.

Medical Control

Medical control of the rheumatoid arthritis process is a critical variable in the rehabilitation of persons with rheumatoid arthritis. For example, if the individual with rheumatoid arthritis is receiving vocational retraining at an area vocational technical center as a part of a comprehensive rehabilitation program and his arthritic condition suddenly flares up and he becomes acutely distressed, the focus of the rehabilitation program changes from one of vocational training and related activities to one of bed rest, medication, and close medical supervision. During this period of hospitalization, the focus of the rehabilitation program must be on the prevention of deformities through positioning the joints in positions of function. As the need for bed rest lessens, the patient becomes involved in a well-balanced program of functional activities and exercise to build up tolerance (Lanyi, 1969). Again the focus of the rehabilitation program shifts as medical control of the disease is gained.

The shifting of focus of the rehabilitation program can be expected by the rehabilitation counselor as medical control changes. This is particularly typical of the younger client— unfortunately, often an event that occurs with those clients who are enrolled in college some distance from the counselor. The rehabilitation counselor has little control over this shift in focus which frequently results in an interruption of vocational rehabilitation services. The rehabilitation counselor should antici- pate that the client will experience feelings of despondency, frustration, and discouragement. The counselor must be prepared to offer supportive counseling and reassurance to the client that he and the agency are still committed to help him reach his rehabilitation goal.

Joint Damage and Surgical Procedures

The extent of damage done to the joint by the arthritic process and the success of orthopedic surgery on the joint are separate, but related, important factors in the rehabilitation of the rheumatoid arthritic. The amount of joint damage and the specific joint or joints damaged have varying effects on the mobility, dexterity, and cosmetic appearance of the individual. For example, consider the vocational implications of ankylosing spondylitis and rheumatoid arthritis of the wrists and hands. Ankylosing spondylitis, which is rheumatoid arthritis of the spine, is characterized by the development of an immobile and fused spine. If the disease process is unchecked, a progressive, incapacitating kyphosis, or hunchback, develops. The client with ankylosing spondylitis will have extremely limited movement of the head and frequently will be unable to look upward. Lanyi (1968) states that clients who have sedentary jobs are more aware of his disability than individuals with standing occupations. The sedentary worker's awareness of his disability is increased by an inability to move his head without rotating his entire body. To look to either side while sitting, he must be in a swivel type chair or he must move the entire chair by lifting and weight shifting motions. Standing occupations, if they do not require lifting, which could place additional stress on the spine and other weight bearing joints, are more suitable for this client .In the Pima Indian culture, for example, where sitting is a rarity, the disability associated with ankylosing spondylitis is less handicapping (O'Brien, Thomas & Bunim, 1963).

Clients who have rheumatoid arthritis of the hands and wrists have severe dexterity problems and fewer mobility and cosmetic problems than the client with ankylosing spondylitis. Dexterity is an important aspect of many occupations and restricted dexterity constitutes a severe vocational handicap. Corrective surgery or arthoplasty offers significant help to these clients. Lanyi (1968) and Tomaszewska (1970) report successful surgical treatment of the metacarpo-phalangeal and interphalangeal joints of the fingers and toes. Carek (1962) states that before surgery for rheumatoid arthritic damaged joints, the patient must be thoroughly evaluated so that all concerned, especially the patient, will know what to expect from surgery because the patient's disappointment with the results of surgery can be detrimental to the success of the rehabilitation plan. If the dexterity is improved by arthoplasty and the prescribed therapeutic activities after surgery, the employability of the client with rheumatoid arthritis of the hands will be changed.

If the rehabilitation goal of the rheumatoid arthritic client includes employment, both the client with rheumatoid arthirtis of the hands and wrists and the client with ankylosing spondylitis will require vocational evaluation, the building of work tolerance, and the development of a work personality. Vocational evaluation is needed to assess the effects of the arthritic process on physical abilities such as dexterity, eye-hand coordination, and the ability to perform work activities in sitting, standing, or bending position. This evaluation can also provide information concerning the client's ability to relate to supervisors, co-workers, and technical personnel. Because the arthritic client has been in a non-work status for a period of time, it will be necessary that his tolerance for work be developed. This is perhaps best accomplished at a comprehensive rehabilitation facility where his personal and physical reactions to the stress of work can be closely monitored by facility personnel and the rehabilitation team. Work assignments can be modified readily in rehabilitation facilities to insure maximum client benefit at minimum risk to further damage of the client's arthritic joints. The dependency which usually accompanies prolonged illnesses such as rheumatoid arthritis does little to develop or maintain the client's worker traits. Therefore, the client's rehabilitation program should be designed to assist the client to develop successful worker traits such as punctuality, consistency of performance, dependability, job skills, and appropriate attitudes towards supervisors and co-workers.

Functional Training

The effects of the rheumatoid arthritis process can be reduced with functional training, thereby increasing the client's rehabilitation potential. Functional training has, as its focus, increasing power in weakened muscles and increasing range of motion in the restricted joints so that these physical gains can be put to use (Rusk, 1971). Rusk (1971) gives as an example of functional training an individual whose quadricep muscle groups are strengthened to provide muscle strength necessary to train him *to climb stairs, curbs, or to arise from a toilet seat* [p. 371]. If the patient-client has not received functional training or has benefitted little from functional training, he will, for example, have limited ability to use public transportation to and from work and to perform in the competitive labor market. Difficulties in getting to and from work constitute an added vocational handicap for the arthritic client, and could become the factor that causes the client to quit or lose his job. For example, the client may not continue working if he must pay a large portion of his salary to hire someone to drive him to work because he cannot drive a care or utilize public transportation. Furthermore, employers do not want employees who are late for work or do not come to work when expected. As can be seen from these examples, the rehabilitation counselor must understand the functional capacities of the rheumatoid arthritic client if he is to be able to successfully place the client in employment.

Self-Help Devices

The functional capacity of the rheumatoid arthritic client can be further increased by self-help devices. Rusk (1971) cautions that special apparatus and self-help devices should be used only when they are essential for increasing function or for protecting the impaired joints. The main goals in the use of self-help devices are as follows:

(1) to provide more dynamic treatment measures (as motivators).
(2) to permit early independence and active participation of the patient in the treatment program.
(3) to provide independence in daily activities despite partial or total loss of function, and
(4) to help build self-esteem and achieve either partial or total economic independence.

(p. 152)

A brief review of the types of self-help devices prescribed for the rheumatoid arthritic client may be helpful to rehabilitation counselors. The types of devices include: devices for dressing, devices for feeding and self care, adapted chairs and toilet seats, wheelchairs, crutches, and energy-saving devices for housework (Rusk, 1971). The selection of the proper device(s) for the rheumatoid arthritic is dependent upon:

(1) the evaluation of the activity to be performed and the physical requirements for it,
(2) the evaluation of the psychologic response to the use of the equipment,
(3) the evaluation of the materials and their design to be used in the construction of a mechanical appliance, and
(4) the role of the device in total rehabilitation of the individual patient.

(Rusk, 1971, p. 153)

At the time the rehabilitation team is considering prescribing or actually is prescribing a self-help device(s) for the rheumatoid arthritic client, the client's vocational plans must be considered. What devices will he need to successfully perform the tasks of the occupation? What devices will he need to be successfully trained for the occupation? It also must be remembered at the time of the prescription that the client's vocational possibilities are dependent on his ability to manage such activities of daily living as eating in a cafeteria, the use of rest room facilities, and travel to and from work (Rusk, 1971).

Psychological Integrity

Because there is so much variability in the psychological adjustment of the rheumatoid arthritic (Kirchman, 1965), the amount of therapy required in this area may also vary extensively. If therapy is indicated, then an individual treatment plan needs to be developed which is based upon a complete case work-up (Moos, Solomon & Lieberman, 1965; Kirchman, 1965). This work-up should include medical, psychological, social, economic and vocational information, motivations and expectations for therapy, interests, effect of the disability on the patient's life situation, and his attitudes toward his disabling condition. In considering avenues for providing psychological therapy, the fact that the patient (client) is receiving medical care from his physician and vocational assistance from his rehabilitation counselor may be sufficient to meet his psychological needs. The solution to his medical and vocational problems may be therapeutic in itself in reducing anxiety and depression which often accompany the physical effects of this condition. Conversely, if the anxiety and the depression associated with the arthritic condition are severe and persistent, the patient may need psychiatric help (*British Medical Journal*, 1969). If psychiatric help is not provided, it is not likely that medical care and vocational assistance will be sufficient enough, in a therapeutic sense, to meet the patient's psychological needs. Therefore, without formal therapeutic measures, the medical treatment, vocational counseling, and the over all rehabilitation plan will, in all likelihood, be unsuccessful for the anxious and depressed client.

One of the dilemmas facing the rehabilitation counselor in attempting to deal with the client's psychological adjustment is that some of the measures instituted in the medical management of the case may foster dependence in the client. The counselor's task is to counsel the client toward acceptance of his role as a person who is dependent in some areas of his life. However, at the same time, the counselor needs to provide opportunities for the client to be independent in certain areas of his life, particularly vocational ones. Hopefully, this independence can be achieved through the vocational rehabilitation process.

The role of the rehabilitation counselor in dealing with the rheumatoid arthritic is a supportive role. In this role, one of the counselor's tasks is to clarify and to help the client integrate the findings of the case study process into a meaningful vocational plan. The counselor needs to review the client's performance in the rehabilitation plan and his progress in the medical management of the physical parameters of the case. The counselor also needs to point out areas of strength and potential which should be utilized as well as circumventing areas of weakness through vocational planning. The counselor must also act as a facilitator for the expression of the client's feelings of hostility, fear, inadequacy, insecurity, and unrealistic goals and expectations which may be the forerunners of inadequate emotional adjust-

ment. When necessary the counselor may also act as a reinforcer
of the client's behavior when he moves toward his rehabilitation
goal and as an encourager of his efforts when he feels despondent
and depressed.

Some of the following suggestions may be applicable in
utilizing psychological information about the rheumatoid arthritic
client (Moos *et al.*, 1965):

1. The client's tendency toward compliance may be capital-
   ized upon by direct reinforcement to maintain a specific
   constructive rehabilitation program. His needs for independence can be partially met through the use of self-
   help training and self-help devices. His need for perfec-
   tionism may be channeled into planning a highly specific
   and ritualized rehabilitation program.

2. The client needs to be counseled toward the acceptance
   of his disability and the resultant physical limitations. This
   can probably be best accomplished by emphasizing that
   the disability does not encompass the whole person. The
   loss the client experiences in physical areas does not
   devalue him as a person. For example, the rheumatoid
   arthritic housewife may no longer be able to perform all
   the household chores she performed previously. Part of
   accepting the disabling condition might be for her to ask
   for assistance from family members and to utilize or
   adapt different working methods and equipment in order
   to make her household chores less physically demanding.

3. The family should participate in the counseling process
   and the treatment program. The members of the family
   should be encouraged to assist the client, but at the same
   time, not to take over the client's role in the family
   structure. It is important that the client see himself as a
   functioning and contributing member of the family unit.

4. Above all, the counselor needs to listen to the client's
   feelings, to provide a warm and accepting atmosphere
   for the expression of these feelings, and to relate to the
   client in a genuine manner.

Vocational and Socioeconomic Factors

The final goal of the rehabilitation process for the rheumatoid arthritic client is the reintegration of the client into society at a level commensurate with his highest potentialities. The achievement of this goal is affected by vocational and socioeconomic factors. Rusk (1971) states that the successful achievement of this goal is directly proportional to two factors:

> (1) the resources of the patient that may be worked with and (2) the extent of positive assistance afforded the patient by the social worker, the psychologist, and the vocational counselor, the latter factor outweighing the former in productive importance (p. 376).

The first factor, client resources, includes financial resources, vocational skills, family resources, community resources, etc. Snorrasen (1951) reported that rheumatoid arthritis is not a disability limited to any one social class or economic stratum nor is its prognosis dependent on social and economic factors. It may be that rheumatoid arthritis attacks all classes equally and that the medical prognosis of rheumatoid arthritis is not related to class stratum. However, the handicapping aspects of rheumatoid arthritis is directly related to the resources of the individual. For example, an assembly line worker who is required to have good eye-hand coordination, manual and finger dexterity, and speed to perform his job will be more severely handicapped by rheumatoid arthritis of the hands and wrists than a minister whose performance requires little use of the hands. It is unlikely the minister would be forced to change jobs; however, it is quite likely the assembly line worker would be forced to change jobs and expect difficulties in locating employment.

The second factor, the extent of positive services available to the client from the rehabilitation team, is crucially important in the achievement of the rehabilitation goal. Positive services to the client may overcome deficits in the client's resources. Since rheumatoid arthritis is a chronic disability, it causes permanent changes in all areas of life. Intensive social services must be provided to the rheumatoid arthritic client and his family. Intensive social services would include detailed analysis of the family structure, living arrangements, and the working environment which the client will encounter when he leaves the rehabilitation facility (Rusk, 1971). A study of the rheumatoid arthritic and the family illustrates the necessity for an analysis of the family structure. Markson (1971) found that among forty-six 30-60 year old female rheumatoid arthritic out-patients that the patients had adapted to the disability by becoming psychologically and physically dependent on the family. Some of the family's members expressed the belief that rehabilitation is useless and the patient should be protected from strangers. Markson (1971) concluded that rehabilitation programs should consider the patient's views on maintaining family stability before a rehabilitation program is initiated. Without family support and encouragement, the rehabilitation program for the rheumatoid arthritic client may be doomed to failure.

Living conditions the client must face can also hinder the rehabilitation process. A member of the rehabilitation team, usually the social worker, must investigate factors in the living arrangement which will promote or retard client independence. Rusk (1971) suggests that what may appear to be of little importance to the nonhandicapped observer may be crucially important to the rheumatoid arthritic client's independent functioning. Ten stairsteps from the house to the sidewalk and the inability to climb and descend these stairs may mean the client is unable to travel independently. Architectual barriers in the home—doors too narrow to permit wheelchairs to pass, poorly arranged bathroom facilities; beds, dressers, etc. at an inappropriate height to permit the client to attend to his needs; kitchen equipment too high or too low to be useful to the client, etc.— may mean the difference between self-care in a private dwelling and professional care in a nursing home. The rehabilitation team member will be required to visit the home several times to identify and take steps to solve these problems. Adequate assessment and the treatment of social factors affecting the achievement of the rehabilitation goal is time consuming, but necessary, if the client is to achieve his rehabilitation goal (Rusk, 1971).

Vocational problems accompanying rheumatoid arthritis are lasting. These vocational problems demand ingenuity and persistence from the rehabilitation counselor if the client is to achieve vocational success. These are problems which with intensive services from the vocational rehabilitation counselor can be solved. Acker (1959), Lowman (1961), and Manheimer (1962) report that forty and fifty percent of those rheumatoid arthritic clients participating in rehabilitation programs are successfully placed in employment. Placement of these clients was secured only after their vocational potential was thoroughly assessed.

The rehabilitation process of the federal-state programs of vocational rehabilitation is well suited for the comprehensive vocational evaluation services needed by the rheumatoid arthritic client. To provide vocational rehabilitation services to any individual, the rehabilitation counselor must determine if a disability is present, if this disability is vocationally handicapping, and if it is reasonable to expect the client to engage in a gainful occupation after vocational rehabilitation services are provided. It is exceedingly difficult for a counselor to determine the client's likelihood of benefitting from rehabilitation services without a thorough vocational evaluation.

Because of the progressive chronic nature of rheumatoid arthritis, the federal-state vocational rehabilitation legislation provides that the counselor shall be allowed up to eighteen months to determine the vocational potential of the rheumatoid arthritic client (Federal Register, 1969). This eighteen month extended evaluation period allows the counselor time to assess adequately the effects of rheumatoid arthritis on the client's vocational potential. To improve the client's vocational potentiality during the period of extended evaluation, services such as psychotherapy, prevocational training, occupational and physical therapy, surgery, medication, etc. can be provided.

Many difficulties are encountered in the vocational evaluation of the rheumatoid arthritic client. Among these is the adequacy of standardized testing for the assessment of the rheumatoid arthritic's vocational aptitudes. Probably the aptitude test most frequently used by rehabilitation counselors is the General Aptitude Test Battery (GATB) which was developed and administered by the United States Employment Service. The GATB yields scores on nine different measures of vocational aptitude. In the case of a rheumatoid arthritic client, the counselor must observe and be aware of certain hazards in using the GATB. First, the test taking time is approximately two and one-half hours, which is likely to be especially fatiguing for the rheumatoid arthritic client. Secondly, the answer must be marked on an answer sheet, and this task involves some dexterity and hand-eye coordination. Thirdly, parts of the GATB are designed to measure manual and finger dexterity. Finally, the GATB is a speed test which depends on quickness of response. Depending on the incapacitating nature of the client's arthritic condition, he may be severely limited in competing with physically normal persons in completing this test. The fact that he may be in such pain or that his fingers and wrists are crippled may well lessen his ability to perform at his highest potential. Although his scores may be an accurate reflection of his ability to function on the GATB, they will likely be much lower than his actual abilities. Consequently, the counselor may obtain a better evaluation of the client's aptitudes by using measuring devices which would not penalize him because of his physical disability.

Methods which appear to be more appropriate in assessing the vocational potential of the rheumatoid arthritic includes the TOWER system (Institute of the Crippled and Disabled, 1959), which utilizes the job sample method and various forms of training such as personal and work adjustment training, on-the-job training, and formal vocational or college training. Using these methods of vocational evaluation, the client and counselor are able to test the client's capacities and abilities in real and simulated work settings. These methods of vocational evaluation can give practical answers to such questions as: How long is the client able to work? Can he stand up for specific periods of time? Can he perform the work required in the job situation? Is he able to get to the rehabilitation facility on time? Can he use public transportation? Is he cooperative? Can he follow instructions? Etc.

In the vocational rehabilitation process, the purpose of the evaluation phase, which may include extended evaluation, is to develop a series of planned services which will lead to the successful job placement of the rheumatoid arthritic client. The rehabilitation services provided the client are based on information secured from intensive medical, social, psychological, and vocational studies of the client. The broad range of services available to the rheumatoid arthritic client are counseling and guidance, physical restoration, and training. Other services which may be used by the counselor to facilitate the client's achievement of his vocational objective include maintenance, prosthetic appliances, transportation, and tools and equipment.

After the client has completed the planned vocational rehabilitation services, job placement becomes the next objective of the rehabilitation process. Placement problems the rehabilitation counselor and rheumatoid arthritic client are likely to encounter include:

(1) joint impairment and limited general mobility,
(2) unpredictable course of the disease,
(3) emotional problems which may interfere with occupational training and performance, and
(4) lack of education among community and employers about rheumatoid arthritis (Acker, 1959, 266).

Pinner (1962) argues that the employability of the rheumatoid arthritic is affected as much by the age factor (in his sample, three-fourths were over forty-five years old) as the physical restrictions of the disability. These problems can be overcome if approached positively and with understanding.

Most rheumatoid arthritics are able to return to work or to continue working if conservation of the client's physical resources is considered when employment is secured for the client (Lowman, 1962). Sedentary work is generally preferred for the rheumatoid arthritic client since it conserves physical resources. Conserving physical resources is crucially important to the rheumatoid arthritic client because it helps maintain psychological integrity and joint function, prevents loss of physical capacity, and contributes to the client's economic well-being. Acker (1959) states the rheumatoid arthritic client/worker must avoid (1) rapid changes in atmospheric conditions; for example, in and out of coolers in the meat packing industry; (2) extremely heavy physical labor, for example, loading trucks or jobs in the construction trades; and (3) work which primarily requires the client to stand, walk, or climb stairs. There is a possibility that some rheumatoid arthritic clients can successfully perform jobs requiring these physical activities. It should be noted that these recommendations must be reviewed for each client on an individual basis. The placement of the rheumatoid arthritic culminates the integration, or reintegration, of the rheumatoid arthritic client into the social and vocational world at his optimal level of performance.

REFERENCES

Acker, M.: Vocational rehabilitation of the rheumatoid arthritic. *Journal of Rehabilitation*, 23:12, 1959.

Acker, M.: Vocational counseling and job placement, In E. W. Lowman (Ed.), *Arthritis: General Principles, Physical Medicine, and Rehabilitation*. Boston. Little, Brown & Co., 1951.

Black, R. L.: The use of synthetic corticosteroids in rheumatoid arthritis. In J. L. Hollander (Ed.), *Arthritis and Allied Conditions: A Textbook in Rheumatology* (7th ed.), Philadelphia, Lea & Febiger, 1966.

Bowie, M. A.: Occupational therapy in arthritis. In J. L. Hollander (Ed.), *Arthritis and Allied Conditions: A Textbook in Rheumatology.* (7th ed.), Philadelphia, Lea & Febiger, 1966.

Brown, R., and Lingg, C.: Musculoskeletal complaints in industry, annual complaint rate and diagnosis, absenteeism and economic loss. *Arthritis and Rheumatism*, 4:283-291, 1961.

Carek, R.: Rehabilitation following surgery for chronic arthritis. *Rehabilitation Counseling Bulletin*, 5:212-214, 1962.

Chalmers, R. M.: The general management of rheumatoid arthritis. *The Practitioner*, 208:5-9, 1972.

Clark, W. S.: Arthritis and rheumatism. *Journal of Rehabilitation*, 31 (5): 10-12, 1965.

Engleman, E. P.: Conservative management of rheumatoid arthritis. In J. L. Hollander (Ed.), *Arthritis and Allied Conditions: A Textbook in Rheumatology* (7th ed.), Philadelphia, Lea & Febiger, 1966.

Federal Register, 34 (No. 200), Part II, 1969.

Felton, J. S.; Perkins, D. C., and Lewin, M.: *A Survey of Medicine and Medical Practice for the Rehabilitation Counselor*. Washington, D.C., U.S. Department of Health, Education, and Welfare, 1966.

Freyberg, R. H.: Gold therapy for rheumatoid arthritis. In J. L. Hollander (Ed.), *Arthritis and Allied Conditions: A Textbook in Rheumatology* (7th ed.), Philadephia, Lea & Febiger, 1966.

Hollander, J. L. (Ed.): *Arthritis and Allied Conditions: A Textbook on Rheumatology* (7th ed.), Philadephia, Lea & Febiger, 1966.

Hylbert, K. W.: *Medical Information for Counselors: An Outline Text.* State College, Penna., Counselor Education, Press, 1965.

Institute for the Crippled and Disabled. *Tower Testing, Orientation, and Work Evaluation in Rehabilitation.* New York, Author, 1959.

Ivght, C. E.; Keefer, C. S.; Lukens, F. D. W., Richards, D. W.; Sebrell, W. H., and Trapnell, J. M. (Eds.): *The Merck Manual of Diagnosis and Therapy* (11th Ed.), Rahway, Merck, Sharp & Dohme Research Laboratories, 1966.

King, S. H.: Psycho-social factors associated with rheumatoid arthritis. *Journal of Chronic Diseases,* 2:287-302, 1955.

Kirchman, M. M.: The personality of the rheumatoid arthritic patient. *American Journal of Occupational Therapy, 19:*160-164, 1965.

Langi, V. F.: Rehabilitation of the arthritic patient. *Modern Treatment,* 5:1010-1012, 1968.

Lesowitz, N.: *Characteristics of Clients Rehabilitation in Fiscal Years 1965-1969. Federal-State Vocational Rehabilitation Program.* Washington, U.S. Department of Health, Education and Welfare, Social and Rehabilitation Service. Rehabilitation Services Administration, n.d.

Lockie, L. M., and Norcross, B. M.: Salicylates, phenylbutazone, chloroguines, and indomethacine in treatment of rheumatoid arthritis. In J. L. Hollander (Ed.), *Arthritis and Allied Conditions: A Textbook in Rheumatology* (7th ed.), Philadephia, Lea & Febiger, 1966.

Lowman, E. W. (Ed.): *Arthritis: General Principles, Physical Medicine and Rehabilitation.* Boston, Little, Brown & Co., 1959.

Lowman, E. W.: Employability of rheumatoid arthritis: Emphasis of physical rehabilitation. *Archives of Environment Health,* 4:502-504, 1962.

Lowman, E. W.: Rehabilitation in arthritis. In J. L. Hollander (Ed.), *Arthritis and Allied Conditions: A Textbook in Rheumatology* (7th ed.), Philadelphia, Lea & Febiger, 1966.

McElven, C.: The diagnosis and differential diagnosis of rheumatoid arthritis. In J. L. Hollander (Ed.), *Arthritis and Allied Conditions: A Textbook in Rheumatology* (7th ed.), Philadelphia, Lea & Febiger, 1966.

Manheimer, R. H.: Arthritics in competitive employment: An eight year experience. *Rehabilitation Bulletin, 5*(3):149-151, 1962.

Markson, E. W.: Patient semeiology of a chronic disease: Rheumatoid arthritis. *Social Science and Medicine,* 5:159-167, 1971.

Mental problems in rheumatoid arthritis. *British Medical Journal,* 4:319, 1969.

Moos, R. H.: Personality factors associated with rheumatoid arthritis: A review. *Journal of Chronic Diseases, 17:*41-55, 1969.

Moos, R. H.; Solomon, G. F., and Lieberman, E.: Psychological orientation in the treatment of rheumatoid arthritis. *American Journal of Occupational Therapy, 19*:153-159, 1965.

Moos, R. H., and Solomon, G. F.: MMPI response patterns in patients with rheumatoid arthritis. *Journal of Psychosomatic Research, 8*:17-28, 1969.

O'Brien, W.; Thomas, B., and Bunim, J.: *A Genetic Analysis of the Occurrence of Rheumatoid Factor (FC) and Rheumatoid Arthritis (RA) in 485 Matings and 1633 Sibling Pairs in Pima and Blackfeet Indians.* Paper read at Tenth Interim session of the American Rheumatism Association. Dec. 6 & 7, Boston.

Pinner, J.: Placement of arthritic applicants. *Archives of Environmental Health, 4*:492-494, 1962.

Polley, H. F.; Swenson, W. M., and Steinhilber, R. M.: Personality characteristics of patients with rheumatoid arthritis. *Psychosomatics, 11*:45-49, 1970.

Potter, T. A., and Kuhns, J. G.: Correction of arthritic deformities. In J. L. Hollander (Ed.), *Arthritis and Allied Conditions: A Textbook in Rheumatology* (7th ed.), Philadelphia, Lea & Febiger, 1966.

Robinson, H.; Kirk, R. F., and Frye, R. F.: A psychological study of rheumatoid arthritics and selected controls. *Journal of Chronic Diseases, 23*:791-801, 1971.

Robinson, H.; Kirk, R. F.; Frye, R. F., and Robertson, J. T.: A psychological study of patients with rheumatoid arthritis and other painful diseases. *Journal of Psychosomatic Research, 16*:53-56, 1972.

Rusk, H. A.: *Rehabilitation Medicine* (3rd ed.), St. Louis, The C. V. Mosby Company, 1971.

Scoth, N., and Geiger, H. J.: The epidemiology of rheumatoid arthritis: A review with special attention to social factors. *Journal of Chronic Diseases, 15*:1037-1066, 1962.

Seidenfeld, M. A.: Arthritis and rheumatism. In J. F. Garrett and E. S. Levine (eds.), *Psychological Practices with the Physically Disabled.* New York, Columbia University Press, 1962.

Tomaszewska, J.: *Rehabilitation of Rheumatics: Selected Problems.* Washington, D.C., Department of Health, Education, and Welfare, 1970. Grant No. 19-P-58318-F-01.

CHAPTER XII

END STAGE RENAL FAILURE:

Considerations for the Rehabilitation Counselor

EVAN JONES

The Kidneys
Diseases of the Kidneys
Treatment of Renal Failure
Peritoneal Dialysis
Kidney Transplants
The Problem of Dialysis
Role of Vocational Rehabilitation Agencies
Counseling Considerations

The Kidneys

EACH OF US HAS two kidneys located on either side of the spine at the lowest level of the rib cage. In the adult each kidney weighs a quarter of a pound and is fist-sized in the shape of the familiar kidney bean. Each kidney contains about 1,000,000 functioning units called nephrons. A nephron consists of a tuft of tiny blood vessels called a glomerulus and an attached tube called a tubule. From blood entering each glomerular tuft a fluid is separated which does not contain either the cellular elements or large protein molecules of the blood. As this fluid passes along the tubule, approximately 99 percent of the water and most of the small molecules are returned to the blood by an extremely delicate and selective series of operations. The remainder is eliminated from the body as urine. Substances needed by your body are returned into the bloodstream, and harmful substances are removed through the urinary system. There are 140 miles of filters and tubes in both kidneys. Thus the kidneys perform their life sustaining job of filtering and returning to the bloodstream almost three times the entire body weight in water and salts every twenty-four hours—about 200 quarts; approximately two quarts are sent to the bladder to be flushed out of your body, and about 198 quarts are retained in the body.

There is one other important point to note about the kidneys. Each kidney has developed the ability to function many times greater than it is called upon to perform in a normal situation. Complete removal of a kidney does not place an undue strain on the kidney remaining in the body. The remaining kidney will do the job of two kidneys.

A simple example taken from the flight of a space ship will illustrate what the kidneys mean to the living human body and will clarify their basic importance in survival. A space ship in flight has apparatus which automatically controls temperature, humidity and oxygen. No matter at what height the space ship flies, the instruments adjust the atmosphere with the space ship automatically so that the internal environment within the space can support life. If the instruments were to fail to function, the environment within the ship would cease.

In the same way, the healthy kidneys within a living organism maintain a constant stable chemical composition of body fluids. They do this despite the introduction of external substances such as food and drink. As long as the kidneys function in a healthy manner, the internal environment can support life. If the kidneys fail to function in this way, the organism will die within a short period of time.

Thus your kidneys are responsible for maintaining the delicate chemical balance required if all other organs in your body are to function in a healthy manner. When your kidneys are functioning in a healthy manner, they dispose of body wastes adequately; they remove substances from your bloodstream that are harmful to you and retain those the body needs. This is why your kidneys are sometimes referred to as "The master chemists of the body" (National Kidney Foundation, 1971).

Diseases of the Kidneys

Many diseases of different types attack the kidneys. Depending on its type, a particular kidney disease may begin by damaging the arteries bringing blood into the kidney, or the nephrons, or the complicated structure of filters and tubes, or other parts of the kidney. Some diseases attack several parts of the kidney at once. Kidney disease may involve one or both kidneys.

While there are several ways of grouping kidney diseases the following are the major types:

Infections: Kidney infections are usually caused by bacteria. Most kidney infections are grouped under the name pyelonephritis. Kidney infections may result from infection of the parts of the urinary tract, or the blood may carry infection to the kidneys from other parts of the body. Infectious kidney diseases must be treated carefully. Inadequate treatment masks the symptoms while the destructive process continues.

Hypersensitivity states: Normally, the body reacts to bacteria, viruses and any other foreign material by producing substances called antibodies that attack and neutralize the foreign material, which is then passed harmlessly out of the body. In one of the most common kidney diseases, glomerulonephritis, it is thought that antibodies formed following a structural coccal infection of the throat or other parts of the body are responsible, in some way not yet understood, for kidney damage. A number of the kidney diseases also appear because of a hypersensitivity state.

Birth defects and hereditary diseases: The exact number of children born with defects of the urinary tract is not known but such disorders may be the most common type of birth defects. One of the more common of these is the narrowing of the ureter and urethra which may cause damage by restricting the flow, or prevention of normal kidney development.

Some urinary tract birth defects are serious and will cause difficulty while others may have no noticeable effect. Many urinary tract birth defects allow infection to develop very easily. It is especially important to detect these abnormalities so that patients who have them can be watched closely for any sign of urinary tract infection.

There are several kidney diseases which are inherited, the most often seen being polycystic. Here cysts are present in the kidneys at birth and grow as the individual matures, eventually affecting kidney function.

Circulatory conditions: Causes of severe hypertension or high blood pressure which may cause or be caused by kidney disease, often result in kidney failure. The other circulatory problems related to kidney disease are fortunately not very common.

Tumors: Benign and malignant tumors may occur at any point along the urinary tract, including the kidney itself. Even benign tumors are dangerous because they may obstruct the normal production and elimination of the urine.

Metabolic diseases: Diabetes, gout and other metabolic diseases usually involve the kidneys. Kidney stones and other obstructions such as enlarged prostate glands may stem from metabolic disturbances. Any obstruction of the urinary tract, if not relieved, lead to destruction of the kidneys.

Injuries: In addition to injuries due to blows, there are various substances such as dry cleaning fluid and antifreeze which, if swallowed or inhaled, are poisonous to the kidneys and may injure them seriously.

Many of the above diseases may result in acute renal failure. It is simply a condition in which both kidneys stop forming urine. This is oftentimes just a temporary condition and if the proper treatment is received the kidneys may start functioning again. The victim may require one or two periods of dialysis to sort of *pinch hit* for the sick kidney.

Endstage renal failure occurs when the kidneys finally stop and there is little hope for any return to function. The kidneys then are unable to preserve the constancy of the chemical composition of the blood by the excretion of body waste products; these wastes accumulate in the blood. As a consequence a series of abnormalities known as uremia, literally, urine in the blood, develops. In its latest stages, uremia is usually associated with headache, nausea and vomiting, blurred vision, and finally convulsions, coma, and death

Treatment of Renal Failure

At the present time there are three recognized forms of treatment for end stage renal disease. These consist of chronic hemodialysis, peritoneal dialysis, and kidney transplanation.

Hemodialysis

Hemodialysis is the process by which an artificial kidney is used to remove from the body accumulated waste chemicals and excess fluid. The word comes from two Greek words meaning *blood* and *to separate* (Webster's Dictionary, 1966).

All artificial kidneys contain cellophane or similar membranes which separate circulating blood from dialyzing fluid. This membrane has a special quality of permeability, in other words, it contains small pores that are able to pass some of the dissolved components of a solution. This membrane is only semipermeable, however, since some other components of the solution are unable to pass through the membrane; in general, these pores are able to pass very small dissolved particles such as sodium, urea, and potassium, as well as water and some other uremic waste products. The pores are too small to permit the passage of red blood cells, white blood cells and certain blood proteins.

There are several different kinds of membranes which differ in the qualities of permeability. Membranes for use in artificial kidneys are carefully selected and studied for this quality.

Consider what happens when one puts sugar in coffee; the small particles of sugar dissolve and spread evenly throughout the cup of coffee. This tendency of particles to spread out to an even concentration throughout a solution is called diffusion. The particles move along a concentration gradient: That is, they move from areas of high concentration to areas of low concentration until they are evenly distributed in the solution, even when separated by the semipermeable membrane from the solution of dialysate. The impurities such as urea, diffuse through the membrane into the dialysate bath. Since the membrane has this characteristic of permitting only very small chemical particles to pass through the pores, other important blood substances do not move in this way.

Osmosis is another term for this process of movement of substances specifically through a semipermeable membrane. Water molecules also move through the membrane in order to equalize the concentration of particles in the blood and in the dialysate solution. In effect, there are two different solutions on opposite sides of the membrane, dialysate on one side, blood on the other. The transfer of water particles and dissolved substances through the membrane is called osmosis.

The combined effect of the chemical functions described above is to produce an effect very similar to an ordinary filter. By circulating blood over the membrane of the artificial kidney, impurities are in much higher concentration in blood than in the dialysate. The dialysate contains normal blood materials in normal amounts, but none of the impurities. These normal materials are not exchanged through the membrane because they are in nearly equal concentraion on each side of the membrane, therefore, there is no force of osmosis and diffusion to move these materials into the dialysate. The impurities, however, are in much higher concentration in blood than in the dialysate, and therefore are removed in proportion to the concentration gradient.

The removal of fluid which has accumulated in your body is one of the most important functions of dialysis. Some water is removed by the process of osmosis, previously described. The efficient removal of water from the blood requires other mechanisms, however, since the concentration of water is essentially the same on both sides of the membrane. Therefore, a pressure gradient is used. One means of doing this is to apply suction, negative pressure, to the dialysate. Since there is a positive pressure in the arterial blood in the blood phase, the pressure gradient between the blood and dialysate is enough to force water through the membrane and remove fluid from the patient. This water carries with it some of the materials present in the plasma, so it not only removes fluid, but it increases the removal of dissolved impurities. This process is called ultra-filtration because it is filtration under pressure through very fine pores.

Dialysate is a solution of carefully measured salts and water.

When properly fixed, the dialysate contains normal concentrations of some salts, roughly equal to the concentration in blood. Dialysate does not contain any of the chemical impurities contained in blood. The ingredients in the dialysate are carefully measured to be mixed with an exact proportion of water.

Dialysate is discarded after a single pass through the artificial kidney. By using a continuous fresh supply of dialysate there is always maximum removal of waste products from blood. The blood, in continuous recirculation into the body will repeatedly pick up more of these impurities and carry them to the dialyzing membrane for removal.

These few chemical principles explain the process of dialysis.

This dialysis process or the artificial kidney machine has been in existence since World War II. It was only used in cases of short term or acute renal failure, because there was no easy way to gain access to a patient's circulation. Long term hemodialysis really became possible around 1960 when Scribner and others devised the external arteriovenous (AV) shunt to provide repeated direct access to the patient's circulation (Quinton, W. E. and others, 1960). More recently Brescia and Cimino described creation of a surgically created fistula, or internal arteriovenous shunt, for the same purpose (Brescia, Michael, and others, 1966).

The external AV shunt consists of two pieces of silastic tubing, each with a teflon vessel tip, which fits firmly without leaking, into a blood vessel. Next to this teflon tip each cannula has two small wings for stabilizing the annula beneath the skin. One piece of tubing is inserted into an artery, the other into an adjacent vein. The two pieces are then connected outside the skin by a teflon connector.

The importance of meticulous care of the external AV shunt cannot be over emphasized. The patient's long term dialysis depends on satisfactory performance of the shunt. Since repeated or severe infection is the major cause of loss of shunts, they should be given the same care as a fresh surgical wound. Read and Mallison have found that with good care a shunt's life may average over a year (Read and Mallison, 1972). Some shunts have been known to last over three years. The second cause of shunt failure is the problem of clotting. Blood color and blood flow should routinely be checked so that any clotting may be dealt with immediately.

The internal shunt is a fistula created between an adjacent artery and vein. The vein receives arterial blood directly and as a consequence, the vein dilates. These dilated veins are easily punctured. However, blood flow, even through large bore needles, is not sufficient for dialysis without addition of a pump to increase flow. This is a major shortcoming of the AV fistula. The obvious advantage is that it does not require the care that an external shunt requires.

The debate still continues as to which is better although patients seem to manage well with either.

Peritoneal Dialysis

Peritoneal dialysis is a second form of treatment and in principle is similar to techniques employing an artificial kidney. However, in place of an artificial membrane, this technique places the patient's own peritoneum, the lining of the abdominal cavity, between the blood and an external solution. The external solution, identical to that normally surrounding body cells, is introduced into the patient's abdominal cavity in the course of peritoneal dialysis, rather than into the bath of the artificial kidney.

This is a painful, discomforting treatment and is not as effective as the other two. Peritoneal dialysis takes approximately eight hours and it takes the patient about a day to recover from the treatment. Accounting for the time just prior to dialysis when a patient is not feeling well, the time for treatment, and the time for recovery, it can be seen that dialysis twice a week leaves the patient with only one or two days a week when he is not completely subdued by his disease. For these reasons peritoneal dialysis is used as a last resort, a temporary method of treatment. It is used as a life saving measure when nothing else is available.

Kidney Transplants

More than 5,000 kidney transplants have been performed in the last decade. In recent years, most patients who have received a kidney from other persons to replace kidneys destroyed by disease have been restored to normal productive life.

Thus, transplantation of human kidneys has graduated from the experimental stage and won wide acceptance as the means of saving the lives of patients whose kidneys can no longer perform the vital function of cleansing the blood of body wastes. Today kidney transplantation is the ideal form of treatment, and the hope of many dialysis patients.

The main problem of kidney transplantation is not the operation; most organ transplant operations are successes, but the problem is the rejection factor. The body's defense system blindly attacks any and all foreign substances, a transplanted life saving kidney as well as an invading life threatening virus.

Because of this rejection reaction, up until a few years ago only about one half of kidney transplants were deemed successful (in that the new kidney withstood the onslaught of powerful antibodies and functioned for more than two years).

However, the rate of successful kidney transplants has considerably improved. This is due to the fact that immunosuppressive drugs which restrain the antibodies attempts to reject the newly transplanted kidney; and also to *tissue typing,* the techniques for the selection of a suitable donor whose tissue *type* matches, as closely as possible, the tissue from the patient and thus arouses less of a rejection reaction.

Dr. John P. Merrill, whose medical-surgical team at the Peter Bent Brigham Hospital, Boston performed the first successful kidney transplant in 1954, and who has witnessed rapid and dramatic advances in this form of therapy to the point where it is now fairly routine:

> When the transplanted kidney comes from a living brother or sister, the chances for long term survival are about 90 percent. Next to siblings, parents generally make the best donors. The survival for kidneys taken from an unrelated dead person is about 50 to 60 percent (Earl, 1971).

When the tissue of the donor and receipient are closely matched, patients usually do well. For this reason, transplants between identical twins are the most successful. However, the patient does not often have a relative suitable to act as a donor, or willing to part with a healthy kidney, although the risk to the living donor is minimal and a person can get along very well with just one kidney. Therefore, kidneys taken at the time of death are increasingly being used.

In order to reduce the rejection factor and improve the chances for success, scientists have established a network of *tissue typing* centers throughout the country. Here donor organs, when they become available, are typed, in much the same way as blood is typed for transfusions, and matched by computer analysis to the most compatible waiting recipient.

It is now possible to preserve organs after death, for brief periods, until a recipient arrives from another part of the country for a transplant. In some cases, organs can be rushed to distant places and planted in the brief time they can be kept *alive* outside the body. Recently, kidneys were flown from Boston to Madison, Wisconsin, and successfully transplanted in twelve hours.

As the chances of finding an excellent tissue match between unrelated persons are small, about one in one thousand, a very large pool of donors is necessary to find *the ideal match.* Until recently, efforts to acquire such a pool were stymied by legal red tape. Outdated and cumbersome laws stood in the way of an individual giving his body upon death for medical and scientific purposes. This contributed to a severe shortage of kidneys and other organs for transplant.

Now, however, the transplant picture has been made much brighter with the passage of an act that greatly facilitates the donation of a human organ.

This uniform anatomical gift act makes available on a national basis the uniform donor card, a wallet size legal document for the disposition for any or all parts of the body at the time of death. Any person of sound mind, eighteen years of age or older, simply has to sign the card with two witnesses, to make it valid in any part of the country. If he should later change his mind about the gift of life he is leaving another, he can just tear up the card.

The Problem of Dialysis

Dr. Adelson, head of Nephrology Service at the Evanston (Ill.) Hospital, an affiliate of Northwestern-McGraw Medical

Center, declares, "I don't think any patient is undialyzable." Yet according to National Kidney Foundation statistics 58,000 Americans died of renal failure in 1970 (Medical World News, 1971). Why must so many people die of renal failure when medical science can treat the disease?

The first reason seems to be that of money, many patients simply cannot afford the high cost of dialysis. While mass production and marketing have helped to reduce equipment costs, dialysis is still expensive. Since many urban hospitals now charge $250.00 per dialysis plus related fees, an annual estimate based on two or three treatments a week is $35,000 to $40,000. At an ambulatory care facility the yearly cost can drop to $14,000 to $20,000 with further reductions anticipated as the centers treat more patients and gain experience. And home dialysis, while eventually cheaper, probably does not save any money over an ambulatory care facility for the first year. Costs for the first year, at home, including equipment and installation plus an in-center training course, can range from $12,000 to $20,000. In subsequent years depending upon complications, the cost might be $4,000 to $6,000. Dr. Belding H. Scribner, Professor of Medicine and Director of the Nephrology Division, University of Washington School of Medicine in Seattle believes the continuing annual cost could be as low as $3,500 for treatment in the home. Dr. Scribner says, "At that price, we can't let a head of family or any breadwinner die" (Medical World News, 1971).

Another reason why people do not receive treatment is because there are not enough qualified staff. Most artificial kidney machines are used only during the day, if the staff were available they could be used twenty-four hours a day.

As mentioned earlier, kidney transplantation is the ideal form of treatment. Due to the difficulties of finding a suitable donor many eligible individuals cannot receive this type of treatment. While these candidates for transplantation are waiting for a suitable donor they must be maintained by dialysis.

According to the National Registry of long term dialysis patients, there were as of April 1, 1973, 3,898 patients being maintained on dialysis (Burton, 1971). Although exact figures are not available it doesn't take much imagination to see that current resources are not meeting the needs of these severely disabled individuals.

As a result of this situation the status quo now includes selection committees or groups of individuals who must decide which renal failure patients are treated and which are left to die. These committees are often referred to as, *death committees* (Medical World News, 1971).

In the past these committees have used several criteria for selecting hemodialysis candidates. The first condition established was that the patient have no other severe medical problems such as cancer, severe cardiovascular disease, or any other irreversible medical condition which would limit recovery. Next psychological considerations were of paramount importance. Emotional stability, past social adjustment patterns, motivation, and intelligence are factors which were investigated. Financial arrangements had to be studied, each individual's financial status along with any community resources were considered. Lastly, if a patient could satisfy the above requirements he was accepted if a dialysis machine was available.

Now though many of these selection committees have consolidated the above criteria into one major assessment, the committee's attempt to determine the relative quality of life a patient will have while on dialysis. As an example, suppose a hospital had two patients who needed dialysis but only one machine or time slot available. Then the committee would select the patient for dialysis who they feel would have the higher quality of life while on dialysis.

Both of the above methods are inhuman if not barbaric. It is difficult to imagine that in this country potentially productive persons are dying of a disease that can be treated. There have been several bills before Congress that would bring some relief to this problem, but none have survived the legislative process. It appears that Americans will have to decide whether or not a human being is entitled to medical service whenever he needs it and as long as he wants it. It also seems that this problem is going to continue until either medical science can find a more economical treatment or some form of relief is provided by the Federal Government.

Role of Vocational Rehabilitation Agencies

Chronic renal failure patients can be rehabilitated. This fact is supported by extensive research and several comprehensive studies. A particularly interesting study was done under a Federal grant at the University of Alabama in Birmingham. The following is a brief quotation from their final report dated 1971:

> Good physical, social and vocational rehabilitation was accomplished in 14 of 16 persons accepted for maintenance dialysis after total loss of renal function. The two patients who did not survive the study period both had extensive disease in addition to renal failure. Such secondary illness, as well as irreversible complications of prolonged uremia, may prevent rehabilitation during dialysis management and must be considered in patient selection.
>
> Those patients who did well medically also functioned well at home and on the job. Even those with major medical complications were able to remain gainfully employed through much of their dialysis experience; 81 percent of this group returned to former employment. However, 31 percent of these required major job adjustments while 57 percent required minor job adjustments. Jobs which limit trauma to the cannulated extremity and avoid heavy physical exertion are essential. Persons who function largely intellectually, such as the two teachers in the group, did best vocationally and were not considered to have a vocational handicap.
>
> The results in this study were comparable to those from other published series (University of Alabama, 1971).

This study leaves little doubt that these individuals enjoyed post-illness lives that were both valuable and productive to themselves and society.

One other point to consider is length of life. This is a difficult thing to determine especially since medical science is making advances in this area daily. Herbert Klarman though, has established via cost-effectiveness analysis, that the average increase in life expectancy with chronic hemodialysis alone is nine years (Klarman, 1968). Nine years is a considerable period of time and certainly valuable enough to justify rehabilitation.

In the past many vocational rehabilitation agencies have avoided renal failure patients. The terminal nature of the disease combined with experimental treatments made most of these victims infeasible for rehabilitation services. Today the situation has changed somewhat, treatments are no longer in the experimental stages, and many renal failure patients have been restored to the point that they may continue in their previous occupations.

Unfortunately vocational rehabilitation agencies have been slow to recognize any responsibility for these individuals. The present state of affairs has been pointed out by a survey of programs and services of state rehabilitation agencies for clients with chronic kidney disease (Virgil Smirnow Associates, 1971). When state agencies were asked the question, "Is there a provision in the state plan of your rehabilitation agency for services of any kind for chronic renal patients in need of hemodialysis?", the results were as follows:

Yes
    3 agencies or 5.7 percent
No, but services are being provided to such patients
    38 agencies or 71.7 percent
No, and no services are provided to such patients
    11 agencies or 20.7 percent
No answer
    1 agency or 1.8 percent
            (Virgil Smirnow Associates, 1971)

When the forty-one agencies who said they provided services were asked, "Does your state agency give all the usual rehabilitation services?" only eight responded, "Yes." Of these eight most required their clients to meet a rather stringent feasibility requirement, which further limited the number of patients served (Virgil Smirnow Associates, 1971).

As can be seen by the above results nation wide service is sketchy and inconsistent. Again Virgil Smirnow has summed up this problem:

> The lack of coordinated national goals or policy relating to kidney disease gives rise to a patchwork of problems, separately funded and administered. As a result, it is difficult to obtain a picture, at any one point in time, of the total resources or activity devoted to kidney problems. While there appears to be a modest growth in resources, it is apparent to most that the need for services far exceeds the capacity to provide them. Cost of hemodialysis treatment has been the largest factor voiced for slowness in closing the

gap, yet the decision as to whether, given the medical know-how available, any human being should be permitted to die for want of financial capability, is one that will plague the consciences of the American people. In the end, it seems inevitable that a greater effort will be made toward preservation of life of patients with end-stage renal disease (Virgil Smirnow Associates, 1971).

The problem of feasibility is one that strictly limits the number of victims that rehabilitation agencies will serve. Once an individual is determined feasible he has usually progressed past the point of major medical expenses and physical complications. As a matter of fact some states that are working with renal failure patients under a special federal grant are having a difficult time using up the grant simply because feasible patients cannot be found.

Counseling Considerations

Counseling an end stage renal failure client is often difficult and challenging. The terminal nature of this disease presents its victims with devastating psychological conflicts that must be resolved if one is to be rehabilitated. As an example, Beard has expressed the paradox that "The fear of dying and the fear of living were an integral part of the whole problem of renal failure and its treatment" (Beard, 1969). The only thing these individuals see in the future is death, or life for an undetermined period, disabled, at the mercy of the disease and the machine (Ebra, 1972).

When a rehabilitation counselor first sees the client, the chances are that he is not yet on dialysis. This makes any type of assessment difficult since the level of uremia has a direct cause and effect relationship with organic brain dysfunction which produces lethargy, impaired judgment, drowsiness, and inability to concentrate for extended periods. During terminal stages of uremia, psychological testing for brain damage has to some degree revealed *organicity* (Short and Wilson, 1969). Possibly the only valid information that can be obtained during the initial interview is background information. This is also a good time to contact relatives and to review medical history. The most important people at this point are the doctors, specialists, and hospital staff since they will be deciding whether or not to treat the individual. If treatment is appropriate they will also prescribe the type of treatment to be used. The rehabilitation counselor should keep in close, direct contact with the hospital staff so that he will be aware of any change in the client's unstable condition. The rehabilitation counselor should also be prepared to consult with hospital staff, since the staff may request his expertise as to the vocational possibilities of a patient.

Depending on the government regulations in the state where the counselor is working he may be asked to help the patient make some financial arrangements for treatment. This could involve contact with insurance companies, use of rehabilitation funds, contact with charity organizations, and contact with other social service groups.

The patient's initial reaction to the disease and its terminal nature is usually severe. Patients often experience severe depression, anxiety, fear of death, feelings of personal inadequacy and insecurity. It may be difficult to make the patient realize the terminal nature of his disease. Reality orientation and weakening of ego functions are common problems at this point (Kemph, 1966). Ebra has summarized this situation:

> Some individuals may necessitate more time and counseling sessions in order to work through these problems and come to the realization that they are, in fact, terminally ill. Until this initial phase of the counseling is successful, the patient cannot be mobilized towards the phase of adaptation and ultimately complete rehabilitation (Ebra, 1972).

An important aspect of the patient's adjustment is how his family, particularly his spouse, views his quandary. It is important that the family include the patient on important decisions. This will help maintain his ego strength and his pre-illness role within the family. As with most disabilities the family should not be over-solicitious or rejecting. The rehabilitation counselor should counsel the patient's family to make them aware of how they can help the psychological adjustment of the patient. The family will also need counseling to facilitate their own adjustment to a new life style. This will help minimize the great burdens of caring for a terminally ill person, and the financial limitations placed on the family.

In order to overcome the rather severe psychological stresses that go along with dialysis many patients employ a series of defense mechanisms. This procedure allows them to maintain some degree of emotional stability and self esteem while on dialysis.

The first defense mechanism used is that of denial. Patients often use this defense mechanism when complications arise, seeing them as one time singular occurrences rather than ongoing problems that develop along with dialysis (Ebra, Toth, 1972). The rehabilitation counselor should alert himself and be aware when a client is using this defense mechanism since he may be covering up serious medical problems. Oftentimes this rationale is recognized in potential transplant patients since they often feel that surgery will solve all their problems.

Another mechanism used by dialysis patients is projection. Patients are quick to recognize mutual problems and setbacks in other patients but not in themselves. Oftentimes a client will project his fears and anxieties on to other family members, for example, he may report his children find his fistula repulsive when he himself finds it repulsive. Ebra and Toth have summarized:

> The patient is not able to attribute certain undesirable emotions or characteristics to himself; instead he attributes his own negative aspects to others. This mechanism is useful in that it can preserve a healthy self-image and prevent massive ego damage. However, its overuse can distort reality and, therefore, cause a significant amount of problems in reality orientation (Ebra, et al., 1972).

An easily recognized defense mechanism in dialysis patients is that of displacement. A patient may displace his fear of death onto a smaller problem such as care of his shunt. He may become overzealous in keeping his cannulus clean. Another more dangerous form of displacement occurs when the patient displaces feelings of aggression and hostility onto his wife and/or family. The problems with this are obvious, a patient's wife and family are important in his adjustment and may play an important part in home dialysis. Any family disagreements can upset the delicate relationship of the family and the dialysis patient.

Lastly, many patients use reaction formations to protect their egos. Patients who are not feeling well may claim that they never felt better. Hostile feelings toward doctors and hospital staff may result in the patient being exceptionally receptive toward treatment and hospital care.

All of the above defense mechanisms are beneficial and help reduce the tumultuous stress that dialysis patients experience. The rehabilitation counselor should be aware that his client is using these defenses and be prepared to counsel if his client begins distorting reality. Depending on the amount of stress and the use of defenses the rehabilitation counselor may want to arrange for some short term psychotherapy (Ebra et al., 1972).

Part of the counselor's job is to help the patient through periods when complications arise. The rehabilitation counselor should keep his client informed as to the ramifications of his disease and its complications. One of the most common problems that dialysis patients experience is infection around the cannula. Unless this infection can immediately be cleared up the cannula will have to be removed and a new one placed at some other point on his body. This is always a considerable setback and requires both surgery and a great deal of expense. The client at this time needs reassurance and counseling, the client should be reminded that this is a part of dialysis and that it cannot always be avoided. Lastly, care of the cannula should be re-emphasized, the client should keep in mind that his cannula must be treated as a fresh surgical wound.

Another complication the patient should be well aware of is the fact that his body can no longer produce blood at the pre-illness level. The kidneys produce a substance which stimulate a person's bone marrow to produce blood. When the kidneys stop functioning production of blood is significantly decreased. Blood loss may rise above production and the patient may require a transfusion. Transfusions are fairly dangerous since an already weak anemic dialysis patient is a prime target for hepatitis. Another consideration is that the transfused blood may contain antibodies foreign to the patient. These antibodies may increase a patient's resistance making a successful transplant difficult.

Patients will need counseling about their reduced sexual function. Some will realize limited sexual activity and others may not be able to perform at all. Females generally stop menstruating, although if they don't they face the problems of blood loss mentioned earlier.

A particularly difficult problem for clients is their change in diet. The rehabilitation counselor should understand why a particular diet was selected for his client and give supportive counseling.

Other common complications and problems include osteodystrophy, neuropathy, hemorrhage, blood clots in and around the cannula, hypertensive and cardiovascular complications, chronic anemia, psychologic and behavioral problems. The rehabilitation counselor must be aware of these problems and be ready to answer questions about them. It is during these times of crisis that the rehabilitation counselor can put his expertise to work. Oftentimes it is this strong supportive counseling that can make a meaningful difference in final rehabilitation.

Throughout this period of time the patient will have questions about his disability. Although the patient's doctors will relate much of this information the rehabilitation counselor must be ready to answer questions about the disability and its future effects. Ebra has found that the rehabilitation counselor is often in a better position to answer questions about the disease than doctors and paramedical staff since patients often withdraw from their doctors and are unable to communicate with them satisfactorily (Ebra, 1972).

As the client's condition (psychological and physical) begins to stabilize, hospital staff will be evaluating him for possible home dialysis. The rehabilitation counselor is often helpful by explaining details of home dialysis and the training that goes with it. The counselor may again be asked to help arrange the financial end of dialysis, as it moves into the home. The patient will have to have an appropriate partner to help him administer dialysis at home. This partner, preferably a family member, will need counseling in order to prepare for the eventual homecoming.

About this time the rehabilitation counselor should be making an assessment of the client's rehabilitation potential. The counselor should consider such things as: will the patient receive dialysis at home or at a neighborhood center? What was his previous job? How much physical activity will a specific vocational objective require? Will he need to be retrained? Does he have any complications? As the counselor answers these questions and lists the client's strengths and weaknesses he should keep in mind some of the general trends that have been observed in rehabilitation renal failure patients. First, the patients that lead the closest to normal lives are those that have had a successful transplantation. These patients are for the most part physically restored and can enter most jobs or training programs. The only employment problem facing transplant patients is that they are predisposed toward disease and infection since they must take considerable amounts of immunosuppressive drugs to combat rejection. A transplant patient should be placed in a job that is not overly taxing physically or a job that would not lower his resistance to the point that he would be dangerously vulnerable to disease and infection.

The patient on dialysis has more serious restrictions placed on his employment. If the client is being dialyzed at the hospital he would need two or three working days a week away from the job since hospital dialysis is done Monday through Friday during the day. If the patient is receiving dialysis at an ambulatory care facility he will still have to schedule work around dialysis. A client on a home dialysis plan usually has the most available time for employment, he can schedule his treatment around his job since he and his partner can administer home dialysis at anytime it fits their schedule. The rehabilitation counselor should remember that oftentimes dialysis patients are anemic which makes physically strenuous jobs very difficult for them. Also these patients should avoid exertion or strain of the cannulated limb. Generally dialysis clients do much better at sedentary or intellectual type tasks rather than labor or physical type jobs. The patients receiving dialysis will have to find an understanding employer who will put up with periodic short term absences from work when the client finds he must be hospitalized for complications.

As stated earlier counseling an end stage renal failure patient is difficult. The rehabilitation counselor needs to know everything about the disability and the client he is counseling. There are many setbacks and frustrations and the rehabilitation process may take a considerably long time. In order to rehabilitate these rather dramatically ill individuals the rehabilitation counselor must develop and utilize truly professional counseling techniques and qualities.

REFERENCES

Beard, Bruce H.: Fear of death and fear of life. *Archives of General Psychiatry,* 21:373-380, 1969.

Brescia, Michael, et al.: Parenteral hyperalimentation. *American Journal of Nursing,* 72:1, 1972.

Burton, Benjamin T.; Krueger, Keatha K., and Bryan, Fred A., Jr.: National registry of long-term dialysis patients. *Journal of the American Medical Association,* 218:718-722, 1971.

Ebra, George, and Toth, John C.: Chronic hemodialysis: some psychological and rehabilitative considerations. *Rehabilitation Literature,* 33:2-10, 1972.

Ebra, George: Rehabilitation counseling considerations in end-stage renal disease. *Journal of Applied Rehabilitation Counseling,* 3:2, 1972.

Kemph, John P.: Renal failure, artificial kidney and kidney transplant. *American Journal of Psychiatry,* 122:1270-1274, 1966.

Klarman, H. E.; Francis, J. O., and Rosentha, G. P.: Cost effectiveness analysis applied to the treatment of chronic renal disease. *Medical Care,* 6:48-50, 1968.

Massachusetts Rehabilitation Commission: *Chronic Hemodialysis and the Vocational Rehabilitation Program.* Third Progress Report, July, 1969.

Medical World News: Hemodialysis for All Who Need It. 12:17:29-36, April 30, 1971.

National Kidney Foundation: *Kidney Transplantation and the Organ Donor Program,* 1971.

National Kidney Foundatin: *The Master Chemists of the Body,* 1964.

Quinton, W. E., et al.: Cannulation of blood vessels for prolonged hemodialysis. *Trans. American Society Artificial Internal Organs,* 6:104, 1960.

Read, M., and Mallison, M.: External Arteriouenous Shunts. *American Journal of Nursing,* 72:1, 1972.

Sapperstien, Michael: Dialysis. *American Journal of Nursing,* 72:1, 1972.

Short, M. J., and Wilson, W. D.: Roles of denial in chronic hemodialysis. *Archives of General Psychiatry, 20*:433-437, 1969.

Smirnow, Virgil, and Colmen, Joseph, G., Ph.D.: *1971 Re-Survey Programs and Services of State Rehabilitation Agencies for Clients With Chronic Kidney Disease,* Virgil Smirnow Associates. Community Health Consultants, Sept., 1971.

University of Alabama in Birmingham: Mogran, Jean M., M.D., Project Director: *Final Report: A Comprehensive Study of the Rehabilitation Process in Patients in a Chronic Dialysis Program,* March, 1971.

Webster's New World Dictionary. Cleveland, World Publishing, 1966.

CHAPTER XIII

PULMONARY DISABILITY

Richard E. Acciavatti

Causes
Symptoms of Respiratory Disease
Chronic Obstructive Ventilatory Disease
Restrictive Ventilatory Defects
General Rehabilitation Considerations
The Pneumoconioses
Testing Pulmonary Function
Definitions of Terms

"I was gasping for air, but there was none to breath, I felt my life pass before me. I was drowning in a sea of air. If I must die, please let me take that last deep breath, I cannot rob my soul from it."

Anom.

Take a deep breath—hold it as long as you can .. . then exhale. If you can feel the satisfaction and relief of breathing deeply you are fortunate. Imagine what it would be like if you were unable to take more than a panting breath or to feel as if you are in a chamber with no air to breathe.

There are over forty million people in the United States who suffer from chronic respiratory disorders. Over two million of these patients must limit their activities and spend up to twelve days a year in bed due to chronic pulmonary conditions (NTRDA, 1969).

Brenda Brown, and Gary Lisak for their help in preparing this chapter.

Body cells require a continuous supply of oxygen and continuous removal of carbon dioxide in order to sustain life. Blood circulates through the lungs and gives up carbon dioxide and takes oxygen which is carried to tissues where the blood gives up oxygen and picks up carbon dioxide. This exchange of gases— oxygen for carbon dioxide—is known as respiration. Interruption of this cycle for more than a few minutes causes irreversible brain damage and even death (PLANS, 1967).

The process of breathing is controlled by the respiratory center of the brain located in the medulla oblongata. The function of the medulla in respiration involves controlling the rate and depth of breathing.

There are three principal parts to the respiratory system: (1) Nasopharynx (nose, throat, larynx); (2) Bronchial tree (trachea, bronchi); (3) Lungs (bronchioles, alveoli).

Causes

Respiratory disorders can be caused by a single factor or a combination of factors.

Causes of pulmonary disease may be classified as intrinsic and/or extrinsic. Intrinsic factors include:

1. Central Nervous System response to an emotional problem causing a bronchial spasm resulting in shortness of breath.
2. Cardiac failure resulting in diminished oxygen in the blood stream and pulmonary edema (flooding of the lungs).
3. Obesity which causes labored breathing with a minimum of activity.
4. Congenital pulmonary abnormalities. In the first twenty-six days after conception certain factors may interfere with lung formation resulting in three different degrees of arrested development which are: (1) Agenesis, a complete absence of one or both lungs; (2) Aplasia, a bronchus which ends in a blind pouch; (3) Hypoplasia, a bronchus which is fully formed but reduced in size (Fraser and Paré, 1970).

Extrinsic factors involve:

1. *Inhalation diseases* due to:
   a. Organic dust or antigens such as pollens, fungus spores

and animal fur. Possible diseases include asthma, farmer's lung, and hen-litter sensitivity.

b. Inorganic dust silicates (asbestos, rock, talc and carbon) causing asbestosis, silicosis, talicosis, and coalworker's pneumoconiosis.

c. Noxious gases and soluable aerosols such as nitrogen oxide, sulfur dioxide, chlorine, and ammonia causing silo-filler's disease and specific chemically related pathology.

d. Aspiration of solid or liquid foreign bodies such as peanuts or other vegetable material, mineral oil, sea water, or foreign matter from the stomach or esophagus. Bronchial obstruction and pneumonia may result from these factors.

2. *Infectious diseases* caused by:

a. Aerobic bacteria (pneumococcus, staphylococcus and streptococcus, hemophilus influenzae, hemophilus pertussis) causing pneumonia, influenza and whooping cough.

b. Anaerobic organisms (bacteroides and spirochetes) causing pneumonia, gingivitis, pharyngitis.

c. Mycobacteria. The major disease produced by pathogen is tuberculosis.

d. Mycotic infections (fungus) include histoplasmosis, coccidiomycosis and candidiasis (Moniliasis).

e. Viruses which cause coryza (the common cold), influenza, ornithosis (Psittacosis), measles and Herpes virus respiratory infection.

f. Protozoan, Metazoan and Arthropod infestation demonstrated as Amebiasis, Toxoplasmosis, Round, Flat Tongue and Hookworm disease.

3. *Residuals of Trauma and Infection*

a. Residuals of an injury to the neck and chest causing pleurisy and/or other pulmonary difficulties.

b. Residuals from an acute infection or prolonged exposure to noxious elements resulting in a chronic infection or irritation of the respiratory tract.

There are numerous diseases of the lung of unknown origin. Sarcoidosis, Diffuse idiopathic pulmonary fibrosis and Hyaline-membrane disease are included in this category (Fraser and Paré, 1970).

The Respiratory System

This chart of the RESPIRATORY SYSTEM shows the apparatus for breathing. Breathing is the process by which oxygen in the air is brought into the lungs and into close contact with the blood, which absorbs it and carries it to all parts of the body. At the same time the blood gives up waste matter (carbon dioxide), which is carried out of the lungs with the air breathed out.

1. The SINUSES (Frontal, Maxillary, and Sphenoidal) are hollow spaces in the bones of the head. Small openings connect them to the nasal cavity. The functions they serve are not clearly understood, but include helping to regulate the temperature and humidity of air breathed in, as well as to lighten the bone structure of the head and to give resonance to the voice.

2. The NASAL CAVITY (nose) is the preferred entrance for outside air into the Respiratory System. The hairs that line the inside wall are part of the air-cleansing system.

3. Air also enters through the ORAL CAVITY (mouth), especially in people who have a mouth-breathing habit or whose nasal passages may be temporarily obstructed, as by a cold.

4. The ADENOIDS are overgrown lymph tissue at the top of the throat. When they interfere with breathing, they are generally removed. The lymph system, consisting of nodes (knots of cells) and connecting vessels, carries fluid throughout the body. This system helps to resist body infection by filtering out foreign matter, including germs, and producing cells (lymphocytes) to fight them.

5. The TONSILS are lymph nodes in the wall of the pharynx that often become infected. They are an unimportant part of the germ-fighting system of the body. When infected, they are generally removed.

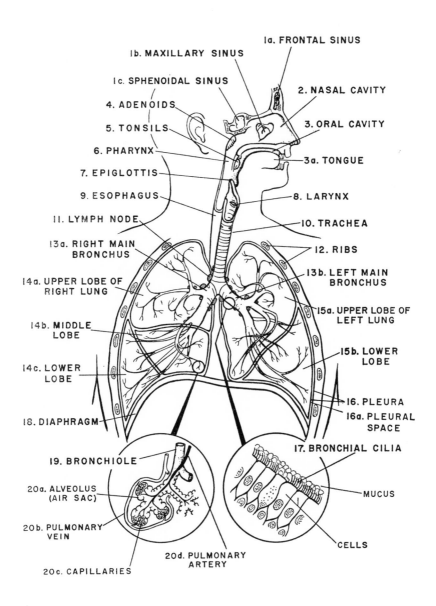

1a. FRONTAL SINUS

1b. MAXILLARY SINUS

1c. SPHENOIDAL SINUS

2. NASAL CAVITY

4. ADENOIDS

5. TONSILS

3. ORAL CAVITY

6. PHARYNX

3a. TONGUE

7. EPIGLOTTIS

9. ESOPHAGUS

8. LARYNX

11. LYMPH NODE

10. TRACHEA

13a. RIGHT MAIN BRONCHUS

12. RIBS

14a. UPPER LOBE OF RIGHT LUNG

13b. LEFT MAIN BRONCHUS

15a. UPPER LOBE OF LEFT LUNG

14b. MIDDLE LOBE

15b. LOWER LOBE

14c. LOWER LOBE

18. DIAPHRAGM

16. PLEURA

16a. PLEURAL SPACE

17. BRONCHIAL CILIA

19. BRONCHIOLE

20a. ALVEOLUS (AIR SAC)

MUCUS

20b. PULMONARY VEIN

20c. CAPILLARIES

20d. PULMONARY ARTERY

CELLS

6. The PHARYNX (throat) collects incoming air from the nose and mouth and passes it downward to the trachea (windpipe).

7. The EPIGLOTTIS is a flap of tissue that guards the entrance to the trachea, closing when anything is swallowed that should go into the esophagus and stomach.

8. The LARYNX (voice box) contains the vocal cords. It is the place where moving air being breathed in and out creates voice sounds.

9. The ESOPHAGUS is the passage leading from mouth and throat to the stomach.

10. The TRACHEA (windpipe) is the passage leading from the pharynx to the lungs.

11. The LYMPH NODES of the lungs are found against the walls of the bronchial tubes and trachea.

12. The RIBS are bones supporting and protecting the chest cavity. They move to a limited degree, helping the lungs to expand and contract.

13. The trachea divides into the two main BRONCHI (tubes), one for each lung, which subdivide into the lobar bronchi—three on the right and two on the left. These, in turn, subdivide further.

14. The right lung is divided into three LOBES, or sections. Each lobe is like a balloon filled with sponge-like lung tissue. Air moves in and out through one opening—a branch of the bronchus.

15. The left lung is divided into two LOBES.

16. The PLEURA are the two membranes, actually one continuous one folded on itself, that surround each lobe of the lungs and separate the lungs from the chest wall.

17. The bronchial tubes are lined with CILIA (like very small hairs) that have a wave-like motion. This motion carries MUCUS (sticky phlegm or liquid) upward and out into the throat, where it is either coughed up or swallowed. The mucus catches and holds much of the dust, germs, and other unwanted matter that has invaded the lungs and thus gets rid of it.

18. The DIAPHRAGM is the strong wall of muscle that

separates the chest cavity from the abdominal cavity. By moving downward, it creates suction to draw in air and expand the lungs.

19. The smallest subdivisions of the bronchi are called BRON-CHIOLES, at the end of which are the alveoli (plural of alveolus).

20. The ALVEOLI are the very small air sacs that are the destination of air breathed in. The CAPILLARIES are blood vessels that are imbedded in the walls of the alveoli. Blood passes through the capillaries, brought to them by the PULMONARY ARTERY and taken away by the PULMONARY VEIN. While in the capillaries the blood discharges carbon dioxide into the alveoli and takes up oxygen from the air in the alveoli. (American Lung Association, 1973.)

Diagnosis of Respiratory Disease

The process of diagnosing respiratory disorders involves precise history taking, x-rays and laboratory testing, and physical examination. Specific details of the patient's complaints are necessary. For example, if shortness of breath is reported, it is necessary to know whether it was sudden or gradual; how severe and under what conditions, such as walking slowly, rapidly, at rest, and at what time during the day.

Past illnesses, occupational history, personal habits, area of residence and travels are additional components that are to be considered in the clinical history.

Symptoms of Respiratory Disease

Cough and Expectoration

One of the characteristic symptoms of respiratory disease is coughing. Coughing is essentially a defense mechanism of the body which clears the airways of mucus and foreign material.

Cough may be classified as dry or productive. A dry cough may develop as a result of a virus infection of the respiratory tracts, nervous habit, or smoking cigarettes. A dry, irritating cough may also be an early symptom of left-sided heart failure which is manifested by pulmonary vascular engorgement. A large number of people with chronic cough complain that it is worse when they lie down at night.

Hoarseness

If this symptom occurs in conjunction with symptoms of infection of the upper respiratory tract, it may be considered to be a viral laryngitis. However, if symptoms persist, the patient should have an examination of the vocal cords to rule out a neoplasm or other pathology.

Shortness of Breath

The symptom of dyspnea or awareness of difficult breathing is due to an increase in the stiffness of the lung, in airway resistance, in exercise ventilation or a combination of these symptoms.

An account of the type of sensation experienced and the circumstances resulting in shortness of breath are of diagnostic importance. These accounts may range from an anxious patient having difficulty breathing because of *nervousness,* the patient with emphysema who has difficulty tying his shoelaces, to an athlete running the 100 yard dash.

There are basically two types of dyspnea: functional (psychoneurotic) or organic. The functional type, related to tension and anxiety, is said to occur in 10 percent of patients attending offices of specialists in internal medicine. Functional shortness of breath is usually described as an inability to take a deep breath or to get air *down to the bottom of the lungs.*

In organic dyspnea, the sensation is more difficult to describe. The patient may say he is *short-winded* or that he *puffs.* Patients who complain of shortness of breath while at rest and not on exercise, with few exceptions, have functional dyspnea. Inability to lie flat due to a feeling of suffocation or waking during the night with shortness of breath, suggests the presence of organic disease (Fraser and Paré, 1970).

Chest Pain

Lung tissue lacks sensory mechanisms which signal pain. Therefore, advanced disease or death can result from conditions involving the lung tissue without any amount of chest pain.

However, the pleura is supplied with sensory nerves. Pleural pain usually suggests inflammatory or malignant disease.

Mediastinal pain may suggest disorders of the trachea, esophagus, pericardium, arota, thymus gland, and lymph nodes since they are located in this area.

Chest-wall pain usually results in local pain and tenderness associated with infection of the upper respiratory tract, and a dry cough. This pain can be differentiated from pleural pain since it increases little or not at all during deep inspiration but may be aggravated by coughing.

Hemoptysis

The expectoration of blood may arise from hemorrhage of the larynx, trachea, bronchi, or lungs. Patients require a chest x-ray and extensive investigation to determine the cause of the hemoptysis (Fraser and Paré, 1970).

Chronic Obstructive Ventilatory Disease

The three major disorders or expiratory airflow obstruction are: (1) Bronchial Asthma; (2) Chronic Bronchitis; and (3) Diffuse Obstructive Pulmonary Emphysema.

In 1970, these disorders accounted for more than 30,000 deaths in the United States.

Emphysema was second to arteriosclerotic heart disease, as the most frequent disorder, for which workers were awarded disability allowances by the Social Security Administration in 1967 (Oregon Thoracic Society, 1972).

The implications for rehabilitation of patients with chronic obstructive ventilatory disease was pointed out by Cohen (1966) in his study of one hundred nineteen patients, 94 men and 25 women, ages 29 to 65 years, referred for examination for social security disability determination because of expiratory airflow disorders. Of this group, thirty-three patients (27.7%) had re-recived no therapy. Only eleven patients (9.2%) had had prior lung function testing. Ninety-seven patients (81.4%) received no therapy or only a single treatment item such as an antibiotic. Cohen concludes that the appraisal of this group of patients suggests defects in measuring the amount of pulmonary function and the application of therapeutic measures readily available. The major impact of Cohen's study for the rehabilitation counselor is his caution that no patient with obstructive ventilation disease should be considered irretrievably disabled before he is afforded the opportunity of an intensive and aggressive treatment program guided by simple ventilation function estimates. (See definition of pulmonary function tests.)

Restrictive Ventilatory Defects

Diseases causing restrictive ventilatory defects are characterized by a significant reduction in the volume of air that can be expelled following full inspiration. This problem is attributed to: (1) decrease in the strength of muscles involved in the respiratory process; (2) scar tissue or fluid outside and inside the lungs; and (3) loss of a portion or total lung.

Diseases and conditions that produce a decrease in the volume of the thorax involve the limitation of rib or diaphragm movement.

A few examples of diseases causing restrictive ventilatory defects are: (1) poliomyelitis; (2) trauma to the cervical spine causing paralysis of all four limbs (quadraplegia) or partial or incomplete paralysis of the limbs (quadriparesis); (3) multiple sclerosis; (4) muscular dystrophy; and (5) certain types of decompensated heart disease.

Non-disease conditions also cause restrictive ventilatory problems. They are pregnancy and massive obesity (Myers, 1965).

General Rehabilitation Considerations

The process of rehabilitation of the patient with any pulmonary disability begins at the time of diagnosis of the condition. When the medical technical aspects have been defined, the patient is to be considered in all dimensions related to his life in the treatment process. Major considerations are:

1. Reaction to the diagnosed condition.
2. Understanding of the disorder in terms of degree or severity of the illness, types of treatment, possible length of illness, and prognosis.
3. The psychological reaction at the feeling or emotional

level, acceptance or denial of the condition and methods of coping with the problem.

4. The effects of the condition in the personal, social, vocational, or occupational and other areas of the patient's life.

The vocational rehabilitation aspects of pulmonary disorders cannot be dealt with in a specific manner which would suggest particular vocational or job objectives for the various types of pulmonary disabilities. A general rule of thumb would be to evaluate each person on an individual basis, regardless of the disease and determine the retrieved functioning capacity which can be utilized to the maximum without jeopardizing the normal course of treatment, and/or cure, arrestation, and maximum restoration of the pulmonary condition.

Bronchial Asthma

Asthma is a condition characterized by shortness of breath and wheezing. This is due to the contraction of the muscle fibers around the bronchial tubes which narrows these airways. *Extrinsic asthma* is caused by allergic reactions to external factors such as pollens, molds, and dust. *Intrinsic asthma* is precipitated by infection in the upper or lower respiratory tract. Asthma is usually found in individuals with an inherited allergic constitution. Emotional stress may also contribute to the onset of an asthmatic attack.

1. Signs and Symptoms

Asthma may develop gradually as a residual of bronchitis or occurs suddenly after exposure to an allergen. Major characteristics are:

    a. Shortness of breath (dyspnea)
    b. Wheezing and coughing
    c. Sense of tightness in the chest
    d. Bluish tint to the skin (cyanosis)
    e. Sensation of asphyxiation
    f. Bronchial constriction and swelling of the mucous membrane

2. Diagnosis

The diagnostic work-up should include:

a. A complete medical history emphasizing family allergies
b. Patient's chief complaints and descriptions of them
c. Chest X-rays (to rule out other causes of bronchial obstruction)
d. Pulmonary function tests and routine laboratory examinations of sputum, blood and urine
e. Bronchoscopy (not routinely done)
f. Tests for sensitivity to allergens
3. Treatment
Treatment modes involve the following:
a. Symptomatic treatment of the acute attack:
   1. Epinephrine or ephedrine
   2. Aminophylline or Oxtriphylline
   3. Adrenocortical steroids
   4. Sedatives and tranquillizers
   5. Oxygen inhalation
   6. Aerosol inhalation
b. Treatment due to extrinsic allergens:

Major factors involved in this process are: 1) avoidance of offending allergens; 2) hyposensitization for specific agents causing asthma.

c. Treatment of infective asthma:

This includes antibiotics in combination with other drugs to reduce the accompanying symptoms (Holvey *et al.*, 1972).

4. Counseling Considerations
Control and management of the condition are main factors to be sought in the total treatment process. These include:

a. Avoidance of specific allergens causing the symptoms of asthma. This could involve a special diet, plastic mattress and pillow covers, removal of rugs from bedroom or home, replacement of wool clothing and blankets with cotton and synthetic material, chemical treatment of the home to reduce bacteria and fungi in the air, avoidance of pets such as dogs, cats and birds, avoidance of tobacco smoke, and chemical fumes.
   Avoidance of offending allergens and other condi-

tions producing asthmatic attacks appears to be the optimum in treatment for the patient. However, it is not possible to control all aspects of the individual's environment and supportive treatment modes must be used.

b. Hyposensitization involving periodic injections of the asthma-producing allergens in graded concentrations is required in order to produce the best possible immunization level for the patient.

c. Reduction in anxiety and other psychological components which produce or magnify an asthmatic attack. Supportive counseling could focus on helping the patient understand the limitations of his disability and to develop confidence in his ability to function in the environment. Geographical relocation to another climate requires careful study and should not be considered solely on the basis that relief of symptoms are eminent.

Chronic Bronchitis

A long standing disease of the tracheobronchial tree which is characterized by excessive mucous secretion typified by a chronic or recurrent, productive cough is known as bronchitis. Some causative factors include bacterial infection, inadequate bronchial drainage, surrounding pulmonary fibrosis or infection, all pollution, and smoking.

There is a significant correlation between the occurrence of chronic bronchitis and pulmonary ephysema. Bronchitis can predispose a patient to emphysema if symptoms persist and remain untreated (Holvey, *et al.*, 1972).

Pulmonary Emphysema

Emphysema is a disease characterized by enlargement or over-inflation of the lungs with destructive changes in the alveolar walls.

Major factors contributing to the obstruction of air flow are the loss of elasticity of the air sacs, stretched and/or ruptured alveolar walls causing air sacs of varying sizes (blebs or bullae), and reduced blood vessels.

The incidence of emphysema in men is ten times greater than in women. It usually occurs in males over forty-five years old. Cigarette smoking, air pollution, and infection are believed to contribute to the development of emphysema (Fraser and Paré, 1970). In addition, another important factor to consider is the occupation of patients with this disease.

1. Signs and Symptoms

This disease is gradually progressive. Patients report a history of chronic cough and wheezing.

The chief symptom is shortness of breath. It can progress to a point where it is difficult to breathe while at rest. Fatigue and irritability are also noted.

2. Treatment

The main thrust of treatment usually focuses on relieving the symptoms and protecting the individual from pulmonary infection.

Bronchodilator aerosols, expectorants, postural drainage and intermittent positive-breathing machines are used singly or in combination to relieve the symptoms of emphysema. Antibiotics are usually administered initially upon diagnosis or maintained as a prophylactic measure to retard the progress of the disease. In selected cases, surgical resection may be indicated.

2. Counseling Considerations

The patient's stage of emphysema may not warrant occupational change or decreased activity. On the other hand, severe disability could necessitate complete bed rest. Selected job placement or modifications are usually difficult due to age and other factors which are attributed to the effects of the disease. Personal and family counseling may focus mainly on reactions to the illness and evaluating coping mechanisms in order to help all individuals maintain optimal daily life activities.

Bronchiectasis

This is a disease of the bronchi which causes the bronchial passageways to become dilated into cylindrical, saccular or cystic forms due to inflammation and ulceration. It can be congenital or acquired.

1. Signs and Symptoms

It is believed that a bronchial obstruction, accompanied by infection is necessary to produce bronchiectasis. Since the advent of antibiotics, there is much less bronchiectasis than formerly. Coughing and profuse expectoration are the chief symptoms. There also may be clubbing of the fingertips and blood in the sputum.

2. Treatment

Treatment includes administration of antibiotics, postural drainage (patient assumes a position permitting drainage from the bronchi), and in selected cases, removal of the lobes or segments of the lung.

3. Counseling Considerations

One of the major problems faced by the patient is the chronic cough which may interfere with his being accepted in a social and employment situation where there is interaction with people (NTRDA, 1969).

Pulmonary Neoplasms

A pulmonary neoplasm is a new growth of tissue which appears in the form of a tumor or growth in the bronchi or lungs. It may be *malignant* or *benign, primary* or *secondary.*

Primary malignant tumors (carcinoma, also known as lung cancer) is more common in men between the ages forty and seventy. It is four to ten times more common in cigarette smokers than non-smokers. From a statistical standpoint, the risk increases in proportion to the number of cigarettes smoked (Fraser and Paré, 1970). Air pollution is also another contributing cause to lung cancer.

Secondary pulmonary carcinoma result from a tumor in other organs which spreads to the lungs through the bloodstream or lymphatic system (metastasis).

1. Signs and Symptoms

   a. The most common complaint is a chronic cough, but may be indicative of a variety of respiratory disorders, making carcinoma difficult to detect.

   b. Scanty and mucoid sputum is another symptom, but—

Severe Disabilities

may or may not be caused by the presence of a neoplasm.

c. Chest pain in the region above or surrounding the affected area occurs in the later stages of cancer. The interior lung areas are not sensitive to consciously felt pain. However, the pleural walls around the lungs are, and neoplasms affect this particular area.

2. Diagnosis

Diagnosis is mainly determined by x-ray techniques. Clinical symptoms are general and similar to other pulmonary conditions, as mentioned earlier. Sputum samples are included in the laboratory tests.

3. Treatment

Surgical removal is the treatment of choice. Other modes of treatment are radiotherapy and chemotherapy which may be used in combination with surgical procedures.

If the disease is diagnosed early, the probability of it becoming terminal is not as great. This indicates the need for regular medical examinations to detect cancer before symptoms occur.

One important area of counseling currently being explored deals with helping the terminal patient and the family adjust and accept the reality of impending death.

The Pneumoconioses

Pneumoconiosis is a general term referring to a pulmonary abnormality resulting from the inhalation of dust particles.

1. Silicosis

This condition is due to inhalation of crystalline free silica (quartz) dust which forms fibrous nodules throughout the lungs. In advanced stages there is marked impairment of respiratory function. Silicosis does not usually cause symptoms of impaired lung functioning until it is advanced or complicated with tuberculosis. Less than 10 percent of patients with this disease ever become sufficiently disabled to require therapy (Holvey, *et al.*, 1972).

a. Signs and Symptoms

The disease may progress for a period of time after

the individual is removed from the silica-producing environment. In uncomplicated silicosis, shortness of breath may be the only symptom and becomes more severe as the condition progresses. In more advanced cases, there are signs of disturbed sleep, loss of appetite, chest pains, hoarseness, bluish tint to the skin (cyanosis), blood in sputum, physical uneasiness, and general discomfort.

Complications of this disease can result in a tendency to develop other pulmonary infections. Two of these that present difficulties are tuberculosis and bronchopneumonia.

b. Diagnosis

A detailed occupational history, chest x-ray findings, ventilatory studies, and a complete physical examination are necessary to arrive at a diagnosis. Silicosis must be differentiated from other disorders resulting in similar x-ray findings. This is accomplished by a careful evaluation of clinical signs and symptoms, as well as occupational history.

c. Treatment

Depending on the severity of the disease, treatment may necessitate alterations in environmental conditions at the site of employment. If the degree of severity is mild or moderate, removal of the individual from work environment may not be required. Bronchodilator medication and use of intermittent positive pressure breathing machines (IPPB) may also relieve symptoms.

d. Special Legislation

Although modern technology has reduced immeasurably the risk of occupational silicosis, the number of victims of this condition was sufficient to justify legislation to aid individuals who are disabled as a result of silicosis. The most recent law is the *Black Lung Benefit Program* which was established by Title IV of the Federal Coal Mine Health and Safety Act of 1969 (Public Law 91-173). Specific information on this program can be obtained from local offices of the Social Security Administration.

2. Siderosis

Cause: inhalation of fumes or dust containing iron particles. Condition is not usually serious and is also known as arc welder's disease.

3. Anthracosis
   Cause: inhalation of soot or carbon smoke having no free silica content. Found in city dwellers.
4. Coal Miner's Pneumoconiosis
   Cause: inhalation of coal dust
5. Silicatoses
   Cause: salts of silica acid involving four silicates: asbestos, talc, kaolin (china-clay), and mica.
6. Byssinosis
   Cause: cotton dust inhalation
7. Bagassosis
   Cause: inhalation of cane fiber dust (after extracting sugar)
8. Berylliosis
   Cause: inhalation of fumes or dust containing beryllium compounds.
9. Sarcoidosis
   Cause: granular tumors or growths of unknown origin present in the lungs and other organs of the body.
10. Farmer's Lung
    Cause: a sensitivity response to fungal spores in moldy hay.
11. Maple Bark Disease
    Cause: a sensitivity reaction to fungal spores.
    (Holvey, *et al.*, 1972).

Pulmonary Tuberculosis

A chronic or acute communicable disease commonly characterized by lung inflammation, causing infiltrations, tubercle formation, caseation, fibrosis and calcification is known as tuberculosis.

There are three types of Mycobacteria which cause this disease. *Mycobacterium tuberculosis* is responsible for ninety-five to ninety-nine percent of the pulmonary mycobacterial infections. *Mycobacterium bovis,* formerly a common cause for tuberculosis of the bones, of the gastrointestinal tract, and other tissues of the body, has nearly been eradicated in the United

States due to control of disease in cattle and the pasteurization of milk. *Mycobacterium avium,* also a rare pathogen, is found in birds and swine.

The disease is contracted mainly by inhalation of the tubercle bacilli which deposits in the bronchi and/or lungs; multiplies, and infects the surrounding tissue. During the primary phase of infection, no symptoms may be exhibited. The body defenses tend to arrest the progress of tuberculosis, leaving small areas of fibrosis or calcification. However, the disease progresses if this initial healing does not take place due to a number of factors including low body resistance, inadequate health status, or virility of the bacilli.

As the disease progresses, symptoms are noted and the areas of lung infiltration may be localized in small areas or spread throughout the lungs. The infected tissue area breaks down and the exudate is expectorated or diffused in the pulmonary system. This causes the sputum to be contaminated with the tubercle bacilli.

Reaction of the body to the tubercle bacilli depends on the natural immunity of the individual. The body will be more sensitive to the bacteria if there was no prior exposure.

1. Signs and Symptoms

The primary phase is usually asymptomatic, but fever and weight loss may occur. Results of x-rays may or may not indicate signs of the illness.

The progressive phase involves fatigue, unexplained weight loss, loss of appetite, low grade fever, sweating (especially at night), and a general feeling of being *"washed out."* In later stages of development, a morning cough may be noted and frequently becomes more severe, leaving the patient exhausted. Sputum is often green, yellow and mucoid in character, sometimes characterized by blood streaking. A massive hemorrhage may occur in some cases. Patients sometimes report chest pain, shortness of breath and hoarseness.

2. Diagnosis

Diagnosis involves chest x-rays, laboratory tests (smear, culture, and guinea pig inoculation of sputum). Other body fluids and tissues removed by biopsy are examined in selected cases. Blood and urine analyses show changes in advanced stages, indicated by a moderate leukocytosis in the blood and albumin in the urine. (For classifications of tuberculosis, see page 276).

A reaction to the tuberculin tests indicates the presence of a tuberculous infection. However, it does not indicate whether the lesion is active or inactive. The Mantoux (Intradermal) test is widely used. The Vollmer patch test is considered to be less reliable and accurate. The Heaf and Tine tests are considered to be accurate tests for screening (Holvey, et al., 1972).

3. Treatment

Treatment modes have changed considerably with more sophisticated use of combinations of anti-tuberculosis drugs. Almost all initial treatment patients who receive a well balanced chemotherapy program rapidly becomes noninfectious and arrestation of the disease should be achieved in at least ninety-five percent of active cases. Rest therapy or surgical resection for pulmonary tuberculosis is required very infrequently in the initial treatment (NTRDA, 1970).

Various drugs used for treatment of tuberculosis are: isoniazid (INH); streptomycin (SM); p-aminosalicylic acid (PAS); dihydrostreptomycin (DHSM); pyrazinamide (PZA); cycloserine; viomycin; ethionamide; rifampin (Holvey et al., 1972).

The current practice in treating tuberculosis is to provide services to patients on an out-patient basis. In-patient care is considered for the symptomatically ill, those with other major diseases, those who need a thorough diagnostic work-up, those who require close monitoring of chemotherapy programs, and patients who have acid-fast bacilli present in their sputum. Recent emphasis is upon the establishment of tuberculosis treatment centers in general hospitals.

Vaccination against tuberculosis is rarely used in the United States. The vaccine is BCG (Bacillus Calmette-Guerin). This method of preventing tuberculosis is a controversial topic. Another subsidiary problem is the development of strains of acid-fast bacilli that resist some of the first-line drugs such as

INH, PAS, and SM. As a result, combinations of other drugs are used with occasional surgical intervention to inactivate the disease.

4. Counseling Considerations

The patient's acceptance and attitude toward the diagnosis determines whether cooperation will be sufficient to effect a successful treatment program. This appears to be more crucial today because of the emphasis on out-patient treatment. This minimizes the monitoring or enforcing of a regularly prescribed dosage of medication.

There are less restrictions on activities of daily living as well as occupational change for the tuberculosis patient. With selected exceptions, individuals can be encouraged to return to their usual activities and occupations after symptoms have subsided.

The fear of relapse is a justifiable response from the patient. This may require special attention in counseling.

The author has conducted research to determine whether the histories of re-admitted tuberculosis patients during the interval between hospital discharge and re-admission were consistent with assumptions of professionals concerning factors related to relapse.

In the investigation of the assumptions, certain factors were found to be related to tuberculosis relapse. These factors were: inadequate diet; incomplete treatment due to leaving the hospital against medical advice; lack of follow-up treatment for non-tuberculosis medical conditions; de-socialization tendencies; and lack of constructive use of leisure time.

Other factors that were not found to be significantly related to relapse were: failure to take antituberculosis drugs; absence and tardiness in meeting clinic appointments; excessive use of tobacco products and alcoholic beverages; unsuccessful work experiences and hazard working conditions; and serious problems with spouse and other members of the household.

Although the study was limited to one of four tuberculosis hospitals in the state of Pennsylvania, the implications for counseling may warrant mention at this time.

The frequency and clustering of factors apparently related to relapse seem to indicate the following areas as foci for attention:

1. Dietary Patterns
   —to help patients obtain more knowledge about the importance of maintaining proper dietary habits.
2. Complete Hospital Treatment
   —if hospitalization is necessary, patients should be given supportive services which include personal and family counseling.
3. Diseases Complicating Tuberculosis Condition
   —to utilize all resources to insure that the patient obtains medical treatment for complicating diseases.
4. Amount of Physical Activity
   —to assure patients an interpretation of the limits (if any) recommended by their physicians and to evaluate possible detrimental physical and environmental factors in their occupations, if applicable.

Strenuous or sustained carrying, pushing, pulling, and working at night were considered to be possible contributors to relapse.

Social adjustment and use of leisure time are also areas that should not be overlooked by the counselor in his work with the tuberculosis patient (Acciavatti, 1962).

The fear of contamination by the patient, family and the public is far greater than the actual infectiousness of the disease. The counselor is in a position to provide information to all concerned so that this stigma will be minimized, enabling the patient and his family to reduce their emotional reactions to the illness.

Tuberculosis Facts in the United States

1. From information in case registers the Public Health Service estimates *known tuberculosis cases under current supervision* as follows:

	Total Cases	On Drug Therapy
Cases in health department TB registers Dec. 31, 1971	260,000	118,000
Active disease cases	44,000	38,000
Hospitalized	13,000	13,000
Unhospitalized	31,000	25,000
All other cases	216,000	80,000

2. Between 1971 and 1972 the new active tuberculosis case rate declined 8 percent; the provisional death rate increased about 5 percent.

Year	New Active Cases of Tuberculosis		Deaths from Tuberculosis	
	Number	Rate Per 100,000	Number	Rate Per 100,000
1972	32,932*	15.8*	4,550*	2.2*
1971	35,217	17.1	4,380*	2.1*
1970	37,137	18.3	5,560*	2.7*
1969	39,120	19.4	5,567	2.8
1968	42,623	21.3	6,292	3.1

*Provisional data.

3. New active case rates per 100,000 population, by age: 1971 and 1961.

Year	All Ages	0-4	5-14	15-24	25-44	45-64	65 and Over
1971	17.1	8.8	3.8	8.3	19.5	28.9	35.7
1961	29.4	11.8	6.6	18.5	34.7	48.3	60.4

4. An estimated 3,000 relapses occur each year.
5. Four out of five new active cases reported in 1971 were contributed by persons 25 years of age or older.
   Three out of five new active cases were found among men. Negroes and other races had a case rate four and a half times that for whites.
6. A total of 1,375 persons whose death certificates listed active tuberculosis as a primary or contributing cause of death in 1971 had never been reported as cases of tuberculosis. This was nearly five percent of all newly reported active cases.
7. Cities of 250,000 or more population accounted for 38 percent of the 32,932 new active cases reported in 1972.
8. There are about 16 million tuberculin reactors in the United States, approximately eight percent of the total population.
9. The Public Health Service estimates that expenditures for the prevention and control of tuberculosis are estimated to be $250 million a year. Income lost due to illllness is estimated at $55 million annually. (American Lung Association, 1973.)

Testing Pulmonary Function

Simple physical tests can be of much help. Asking the patient to breathe deeply in and out can reveal some measure of his ability to move air with his lungs. A second simple test is the Snider Match Test. The patient is asked to blow a lighted match out at a distance six inches away from his open mouth. A normal individual can blow the match out at nine inches; the one with obstructive pulmonary disease is unable to accomplish this at six inches and often as close as three inches.

More sophisticated measurements are made with a spirometer, a machine which records certain significant functions of the lung. Measurements are made as follows:

> Vital Capacity (VC) which is the maximum volume expired after the deepest inspiration.
> Forced Vital Capacity (FVC), the vital capacity performed as rapidly as possible. This is measured by time segments such as ½, 1, 2, and 3 second intervals.
> Maximal Voluntary Ventilation (MVV), the largest volume of air which can be breathed in a specfiic period of time.

These measurements are useful to determine the presence or absence of pulmonary insufficiency, the extent of disability and the type of pulmonary insufficiency, i.e. obstructive or restrictive (Lev, 1973).

Definitions of Terms[1]

A. *Diagnostic Terms:*

Lungs

1. abscess of lung—a localized area of suppuration in the lung with or without cavitation. It is accompanied by necrosis of tissue.
2. anthracosis—a disease of the lungs caused by the prolonged inhalation of fine particles of coal dust.
3. aplasia of lung—incomplete development of the lung.

---

[1] Frenay, Sister Agnes Clare, *Understanding Medical Terminology,* The Catholic Hospital Association, St. Louis, Missouri, 1969, pp. 105-112. (Reproduced with permission of publisher.)

4. asbestosis—occupational disease due to protracted inhalation of asbestos particles.
5. atelectasis—a functionless, airless lung or portion of a lung.
6. blast injury—internal trauma of lungs, ears, and intestines due to high pressure waves following explosion. It may result in extreme bradycardia, severe cyanosis, dyspnea, hemorrhage and deafness.
7. carcinoma of the lung, primary, secondary or metastatic—malignant new growth and the most important of the neoplastic diseases of the lung.
8. cystic disease of the lungs—condition characterized by the presence of air or fluid containing spaces within the lung. Most cystic lesions are secondary to obstructive emphysema, partial bronchial obstruction and tuberculous infection.
   Air cysts may enlarge tremendously and form tension cysts due to the development of a check-valve mechanism in the draining bronchus. Solitary cysts occasionally balloon to such a large size that they dislocate the mediastinal structures and produce dyspnea and cyanosis. Rupture of the cyst leading to pneumothorax is not infrequent.
9. histoplasmosis—fungus disease caused by Histoplasma capsulatum; sometimes associated with calcified pulmonary lesions.
10. pneumoconiosis—a disease of the lungs due to injury by dust from any source.
11. pneumonia—inflammation of the lungs with exudation into lung tissue and consolidation. Predominant etiological agents are pneumococci and mycoplasmas or pleuropneumonia-like organisms (PPLO). Many other bacteria may cause pneumonia.
    a. bronchopneumonia—inflammation of bronchioli and air vesicles with scattered areas of consolidation.
    b. lobar pneumonia—acute inflammation of one or more lobes of the lung or lungs.
    c. primary atypical pneumonia—infection due to Mycoplasma pneumoniae varying from mild to fatal disease.
    Etiology of pneumonia: the pneumococcus is generally the

source of the infection, but sometimes respiratory viruses and tubercle bacilli cause the disease and, rarely, streptocci and staphylococci are the etiological bacteria.

12. pneumonitis—inflammation of the lung—a virus form of pneumonia.

13. pneumonocele, pneumocele—a pulmonary hernia.

14. pulmonary edema—excess of intraalveolar and intrabronchial fluid in the lungs inducing cough and dyspnea; common in left heart failure.

15. pulmonary embolism—lodgment of a clot or foreign substance in a pulmonary arterial vessel cutting off the circulation.

16. pulmonary or vesicular emphysema—overdistention of alveoli and smaller bronchial tubes with air.

17. pulmonary hypertension—condition due to increased pressure in the pulmonary artery resulting from obstruction by pulmonary embolism or thrombosis, tuberculosis, emphysema or pulmonary fibrosis.

18. pulmonary infarction—necrosis of functional lung tissue (parenchyma) due to loss of blood supply usually caused by embolism.

19. pulmonary thrombosis—clot formation in any pulmonary blood vessel resulting in circulatory obstruction.

20. pulmonary tuberculosis, phthisis—a specific inflammatory disease of the lungs caused by tubercle bacillus and characterized anatomically by a cellular infiltration which subsequently caseates, softens, and leads to ulceration of lung tissue; manifested clinically by wasting, exhaustion, fever and cough.

   a. classification according to extent of lesions:[1]

     (1) minimal—the lesions are of moderate density without cavitation and either limited to one lung or affecting both lungs. The total extent of these tuberculous infiltrations, regardless of their distribution, does not exceed the equivalent of lung

---

[1] For classification of tuberculosis according to activity status see *Diagnostic Standards and Classification of Tuberculosis*, 12th ed. New York, National Tuberculosis Association, 1969.

tissue which lies above the level of the second rib.

(2) moderately advanced—either unilateral or bilateral lung involvement is present. The extent of the lesions is limited to

    (a) the dissemination of infiltrates throughout one lung, or its equivalent in both lungs.

    (b) confluent, dense infiltrations which do not exceed one-third of the volume of one lung.

    (c) cavitation less than 4 cm in diameter.

(3) far advanced—lesions are more extensive, dense and confluent and cavitation exceeds 4 cm in diameter.

  b. some forms of tuberculosis:

    (1) endobronchial tuberculosis—implantation of tubercle bacilli in the bronchial mucosa followed by the development of irregular necrotic ulcers or by extensive fibrosis with a gradual occlusion of the bronchial lumen.

    (2) fibrocaseous, fibroulcerative—form characterized by reparative fibrous and destructive caseous elements representing the two extremes in the way of the healing and progression—the most frequent form of tuberculosis in the ages of 20 to 40.

    (3) miliary—symmetrical distribution of minute tubercles in both lungs—generally hematogenous in origin. Seeding elsewhere may occur resulting in dissemination of tubercles in various organs.

21. silicosis—occupational disease due to inhalation of silica dust usually over a period of ten years or more.

Bronchi

22. aplasia of bronchus—undeveloped bronchus.

23. bronchiectasis—dilation of a bronchus or bronchi, secreting large amounts of offensive pus.

24. bronchiectatic—pertaining to bronchiectasis.

25. bronchitis—inflammation of the bronchial mucous membrane; endobronchial tuberculosis or tuberculous bronchitis due to tubercle bacillus.

26. bronchogenic, bronchiogenic—originating in a bronchus; for example, bronchogenic carcinoma—lung cancer having its origin in a bronchus.
27. bronchopleural fistula—open communication between a bronchus, a cavity and the pleura. This may be a complication of pulmonary resection.

Pleura

28. empyema of pleura, pyothorax—pus in pleural cavity.
29. hemothorax—blood in pleural cavity due to trauma or ruptured blood vessel.
30. hydropneumothorax—watery effusion and air in pleural cavity.
31. pleural effusion—excessive formation of serous fluid within the pleural cavity.
32. pleurisy, pleuritis—inflammation of the pleura.
33. pyopneumothorax—pus and air in the pleural cavity.
34. spontaneous pneumothorax—entrance of air into the pleural cavity resulting in a collapse of a lung.
35. tension or valvular pneumothorax—entrance of air into pleural cavity on inspiration; air exit blocked by valve-like tissue on expiration; enlargement of pleural cavity and collapse of lung as positive pressure increases resulting in mediastinal shift and depression of diaphragm.

B. Operative Terms:

Lungs

1. collapse surgery—surgical procedure which aims to put the diseased lung at rest by causing it to relax. The tuberculous lesion remains within the lung, but becomes nonactive and rarely develops into a focus of reinfection. Most collapse procedures have been abandoned since the advent of antituberculous chemotherapy. The only operations occasionally performed are
   a. extrapleural thoracoplasty—multiple rib resection without entering the pleural space.
      (1) primary—to effect permanent collapse of the diseased lung and cavity closure.

(2) postlobectomy or postpneumonectomy—to oblite-
rate dead space subject to infection or to reduce
empyema space.
b. plombage—packing the space between chest wall and
lung with foreign material to collapse the lesion.
2. excisional surgery (extirpative, definitive)—partial or complete removal of the diseased lung.
a. lobectomy—removal of a pulmonary lobe.
b. lung resection, pulmonary resection—partial excision of
the lung, such as
(1) segmental resection—removal of a broncho-
pulmonary segment.
(2) subsegmental resection—removal of a portion of a
segment.
c. pneumonectomy—removal of an entire lung.
d. wedge resection—removal of a triangular portion of
the lung, usually a small peripheral lesion, such as a
tuberculoma.

Bronchi

3. bronchoplasty—plastic operation for closing fistula.
4. bronchoscopy—examination of the bronchi through a
bronchoscope.
5. bronchotomy—incision into a bronchus.
6. closure of bronchopleural fistula—bronchoplasty with post-
operative drainage of pleural cavity.

Pleura

7. artificial or therapeutic pneumothorax—the introduction
of a measured amount of air into the pleural cavity through
a needle in order to give the diseased lung temporary rest.
8. pleurectomy:
a. partial—removal of a portion of the pleura.
b. complete—removal of the entire pleura. This is generally associated with pneumonectomy.
9. pulmonary decortication—removal of fibrinous exudate or
pleural peel from the visceral surface of the imprisoned

lung to restore its functional adequacy.

10. thoracentesis—tapping of the pleural cavity to remove pleural effusion for diagnostic or therapeutic purposes.

C. *Symptomatic Terms:*

Lungs

1. apnea, apnoea—temporary absence of respiration—also seen in Cheyne-Stokes respiration.
2. bronchial or tubular breathing—harsh breathing with a prolonged high pitched expiration which may have a tubular quality.
3. Cheyne-Stokes respiration—irregular breathing beginning with shallow breaths which increase in depth and rapidity to a certain degree; then they gradually decrease and cease altogether. After 10-20 seconds of apnea, the same cycle is repeated.
4. cyanosis—bluish color of skin due to deficient oxygenation.
5. dyspnea, dyspnoea—difficult breathing.
6. expectoration—act of coughing up and spitting out material from the lungs, trachea and mouth.
7. hemoptysis—expectoration of blood.
8. hiccough, hiccup, singultus—spasmodic lowering of the diaphragm followed by spasmodic, periodic closure of the glottis.
9. Hyperpnea—respirations increased in rate and depth.
10. hyperventilation hyperaeration—excessive movement of air in and out of the lungs.
11. hyperventilation syndrome—prolonged heavy breathing and long sighing respirations causing marked apprehension, palpitation, dizziness, muscular weakness, paresthesia and tetany. The attack may result from biochemical changes in neuromuscular and neurovascular function.
12. hypoxia—oxygen want due to decreased amount of oxygen in organs and tissues.
13. orthopnea, orthopnoea—breathing only possible when person sits or stands.

14. rales—bubbling sounds heard in bronchi at inspiration or expiration.

Pleura

15. pleural adhesions—fibrous bands which bind the visceral pleura to the parietal pleura. They may be loose, elastic, avascular or firm, inelastic and vascular.
16. pleural effusion—abnormal accumulation of fluid within the pleural space.
17. pleural exudate—pus or serum accumulating in the pleural cavity. Fibrinous exudate may lead to the formation of adhesions.
18. pleural peel—abnormal layer of fibrous tissue adherent to the visceral pleura and underlying diseased lung. The ever thickening peel may inhibit respiratory function.
19. pleuritic pain, pleurodynia—sharp, intense pain felt in intercostal muscles.

Radiology

A. *General Terms Used in X-Ray Reports:*

1. aerated—filled with air.
2. calcification—deposit of lime salts in the tissues.
3. consolidation—solidification of the lung as in pneumonia.
4. density—the compactness of structure of a substance.
5. discrete—well-defined and clear-cut in appearance.
6. fibrosis—replacement of normal tissue with fibrous tissue.
7. infiltration—the permeation of a tissue with substances that are normally absent.
8. infraclavicular—below the clavicle or collar bone.
9. infrascapular—below the scapula or shoulder plate.
10. inspissated—thickened by absorption of fluid content.
11. peribronchial—pertaining to area around the bronchial tubes.
12. rarefaction—process of decreasing density.
13. rarefied area—area of lessened density.
14. subdiaphragmatic—below the diaphragm.

15. substernal—below the sternum or breast bone.

B. *Terms Related to X-Ray Examination of Chest:*

1. bronchography—radiographic examination of the bronchial tree following the intratracheal injection of an opaque solution.
2. laminograms of lung—body section radiograms which delineate sharply a thin layer of lung tissue; thus, the structures lying anteriorly and posteriorly are more or less blurred out. Laminograms demonstrate the presence of a cavity.
3. selective segmental bronchography—bronchographic examination of selected parts of the lungs; for example, the apices. Under local anesthesia a Metras catheter is inserted for the injection of a radiopaque substance. Aided by fluoroscopic guidance, the contrast medium is allowed to fill the bronchial branches of the pulmonary segments. Abnormalities are recorded instantly by spot-films.
4. planigrams of lung—same as laminograms.
5. teleradiographic examination—x-ray examination made at a distance of 6 feet.
6. tomograms of lungs—same as laminograms.

Clinical Laboratory

A. *Terms Related to Some Essential Bacteriological Studies:*

1. examination of sputum and gastric washings—tests for demonstrating pathogenic organisms. Three methods are used:
   a. animal inoculation—injection of prepared material from specimen into a laboratory animal; for example, either a guinea pig or a white mouse. Smears are made from sacrificed animal after a definite time has elapsed.
   b. culture—material inoculated into an appropriate medium for the purpose of growth and possible identification of the organism.
   c. smear—material spread on a slide for microscopic study of organisms.

2. sensitivity studies on Mycobacterium tuberculosis—tests for determining the susceptibility of tubercle bacilli to various antimicrobial agents in an effort to evaluate the effectiveness of the therapeutic regime. Results indicate:

   a. drug sensitivity or
   b. drug resistance.

3. skin tests—tests for detecting previous exposure and sensitization to tubercle bacilli.

   a. Heaf—intradermal tuberculin test by multiple puncture technique.
   b. Mantoux—intradermal tuberculin test.
   c. Tine—intradermal tuberculin test by puncture with four tines dip-dried with old tuberculin.
   d. Vollmer—patch test; adhesive impregnated with tuberculin applied to skin.

4. vaccine for tuberculosis, BCG—attenuated vaccine composed of avirulent tubercle bacilli. BCG vaccination produces immunity against tuberculosis, variable in effect and duration.

REFERENCES

Acciavatti, Richard E.: Rehabilitation of tuberculous students by the health services of land-grant colleges and universities in the United States. Unpublished, 1954.

Acciavatti, Richard E.: Factors related to hospital readmission of tuberculosis patients. Ann Arbor, Michigan, University Microfilms, 1962.

American Lung Association: Tuberculosis Facts in the United States.

Cohen, Burton M.: Therapeutic opportunities in chronic ventilatory disease. *Journal of Applied Therapeutics, 8*:340-345, 1966.

Cohen, Burton M.: Clinical estimation of breathlessness. *The Journal of the Medical Society of New Jersey, 61*:23-26, 1964.

Fraser, Robert G., and Paré, J. S.: *Diagnosis of Diseases of the Chest.* Philadelphia, W. B. Saunders Co., 1970.

Frenay, Sister Agnes Clare: *Understanding Medical Terminology.* St. Louis, Catholic Hospital Association, 1969.

Holvey, David N. (Ed.) *et al.*: *The Merck Manual of Diagnosis and Therapy* (12th Edition). Rahway, N.J., Merck, Sharp & Dohme Research Laboratories, 1972.

Hylbert, Kenneth W.: *Medical Information for Counselors: An Outline Text.* State College, Pa., Counselor Education Press, 1965.

Langley, L. L.; Cheraskin, E., and Sleeper, R.: *Dynamic Anatomy and Physiology*. New York, McGraw, 1958.

Lev, Ralph: Lecture on Pulmonary Disabilities, Seton Hall University, January, 1973.

Lyght, Charles E. (Ed.), *et al.*: *The Merck Manual: Diagnosis and Therapy* (10th ed.). Rahway, N.J., Merck, Sharp and Dohme Research Laboratories, 1961.

Myers, Julian: *An Orientation to Chronic Disease and Disability*. New York, Macmillan, 1965.

National Tuberculosis and Respiratory Disease Association. *Introduction to Respiratory Disease*. New York, NTRDA, 1969.

National Tuberculosis and Respiratory Disease Association. *Facts About Selected Respiratory Conditions in the United States: Epidemiology and Statistics Division*. New York, NTRDA, 1969.

National Tuberculosis and Respiratory Disease Association: *Standards for Tuberculosis Treatment in the 1970's: A Statement by the Ad Hoc Committee on Quality Care for Tuberculosis*. New York, NTRDA, 1970.

National Tuberculosis and Respiratory Disease Association: *Tuberculosis Facts in the United States*. New York, NTRDA Planning Office, 1972.

Orgeon Thoracic Society, Medical Section of the Oregon Tuberculosis and Respiratory Disease Association: *Chronic Obstructive Pulmonary Disease —A Manual for Physicians*, NTRDA, N.Y., 1972.

Pharmacy Lecture and Note Series. Philadelphia, Smith, Kline and French Laboratories, 1967.

Rusk, Howard A., and Taylor, Eugene J.: *Rehabilitation Medicine: A Textbook on Physical Medicine and Rehabilitation* (2nd ed.), St. Louis, C. V. Mosby, 1964.

Taber, Clarence W.: *Taber's Cyclopedic Medical Dictionary*. Philadelphia, F. A. Davis, 1963.

CHAPTER XIV

HOW MECHANICAL ASSISTIVE DEVICES AND ADAPTIVE BEHAVIOR CAN AID IN THE REHABILITATION OF SEVERELY DISABLED PERSONS

A. G. GARRIS

~~~~~~

Conservation of Energy with Adaptive Techniques
Expand the Use of Your Devices
Mechanical Assistive Devices
Who Is Likely to Use Aids?
Uncover the Expectancies
Commercially Available Devices
Custom Designed Devices

~~~~~~

Conservation of Energy with Adaptive Techniques

THE EFFICIENT USE of adaptive techniques may well be the most significant difference between a successfully employed severely disabled worker and an unsuccessful, unemployed disabled person.

Nearly everyone uses adaptive techniques of one type or another. Often they are not obvious and persist as a habit. The techniques people adapt may have been learned in treatment centers or they may have been devised by the person himself to meet a particular need. Some techniques are efficient and some are not. But to the severely disabled person they become increasingly important if they enable him to perform a task or do it easier.

Every meeting a counselor has, then, with a physically disabled person is an opportunity to learn about adaptive techniques. Most disabled persons are glad to share their innovations with interested counselors because they realize the information may be passed on to help other disabled persons.

Able bodied persons often do things the hard way. Usually they have a surplus of energy so wasting it doesn't matter. With the severely physically disabled person, however, adaptive techniques are mandatory and become a pathway back to independence and dignity.

Some severely disabled persons don't have much energy available in the first place, so the things they do may have to be done in other ways with their damaged muscles. Consequently they may have to expend more energy than what would be required normally. For example, a paraplegic with poor strength in his upper extremities may transfer himself from one chair to another with great effort and temporarily exhaust himself in the effort. On the other hand a normal person can change from one chair to another without noticeable effort and without any danger of exhausting himself. It is imperative, then, that the disabled person devise the best ways to accomplish his necessary tasks.

The adaptive techniques the disabled person uses in his home and the extent and quality of his personal care becomes a proper field of inquiry for the counselor. The time the client spends in these preparations, particularly his morning chores, may determine if he can be ready for training on schedule and later be able to get to work on time.

The energy the client expends is of paramount importance because any energy he saves can be used later on the job. Whenever the energy needed by the client in training or working diminishes the reserve energy he needs for breathing, seeing, self-care and other basic physiological demands, the vocational plan is doomed to failure.

So, conservation of energy becomes mandatory for the client. Such a simple innovation as placing furniture in strategic places in the home helps the client to conserve energy he needs in dressing, standing up and getting in and out of the bathtub.

Conversely, the movement of furniture ordinarily used by the handicapped person often causes difficulties for him. Therefore, a stable environment contributes to the success of adaptive behavior.

The need for adaptive behavior varies and the methods or techniques adapted also vary. One purpose of this chapter, then, is to help the counselor recognize and become more aware of these variations. He can also evaluate the efficiency of the techniques his clients have adapted. Clients demonstrate these techniques in their work, in their home life, in their use of tools, in their acceptance of suitable and useful orthotic devices and even their willingness to accept the help of others.

The amputee who has lost both hands probably has to devise the most detailed adaptive techniques and then rigidly follow them. His day starts with getting into his prostheses and following carefully devised procedures that enable him to complete his self-care efficiently.

Actually his day started the evening before when he arranged his prostheses on a platform or at a suitable height where he backed out of them. He took off his undershirt and put on his pajamas without his prostheses.

The process is reversed in the morning. He sheds his pajamas and wiggles into his bathing prosthesis. This set is especially designed for bathing because his regular prosthesis would deteriorate from the water.

The bathing prosthesis enabled him to handle soap, brush and toweling. After drying off, he removes his bathing prosthesis carefully, arranging it so he can put it back on independently.

His next step is to wiggle into his undershirt and then into his regular prosthesis. Following the pattern he has devised so successfully, he puts on the rest of his clothes. After shaving he slips into his shirt and puts on his tie. Then he transfers things from the pockets of yesterday's clothes and he is ready to prepare breakfast.

These adaptive techniques vary little from day to day. After many trials he discovers the most efficient ways and the process becomes an ingrained habit.

A disabled person appears to learn a specific procedure or

technique quicker when it is the only way to perform a task. When there are alternate ways, he may vaccilate considerably before accepting one way over another.

The adaptive behavior of a wheelchair user is often limited by his sitting balance, the strength of his arms and hands and other physiological factors. A desirable goal for a wheelchair user is the development of skills in handling the equipment as efficiently as possibly. The new wheelchair user soon learns that the chairs have to be steered. This is an obvious requirement. Until he masters it, doorways and furniture will bear evidence of his poor aiming.

Street curbs can often be negotiated if the wheelchair user is properly trained. If a driveway isn't handy, a paraplegic may use a parking meter in getting the wheelchair up over the curb. He does this by tipping the chair back and balancing it on the two large wheels and putting the small casters up on the curb. Then by pulling on the parking meter pole with one hand and turning the opposite wheel with his other hand, he can pull the wheelchair up over the curb.

The most dangerous part of this maneuver is tipping and balancing the wheelchair. In this instance strong hip muscles are desirable. A good sense of balance and quick reaction are also required. This method should not be attempted without assistance at first to prevent falling over backwards.

There is also a relatively easy way to place a wheelchair behind the front seat of a two-door automobile. If a handicapped person is taught the proper method and uses it, he should have little difficulty. A physical therapist or occupational therapist can teach him this adaptive technique quickly. Where a therapist is not available, a trained and experienced paraplegic can usually be found to give the instruction.

It takes a certain kind of discipline to get a routine perfected to the habit stage. When that point is reached, the act is performed automatically because it has become the way to do it. Why many persons quit before reaching this threshold of efficiency may be due to many reasons. One cause may be the number of ways he uses instead of settling on the most effective method and refining it into a habit.

Expand the Use of Your Devices

The successful disabled person tries to find additional uses for his assistive devices. A cane, for instance, is a useful tool. The person who uses a cane soon learns that it can be used to operate light switches, and thereby save steps; to extract articles from high shelves; to pick up clothes and shoes; to push and pull objects and otherwise manipulate things.

A cane, when used properly, can lessen weight bearing on unstable knees or damaged hips, restore equilibrium and help the blind to walk. It can be used to fend off mean dogs and as a weapon. It can be used to measure the height of fluid in a container. By removing the rubber tip it can be used as a stethoscope to locate a knock in an automobile engine.

Two canes can be even more useful. In addition to adding more stability to the client's gait and removing a greater load of weight bearing on unstable or damaged joints, two canes, used together, can be used to pick up small objects.

Mechanical Assistive Devices

A mechanical assistive device is a term applied to any device that helps the user. It may be a simple lever used to lift a heavy object.

Pertinent personal tools are custom designed assistive devices used to overcome some personal problem. An example is a fork with an enlarged handle to permit its use by an arthritic person who cannot make a grasping fist.

Timing is important in prescribing the use of assistive devices. They may become a little more acceptable by the client as he recognizes their need. Too often the patient is fitted with devices he discards after leaving the treatment center. Other adaptive techniques may be developed to supplant these mechanical aids. Such aids, even if they are discarded later, may have served a useful purpose in selling the basic idea to the patient of learning new ways to do certain things. Our evaluation of aids must rely on the user's experience. The assistive devices that survive and continue to be used are those that are the most simple.

Who Is Likely to Use Aids?

There are some indications of a person's ability to use aids. Questions such as "How long did it take you to get used to wearing glasses?" (or dentures or any other appurtenance) will give an indication of a person's adaptability. Patients whose approach to life has been rigid, such as a perfectionist, rarely make a good user of adaptive devices because nearly all aids have built-in imperfections.

The successful use of aids appears to relate the life styles. If a person habitually leaves for appointments at the last moment, he is not likely to be a good user because the assistive device takes time to put on. The same is true for adaptive techniques. A good deal of trouble in using aids has to do with taking time to use them correctly. Short cuts in procedure (until perfected) are usually disastrous. I would rather design a device for an impulsive person than for a compulsive one because, I have found, the chances appear to be better for the device to be used by the impulsive person.

The provision of mechanical assistive devices, pertinent personal tools and training in adaptive techniques helps to create a therapeutic environment for the client. It strengthens his hope of becoming useful not only in his own self care, independence and performance of work but also in his being helpful to others.

Uncover the Expectancies

The client's use of mechanical assistive devices and adaptive techniques does not always indicate that he is making a good adjustment to his disability. Too often in treatment centers the patient uses equipment and adaptive behavior simply to please a therapist or someone else who has worked hard on developing the device or otherwise helped him. It may only be a reflection of the observer's expectancies of how the patient should act under the circumstances. In some cases the stroke patient, for example, who refuses to use mechanical assistance and who is stubborn and irascible may have the ego strength to achieve vocational rehabilitation.

Nevertheless, the expectancies of others play a leading role in the rehabilitation of a disabled person. If a disabled person learns how to cope with these expectancies, he makes faster progress. Some of the general expectancies should be explored by the counselor. One is the expectancy that the client should always present the face of a smiling Cheshire cat. For a client to do otherwise seems to indicate that he is having trouble coping with his disability.

Another expectancy is that help is always welcomed or needed. For those who walk with a precarious balance, any help, however slight, may throw their equilibrium into a spin and cause them to fall. Many well-meaning helpers like to push wheelchairs. The disabled occupant may be getting along quite well until he meets a person who wants to push him. In this case the client must never assume that the pusher is experienced enough to foresee objects that will bump the footrests and send him sprawling out of his chair.

So, one adaptive technique is for the disabled person to tell those who want to help, how to help.

Commercially Available Devices

Mechanical assistive devices that have been useful to a large number of disabled people have been manufactured for sale and are available. There are many varieties of the same kind of device. Therefore, a decision has to be made on the priority of needs and the best device for the need.

A good example is the large number of electrically powered wheelchairs on the market. They differ in appearance. Some have variable speeds. On some the climbing power is inadequate. On others the steering control bar prevents getting the chair up close to a working area. The turning radius of some of the leading models leaves much to be desired. Turning radius is the amount of space required to turn the chair. The smaller the radius, the more maneuverable the chair. And all chairs present problems of transportation from one place to another.

Custom Designed Devices

Providing clients with custom designed assistive devices lags far behind the need. The creation of specially designed aids must often wait until a counselor or client becomes aware of the need for a special device and believes that device can meet the need. Unfortunately, the talent of creative imagination is not equally distributed among all counselors, particularly those who lack experience and awareness of what can be accomplished with assistive devices. Neither have engineers in various fields been asked by many counselors to help solve the problems of the disabled.

As to the availability of devices, some custom-made devices that solve the urgent needs of hundreds of persons constitute such a limited sales market that manufacturers are hesitant to produce them. One such device, a hold-down clamp to prevent a wheelchair from bouncing around in van type vehicles, prompted inquiries from over seven hundred persons. Yet no manufacturer has tooled up to produce the clamp.

Another device used to load and unload a wheelchair into an automobile prompted a large number of requests from disabled persons for a *do-it-yourself* drawing. This device, too, is not in production. The exchange of information and do-it-yourself designs may continue to be a partial answer to the problem unless some means of subsidy can be arranged to help a manufacturer with his production and distribution costs.

The following case histories demonstrate the variety of mechanical assistive devices that were designed to meet special needs of severely disabled persons.

Case History No. 1

This client, an employed quadriplegic (poliomyelitis), was referred to us by her employer. She had been hired as a job interviewer for the State Department of Employment.

As a quadriplegic, she was confined to her wheelchair. Since she was unable to propel an ordinary wheelchair, she was fitted with a two-speed, electrically powered chair. Even so, it moved too slowly to keep up with the flow of foot traffic in the narrow halls that led to the cafeteria in the office building.

Her arms were supported by *flying saucer* supports attached to the wheelchair. The combination of the supports sticking out from both sides of the chair and the narrow aisles separating the desks in the office prevented her from using one of the arm supports.

Having only one wheelchair, she had no backup equipment to use in case her chair needed repairs and all electric wheelchairs need monthly maintenance to prevent breakdowns.

Her job required her to perform other duties in addition to conducting interviews. She was required to fill out forms, maintain records, use reference books, and use the telephone. Her clients had to be escorted to her desk through the narrow aisles.

She worked from a wheelchair tray in front of a conventional desk, using only her right arm and hand. She couldn't use her left arm because she couldn't wear the arm support.

On her right hand she wore a tenodesis splint. Upon bending the wrist muscles, this device closed her fingers in a *three-jawed chuck*, allowing her to write with the tip of her fingers grasping the pen. Her job required her to write for long periods of time. This caused pain in her tired wrist muscles. These muscles are not designed for such tedious tension.

Being a quadriplegic, she needed the help of her supervisor to place her work materials within her reach on the tray. She needed this assistance several times a day. Since the tray prevented her wheelchair from getting near the desk, there were parts of the desk she couldn't reach.

The major problem appeared to be her inability to reach things on her desk. She demonstrated satisfactory control, however, over a working space of about one square foot in front of her. The problem was to devise some way to bring a larger working space under her control.

The solution was designing a *lazy Susan* type desk. It consisted of a revolving desk top that was electrically powered and controlled by microswitches. It could be moved in both directions. The revolving desk top increased her working space over 1,000 percent. All the things she needed during the day were placed in strategic places on the desk and as she needed them, she pressed the switch and the revolving top brought the item around in front of her. The front of the desk was entirely open. The desk was skirted and finished to match the other furniture in the office.

The wheelchair tray could now be discarded and the client could approach the desk closer in her wheelchair.

The problem of the wheelchair in the narrow aisles was solved by a new type of arm support designed by the upper extremity brace shop of the Los Angeles County Rancho Los Amigos Hospital. The new arm supports do not protrude from the sides of the wheelchair.

The old electric wheelchair was replaced with a speedier model which permitted the client to keep up with the flow of traffic through the halls at a variety of speed. With a second wheelchair, the client was now able to leave the new model at work and use the old one at home. She now had backup equipment at the office when repairs were needed.

All these improvements resulted in a 50 percent improvement in the client's work.

Case History No. 2

A triple amputee of both legs and the upper right arm was successfully employed as a clerk in a motorcycle parts store. He wore a prosthesis on the stump of his right arm. With it he could propel a regular wheelchair. But his left arm and hand had to do everything else. That put a heavy burden on the one arm. The client was also able to drive his automobile with hand controls.

There was only one major problem. At work he couldn't reach up to the top shelves to get spare parts for customers. All the parts were placed in cardboard boxes of similar size and strength. To solve his problem a reaching device had to be designed to meet the following specifications:

1. The device had to be lightweight.
2. It had to be operated by one hand, the left one.
3. It had to be able to hold a box of parts securely while the client lowered it to within his reach.
4. The device had to be well constructed as it would be used many times a day.

The solution was a spring-loaded clamp secured to the end of a lightweight pole. When the client pressed a control lever in his hand, the clamp opened and grasped the box. The client then permitted the device to slip through his hand, bringing the box down to within his reach.

This device was designed, constructed and tested on the job within a week and contributed to the continued employment of the client.

Case History No. 3

A client on crutches was being trained on the job as a television repairman. But the TV chassis were too heavy for him to lift to the workbench. He needed help.

A visit to the shop revealed what had to be done.

1. An elevator-type work platform was needed to enable the client to pick up a TV set from the floor and raise it to a height which was convenient and comfortable for him to work on it. The platform also needed to rise high enough to enable the client to pick up other chassis from conventional workbenches and lower them to the floor.
2. The device should support weights up to one hundred pounds.
3. The lifting mechanism should be electrically powered by regular 115 volt house current.
4. It should have a fail-safe mechanism to freeze the load in place and thereby prevent the platform from falling in event of a power failure or the loss of power should the electric cord be accidentally pulled from the plug.
5. The device should be mounted on casters that permit it to be rolled easily.
6. Extra power outlets should be provided for a soldering iron and test equipment near the switch used for raising or lowering the work platform.

The device was designed to employ an electrically powered worm gear to lift or lower the work platform. The platform could be stopped at any height, ranging from the floor level to the level of other work benches.

Another safety feature was added. The surface of the elevated work platform was covered with a non-conductive material and covered with glass cloth that had been impregnated with several coats of resin to provide a smooth, sliding work surface.

The device solved the client's lifting problems. It had an added feature: it could be used by able-bodied repairmen, too, to make their job easier.

Case History No. 4

How does a person confined to a wheelchair weigh himself? He can't stand on bathroom scales. And scales that accommodate wheelchairs are generally found only in rehabilitation centers. A simple solution was to construct a frame with two channels over a regular bathroom scales and ¼″ off the floor. The weight of the empty wheelchair was then registered on the scale. Getting in his wheelchair, the occupant rolls the chair on the channels. He reads the weight registered on the scale and subtracts the weight of the wheelchair.

Plans for this simple device are available free from the author.

Case History No. 5

A severely disabled client had to be transported in a van-type vehicle that had been equipped with a lift gate attached to the rear of the van. He lived at the end of a rough dirt road. Nothing he had used to hold down the wheelchair securely had succeeded. After studying the problem we developed a method that worked. We modified a standard over center clamp that we secured to the floor of the van on each side of the wheelchair and to the frame of the wheelchair. The device prevented movement of the chair in any direction. Seat belts were added later and attached to the van's frame.

A sketch of this *do-it-yourself* device is also available free from the author.

Case History No. 6

A counselor for the blind was confronted with this problem. He could train a number of legally blind typists if a suitable copy holder could be devised. The device needed to be adjustable and hold copy within two or three inches from the typist's eyes. It needed to be adaptable to fit a number of different typing desks and to permit attaching it to the desk on either side of the typewriter. At first the counselor experimented with a wooden model. After proving its usefulness, he constructed a permanent device of metal. Later he added a small, high intensity lamp to improve lighting the copy. His ingenuity solved the problem and pleased the clients.

Other Assistive Devices

Several modifications were made to solve unique problems of clients using sewing machines. In the case of a little person, a dwarf, an extension on the foot control enabled her to operate the machine. In other cases arm controls were devised for paraplegic clients.

Almost any mechanism controlled by the foot can be converted to hand operation. Hand controls for paraplegic automobile drivers are an example.

The movement of switches or levers to solve reaching problems are generally known and such modifications are easily made.

Using one part of the body to perform a task usually done by another part is not an uncommon practice. A quadriplegic who is completely paralyzed, except for moving his head from side to side, operates a nurses' registration service by telephone from his bed. He actuates the telephone by turning his cheek against an extension to the operating switch.

Even the neck muscles can be used. One device invented in Canada fits around the client's head. It has an extension that reaches down to a desk. By attaching a pen to the end of the extension, the client can write.

The tongue, too, can be used. The muscles regulating the position and movement of the tongue are exceptionally well developed. Consequently the tongue has a larger potential than is realized. Its versatility is amazing. The Rancho Los Amigos Hospital has successfully experimented with using the tongue to control a powered, arm prosthesis.

New and unusual assistive devices continue to be invented.

Some astonish persons engaged in the rehabilitation of the severely disabled. The success of the devices prove that instead of counselor's traditional approach of looking at his client's medical diagnosis and list of things he supposedly can no longer do, the time has come to search for new ways of helping him. Therefore, counselors should try to develop an expertise in the use of assistive devices and adaptive behavior. If he is unimaginative, the counselor should solicit the help of an adaptive device specialist. Mechanical assistive devices and the proper adaptive behavior hold rich rewards for the client whose counselor has a creative mechanical imagination or an appreciation of this field.

As a guide in helping you to evaluate your awareness of a disabled person's need for and use of mechanical assistive devices and adaptive behavior, the following tests are furnished.

Test No. 1

Perform the tasks indicated and check your responses with the answers given on page 304.

In the following case

A. Circle three geographical areas to check for adaptive devices.

B. *Underline* at least three activities that could be improved by training.

A client has been unable to adjust himself satisfactorily to work. He is a paraplegic as the result of a recent spinal cord injury. He sits solidly in his wheelchair which appears to fit him very well. His feet are properly positioned on the footrests. During an hour long interview, he made no attempt to change his position.

His replies to my questions indicate that he gets up at six in the morning. He transfers from his bed to his only wheelchair and then wheels himself to the bathroom. He completes his toilet activities, shaves, bathes, and dresses himself in that order.

At eight o'clock he is ready for breakfast. After breakfast he brushes his teeth, puts on his tie and coat.

He says he experiences the most difficulty in getting into and out of the bathtub. He also has to struggle to put on his trousers and shoes. His shoes are laced and tied with a granny knot.

I watched him back his wheelchair down a six inch step from the porch to the sidewalk. In doing this he leaned forward in the chair to keep from turning over. He landed with a resounding bump. He then wheeled over to the garage door and unlocked it. Returning to the center of the door, he gave it a mighty pull and it opened up over him.

Entering the car on the side opposite the steering wheel, he reached down, folded up the footrests, and then lifted and pulled the wheelchair into the front seat. After closing the door, he slid over behind the steering wheel. The footrests extended over into the driver's area. By this time his face was flushed and he was perspiring profusely. By 9 a.m. he was ready to travel.

Turn to page 304 to check your responses. Your answers should cover the items mentioned and reinforce the idea that there is no adequate substitute for proper training. The proper aids or devices should be provided and the client should be trained in their use.

Test No. 2

To test your skill of observation, circle at least three adaptive devices to be found in the following account and *underline* at least five orthotic devices or pertinent personal tools.

Mary is a successful worker. Her job requires her to answer telephones and write messages for later transmission. She walks with the use of two Canadian crutches. Her gait is stable. An automobile accident had damaged her spinal cord. Only because her leg muscles go into spasm is she able to walk. Her hand grasp is poor and she often picks things up by using one hand on one side of the object and the other hand in opposition.

The range of motion in her shoulders is limited but she can comb her hair by using a comb on an extension. She is able to put her lipstick on by bending her neck and lowering her head within reach of her hand. She holds her lipstick in her hand by use of a gadget that has two round bands which fit around her fingers.

To save time in loading and unloading her wheelchair in her two door, hardtop car, she had two wheelchairs. She leaves one at home and one at work. This requires her to walk a necessary, but minimum distance each day. As with many persons who walk with aids that require the use of both hands, she can work only in a sitting position. A tight heelcord on her left foot is corrected by a short leg brace.

The telephone she uses at work is placed on an adjustable arm which she arranges after she sits down. She answers the telephone by flipping a switch. In writing she uses a ballpoint pen that has a small receptable on it for her fingers. She files her messages in spring-loaded clips which she opens with the lower part of her hand. She then inserts the paper she holds between her first and second fingers.

Mary is quite independent in her work and only rarely does she require help from others. When she needs help, she asks for it in a matter-of-fact way, making it easy for others to assist her.

Turn to page 305 to check your responses.

Answers to Test No. 1

Areas   Devices probably needed
A. Bathroom: shower facilities, handrails, bathtub seat, etc.
   Porch: ramp
   Garage: electric door opener or a stronger counterbalance
B. *Activities that could be improved by training*:

1. *Proper use of a wheelchair*
   - to change position in the chair frequently, thereby preventing pressure sores
   - to avoid jumping curbs or steps
   - to avoid bruising jolts to the buttocks.
2. *Getting into the automobile*
   - to enter from the driver's side
   - to avoid scraping or abrading the buttocks
3. *Loading the wheelchair*
   - to utilize the pivotal action of the rear wheels by picking up the front casters first and then starting the chair into the car behind the front seat.
   - to hold the chair securely with the left hand; grab the driving rim of the wheelchair with the right hand; turn

the wheel and use the wheel to help load the chair into the car. This method uses much less energy.

Practically every activity of this client can be improved. With proper planning and suitable equipment, the time required for the activities the client has to perform may be cut in half with the saving of much of his energy.

Answers to Test No. 2

Mary is a successful worker. Her job requires her to answer telephones and write messages for later transmission. **She walks with the use of two Canadian crutches.*** Her gait is stable. An automobile accident had damaged her spinal cord. Only because her leg muscles go into spasm is she able to walk. Her hand grasp is poor and **she often picks up things by using one hand on one side of the object and the other hand in opposition.**

The range of motion in her shoulders is limited but she can comb her hair by using a comb on an extension. **She is able to put her lipstick on by bending her neck and lowering her head within reach of her hand.** She holds her lipstick in her hand by use of a gadget that has two round bands which fit around her fingers.

To save time in loading and unloading her wheelchair in her two-door, hardtop car, she has two wheelchairs. **She leaves one at home and one at work.** This requires her to walk a necessary but minimum distance each day. As with many persons who walk with aids that require the use of both hands, she can work only in a sitting position. A tight heelcord on her left foot is corrected by a short leg brace.

The telephone she uses at work is placed on an adjustable arm which **she arranges after she sits down. She answers the telephone by flipping a switch.** In writing **she uses a ballpoint pen that has a small receptable on it for her fingers.** She files her messages in spring-loaded clips which **she opens with the lower part of her hand.** She then inserts the paper she holds between her first and second fingers.

––––––

* Boldface type has been used to denote encircled material.

Mary is quite independent in her work and only rarely requires help from others. When she needs help, **she asks for it in a matter-of-fact way,** making it easy for others to assist her.

TABLE III

TABLE FOR MALE PATIENTS

	Employment	Hours	% Pre-Illness Earnings
HF	Fork lift operator	40	100%
RS	Counter Work	24*	100%
TS	Air Conditioner Assembler	32	80%
RR	Welding Supervisor	40	107%
JB	Painter	40*	60%
CR	Butcher	40	70%
TH	Repairman	32	80%
	AVERAGE:	35	85%

(University of of Alabama, 1971.)

TABLE IV

REHABILITATION: COMPARISON WITH PRE-ILLNESS EFFORT

This is the table for women, the first or left hand column of percentages represents the amount of effort put into housework compared with pre-illness effort

PS	Household	60%	Clerical	6%
WW	Household	100%	Clerical	80%
RG	Household	100%		
JH	Household	100%	Teacher	100%
MR	Household	100%		
VG	Household	90%		
PW	Household	60%	Clerical	50%
BJ	Household	90%	Teacher	100%
AVERAGE:		88%		67%

(University of Alabama, 1971.)

INDEX

307